Intermediate Microeco

MW01131958

Intermediate Microeconomics: A tool-building approach is a clear and concise calculus-based exposition of current microeconomic theory that is essential for students pursuing degrees in economics or business. This beautifully presented and accessible text covers all the essential topics typically required at the intermediate level, from consumer and producer theory to the market structures of perfect competition, monopoly, duopoly, and oligopoly. Other topics include general equilibrium, risk, and game theory, as well as chapters on externalities, asymmetric information, and public goods.

Through numerical examples as well as exercises, the book aims to teach microeconomic theory via a process of learning-by-doing. When there is a skill to be acquired, a list of steps outlining the procedure is provided, followed by an example to illustrate how this procedure is carried out. Once learned, students will be able to solve similar problems and be well on their way to mastering the skills needed for future study.

Intermediate Microeconomics presents a large amount of material in a concise way, without sacrificing rigor or clarity of exposition. Through use of this text, students will acquire both the analytical toolkit and theoretical foundation necessary in order to take upper-level field courses in economics such as industrial organization, international trade, and public finance.

Samiran Banerjee is Senior Lecturer in the Department of Economics at Emory University in Atlanta, USA.

Intermediate Microeconomics
A tool-building approach

Samiran Banerjee

Routledge
Taylor & Francis Group

LONDON AND NEW YORK

First published 2015
by Routledge
2 Park Square, Milton Park, Abingdon, Oxon OX14 4RN

and by Routledge
711 Third Avenue, New York, NY 10017

Routledge is an imprint of the Taylor & Francis Group, an informa business

© 2015 Samiran Banerjee

The right of Samiran Banerjee to be identified as author of this work has been asserted in accordance with the Copyright, Designs and Patent Act 1988.

All rights reserved. No part of this book may be reprinted or reproduced or utilised in any form or by any electronic, mechanical, or other means, now known or hereafter invented, including photocopying and recording, or in any information storage or retrieval system, without permission in writing from the publishers.

Trademark notice: Product or corporate names may be trademarks or registered trademarks, and are used only for identification and explanation without intent to infringe.

British Library Cataloguing in Publication Data
A catalogue record for this book is available from the British Library

Library of Congress Cataloging in Publication Data
Banerjee, Samiran.
Intermediate microeconomics: a tool-building approach/Samiran Banerjee.
pages cm
Includes bibliographical references and index.
1. Microeconomics. I. Title.
HB172.B26 2014
338.5–dc23
2014018108

Publisher's Note
This book has been prepared from camera-ready copy provided by the author.

ISBN: 978-0-415-87004-7 (hbk)
ISBN: 978-0-415-87005-4 (pbk)
ISBN: 978-0-203-79755-6 (ebk)

Typeset in Palatino

Dedicated to the memory of Leonid Hurwicz and Marcel K. Richter

Contents

Preface

To the instructor

The primary purpose of the intermediate microeconomics class at Emory University (and I imagine elsewhere) is to provide the theoretical foundation and tools that economics majors need in order to take upper-level field courses. It is not a terminal class, nor is it a mere continuation of a principles-level class where the emphasis is on applications and understanding items in the news. This book reflects those priorities.

Undergraduate students have an easier time going from the specific to the abstract rather than the other way around. My approach has been to teach theory indirectly, by presenting specific numerical examples or models that instantiate the theory, by solving related problems, and learning by doing. Because tool-building is time-consuming in itself, I have on purpose downplayed applications, relegating them to end-of-chapter problems when appropriate. Many of these go beyond the run-of-the-mill problems that are found in most books and are challenging, yet still within the student's ability.

This is a calculus-based text for students who are only assumed to know elementary differential calculus and unconstrained optimization for a function of a single variable. While I use partial derivatives throughout (which can be learned from the mathematical appendix), all constrained optimization problems — for instance, utility maximization, or maximizing a firm's profit subject to individual rationality and incentive compatibility constraints — are solved without the use of Lagrangians.

In teaching at the intermediate level, the personal preferences of the instructor play a large role in the selection of topics as well as the level, depth, and treatment of coverage. Even though it is probably impossible to write a short book that serves everyone's teaching preferences, I have tried to concentrate on what I consider to be the *basic* foundation material of modern microeconomics commonly taught by most instructors. This material includes consumer theory, producer theory, the market structures of perfect competition, monopoly, and oligopoly, as well as some exposure to risk, game theory, and general equilibrium. The final three chapters provide a tour of optional topics in increasing order of sophistication: externalities, asymmetric information, and public goods. Many sections are marked with the degree symbol (°), signifying "optional" or extra material that may be omitted.

I believe that a student who is an economics major in the 21st century should have a good understanding of competitive equilibrium, and be able to express in lay terms the insight of the First Welfare Theorem. I have therefore covered the Edgeworth-box economy in some detail and use the idea of Pareto efficiency and general equilibrium in later chapters as well, in producer theory, risk-sharing, externalities and public goods.

Throughout, I have attempted to be concise without compromising rigor and, I hope, clarity. I look forward to receiving feedback and suggestions for improvement at *banerjeemicro@gmail.com*.

To the student

The purpose of this book is to provide a foundation of the tools of microeconomic theory necessary to take upper-level electives in economics, such as public finance, international trade, or industrial organization. You are expected to have had a semester of calculus, be familiar with the contents of a principles of microeconomics class, and recall some of the basic ideas involving demand, supply, and market equilibrium. Chapter 1 begins with an overview of this material. Chapters 2–13 covers core material of intermediate microeconomics. Chapters 14–16 provide an introduction to optional topics in increasing order of difficulty; many universities offer semester-long courses in welfare economics, the economics of information, and public economics that include the material in each of these chapters.

Because the focus is on the acquisition of tools, applications are downplayed, though a few appear in the end-of-chapter problems. An unavoidable consequence is that you may not know exactly why you are learning something. Realistic applications take longer to develop than the time available in a theory class and will be covered in your field courses that take up an entire semester. In the interim, your instructor can help you to supplement your reading.

This book, alas, cannot be read passively! It is fairly dense, with complicated graphs and detail that may be difficult to follow in the beginning. It is based on the premise that people learn by doing, so you will have to dedicate some time and effort to get the most out of it. Here is some advice on how to use this text.

The very first time you read, skim through the chapter without being too concerned about understanding everything — it is normal for your grasp to be a bit shaky at this point. The goal of this first reading is akin to tilling the soil, to familiarize yourself with economic terms and the broad ideas of that chapter. Revisit the same sections with patience a second time, going into greater depth and working through all the derivations using a pencil and scratch paper. Any time you encounter the red "writing hand" (✍ symbol) in the margin, work through the derivations in that paragraph. Definitions and insights are often highlighted. In many chapters, there are light blue boxes with numbered steps.

1. These steps provide a general algorithm to derive something or to solve a particular kind of problem.

2. They are accompanied by a numerical, worked-out example.

3. These steps are part of your theory toolkit; make sure you understand how they are utilized in the numerical example. Many end-of-chapter problems require you to apply these steps, either directly or with appropriate modifications.

Finally, several miscellanea.

(a) Sections marked with the degree symbol (°) are less important to your theory toolkit and may be skipped with no loss of continuity. If you are enrolled in a class, be sure to ask your instructor if she or he intends to cover this material.

(b) Regarding font styles, an economic term is **bolded** in blue the first time it is used, and an English word is *italicized* at times for emphasis or to draw your attention.

(c) Slopes of straight lines are indicated with an angle symbol ∡, and a black arrow pointing to the value of the slope.

(d) In many of the graphs, there is a background grid. Its purpose is to help you figure out why certain lines look the way they look or why they pass through certain points.

(e) If you see any errors, typos, or any other discrepancies, please alert me at *banerjeemicro@gmail.com.*

Acknowledgments

This book was written over five years while teaching at Emory University in Atlanta during the regular academic year, and Korea University's International Summer Campus in Seoul, South Korea, during the summer. I am grateful to Emory University's 2013–14 Winship Award which gave me the Fall 2013 semester off to bring the book to the finish line. Thanks are also due to my past and present department chairs, Elena Pesavento and Hashem Dezhbakhsh, for their support, as well as Sue Mialon whose encouraging comments at an early stage made me think that perhaps there was something worthwhile in this endeavor.

The suggestions and corrections by many students have been invaluable. Thank you Brenda Chew, Alvin Jun Young Choi, Veronica Chua, Mingyan Fan, Naomi Giertych, Hyun Hwang, Parth Jariwala, Geunyoung Kim, Jung Hwan Kim, Jiho Lee, Howard Riady, Regina Bong Sun Seo, Uma Veerappan, and especially Minji Lee and Aashka Patel. Thanks also go to Elena Antoniadou, Taradas Bandyopadhyay, Ahanu Banerjee, Anne Hannusch, Hugo Mialon, and Eliška Oller.

This book was typeset in LaTeX using TeXShop on a MacBook Pro. All graphs were drawn using EazyDraw for Mac. I thank Srinivasa Rao Kotte of Aditya Infotech, Hyderabad, India for promptly addressing my typesetting questions, and Dave Mattson from EazyDraw tech support for helping me through some graphical challenges.

My editors at Routledge, Rob Langham and Emily Kindleysides, have been friendly, warm and supportive throughout. I am especially grateful for the latitude they gave me to write the book that I wanted.

The bulk of the problems in this book are either my own, or drawn from the literature, or variants of problems in the public domain. If I have inadvertently violated anyone's intellectual property, please let me know and I will be happy to post an acknowledgment on the publisher's website.

Last but not least, I owe a tremendous debt to my teachers, especially my erstwhile co-advisers and mentors at the University of Minnesota, the late Professors Leo Hurwicz and Ket Richter, whose influence on my life transcends economics. I hope I have been able to do justice to their pedagogical clarity. I alone am responsible for all errors and any opacity in my presentation of the material.

Chapter 1

Markets

As a segue into the material of intermediate-level microeconomics, we begin with some familiar material from your introductory microeconomics class: market demand, supply, and equilibrium. We cover the same material but utilize algebra in addition to graphs. Then, we take up taxes and subsidies, topics which should also be somewhat familiar to you. Finally, we look at various elasticity concepts in greater detail than is usual in a principles-level class.

1.1 Market Demand and Supply

Consider a single product (say, the market for steel) over a specific geographical area and a relatively short time period, such as a few months.

1.1.1 Plotting a market demand function

A **market demand** function shows how much is demanded by all potential buyers at different prices and is written generically as $Q^d = D(p)$. Here, Q^d is the total quantity demanded and is the dependent variable, while the per-unit price, p, is the independent variable. An example of such a market demand function is given by the equation

$$Q^d = 120 - 2p \qquad (1.1)$$

where Q^d is measured in thousands of tons and p in dollars per ton. The fact that the derivative dQ^d/dp is negative means that this market demand

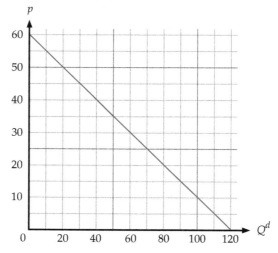

Figure 1.1 Market demand

embodies the so-called 'Law of Demand': keeping all other factors fixed, as the price of a product increases, its quantity demanded decreases.[1]

Since an independent variable is measured along the horizontal axis and the dependent variable along the vertical, the variable p ought to be on the horizontal axis and Q^d on the vertical. However, economists customarily put p on the vertical axis and Q^d on the horizontal axis, thereby depicting the **inverse market demand** by switching the variables in equation (1.1) and writing the price as a function of the quantity demanded:

$$p = 60 - \frac{Q^d}{2}. \tag{1.2}$$

This tradition follows Alfred Marshall's classic text, *Principles of Economics,* which was published in 1890 and was very influential in educating genera-tions of economists worldwide over eight editions spanning 30 years. Mar-shall's interpretation of the inverse demand is that it shows the maximum price (the dependent variable) that someone is willing to pay for a certain quantity (the independent variable). The inverse market demand given by equation (1.2) is therefore linear with a vertical intercept of 60 and slope of –0.5,[2] as shown in Figure 1.1.

---

[1]Traditionally, the Latin phrase *ceteris paribus* (sometimes abbreviated as *cet. par.*) is used instead to mean "keeping all other factors fixed".

[2]See section A.1 in the Mathematical appendix. The units of measurement will generally be omitted from the graphs to minimize clutter.

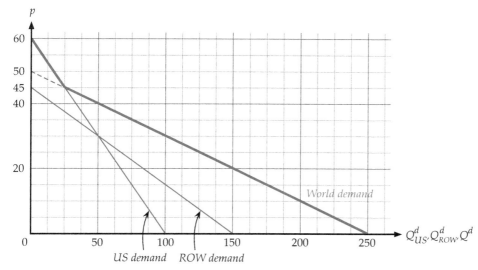

Figure 1.2   Aggregate demand

1.1.2   Aggregating demand functions

Suppose we are given the market demand curve for steel in the US as

$$Q_{US}^d = 100 - \frac{5}{3}p,$$

while the demand for steel in the rest of the world (ROW) is given by

$$Q_{ROW}^d = 150 - \frac{10}{3}p.$$

The corresponding inverse demand curves then are

$$p = 60 - 0.6Q_{US}^d \quad \text{and} \quad p = 45 - 0.3Q_{ROW}^d,$$

shown in Figure 1.2 by the thin blue lines. For a price between \$45 and \$60, the only demand for steel in the world comes from the US as the ROW demands zero at such a high price. But for $0 \leq p < 45$, there is a positive demand from both the US and the ROW — for instance, at a price of \$30, the US demands 50 thousand tons as does the ROW, for a total world demand of 100 thousand tons.

Then in the global market for steel, the quantity demanded by the entire world, Q^d, can be graphically derived as the piecewise-linear heavy blue line shown in Figure 1.2. For $45 \leq p \leq 60$, the world demand follows the US demand, but for $0 \leq p < 45$, the aggregate demand is given by the horizontal sum of the US and ROW demands:

$$Q^d \equiv Q_{US}^d + Q_{ROW}^d = 250 - 5p.$$

Thus the world demand is found by aggregating the demand functions of the US and the ROW and can be written as

$$Q^d = \begin{cases} 250 - 5p & \text{if } 0 \leq p < 45 \\ 100 - \frac{5}{3}p & \text{if } 45 \leq p \leq 60, \end{cases}$$

while the corresponding *inverse* aggregate demand is

$$p = \begin{cases} 60 - 0.6Q^d & \text{if } 0 \leq Q^d \leq 25 \\ 50 - 0.2Q^d & \text{if } 25 < Q^d \leq 250. \end{cases}$$

Note that the first line of the inverse aggregate demand is the equation for the linear segment that overlaps exactly with the US demand for prices above $45, while the second line is the equation for the flatter linear segment that consists of the horizontal sum of the US and ROW demands for prices below $45. For plotting purposes, note that the vertical intercept of the flatter linear segment of the inverse aggregate demand is at 50, as given by the equation $p = 50 - 0.2Q^d$ and shown by the dashed line in Figure 1.2.

1.1.3   Plotting a market supply function

Just as in the case of a market demand, we can write a generic **market supply** function as $Q^s = S(p)$ where Q^s is the quantity supplied by all the sellers in this market at the price p. Suppose the world supply curve is given by

$$Q^s = 5p,$$

from which the inverse world supply is

$$p = \frac{Q^s}{5}.$$

Plotting this in Figure 1.3 along with the inverse world demand from Figure 1.2, we see that they intersect at a price of $p^* = \$25$ and a quantity of $Q^* = 125$ thousands of tons.

Algebraically, this intersection point can be found by setting the inverse world demand $p = 50 - 0.2Q^d$ equal to the inverse market supply $p = Q^s/5$ and solving for Q^*. Substituting Q^* into either the inverse demand or the inverse supply yields the price p^*.

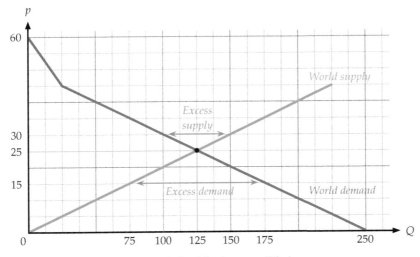

Figure 1.3   Market equilibrium

1.1.4   Market equilibrium

A market is said to be in **equilibrium** if there is a price, p^*, at which the quantity demanded equals the quantity supplied, i.e., if there is a p^* such that $D(p^*) = S(p^*)$. We refer to p^* as the **equilibrium price** and Q^* as the **equilibrium quantity**, where $Q^* = D(p^*) = S(p^*)$.

Even though the notion of market equilibrium is a static one, economists often tack on a dynamic story to drive the intuition that this is a **stable equilibrium**, i.e., any deviation from equilibrium will be automatically redressed by market forces to restore the price back to its equilibrium level. Suppose, for instance, that the market price is above p^*, say, at $30. At this price, there is **excess supply**: the 150 units supplied exceeds the quantity demanded of 100. Since the sellers have more of the product on their hands at this price than what buyers are willing to buy, this excess supply exerts downward pressure on the market price back towards the equilibrium price of $25.

Likewise, at a price that is lower than p^*, say $15, there is **excess demand** because the quantity demanded exceeds the quantity supplied. Here, the shortage of the product exerts upward pressure on the market price towards the equilibrium price, p^*.[3]

---

[3]The presumption is that this price adjustment process works smoothly and that the convergence to the equilibrium price happens relatively quickly.

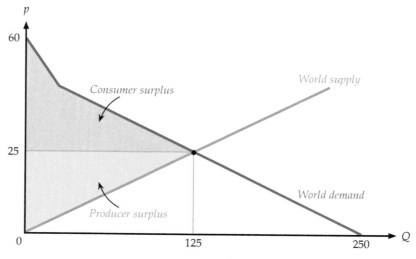

Figure 1.4   Consumer and producer surplus

1.1.5   Consumer and producer surplus

In any voluntary transaction between a buyer and a seller, trade takes place at some price in between the maximum price a buyer is willing to pay and the minimum price a seller is willing to accept. The difference between a buyer's maximum price and the actual price paid measures the buyer's gain from making this trade and is called the **individual consumer surplus**. The difference between the price received by a seller and the minimum price this seller is willing to accept is an index of the seller's gain from the sale and is called the **individual producer surplus**.

In Figure 1.4, the buyers who purchase steel value it somewhere between $60 and $25 per unit, as reflected by the portion of the world demand curve above $p^* = \$25$. Since these buyers each pay $25, their total gain from trade or **consumer surplus** is the blue shaded area below the world demand and above the equilibrium price of $25. Similarly, the sellers who receive $25 for each unit sold value it at somewhere between $0 and $25, as can be seen from the world supply. Therefore, the **producer surplus** is given by the orange shaded area below the equilibrium price and above the world supply.

In an introductory microeconomics class, the sum of consumer and producer surpluses is a measure of the gains from trade in this market and regarded as an index of **market efficiency**.

1.2 Determinants of Demand and Supply

From your introductory class, you may recall that the market demand for any product depends on several variables other than the price of that product. These include (a) the income levels of potential buyers, (b) the prices of other goods, (c) the tastes or preferences of buyers, and (d) the number of buyers. A change in any of these determinants, keeping all other factors fixed, causes a shift in the market demand curve. A rightward shift is called an increase in demand while a leftward shift is a decrease in demand.

When an increase in the income levels of buyers leads to an increase in demand — consumers buy more of the product no matter what the price level is — we say that such a good has a positive income effect. A good with a positive income effect is called a normal good. On rare occasions, the opposite may occur: a good may have a negative income effect. For instance, it is possible that consumers at low levels of income will reduce their purchase of cheap cuts of fatty red meat when their incomes increase, perhaps by buying more expensive lean cuts or switching to chicken instead. A good like this, where the demand shifts to the left when incomes rise, is called an inferior good.

The demand for a product depends on the prices of related goods: substitutes and complements. An increase in the price of a substitute good would make consumers buy more of the good under consideration, thereby increasing its demand. An increase in the price of a complement is likely to cause a decrease in the demand for this product.

On the supply side, the market supply for any product primarily depends on (a) the prices of inputs that go into producing the good, (b) the technology that underlies the production process, and (c) the number of firms. A change in any of these determinants causes an increase or decrease in supply. Thus, an innovation in technology that raises the productivity of inputs, or an increase in the number of firms is likely to cause an increase in supply, i.e., a rightward shift of the supply curve. An increase in the price of an input would have the opposite impact, causing a decrease in supply or a leftward supply shift.

1.3 Market Interventions

In this section, we recap some of the material from an introductory microeconomics class concerning interventions in markets. These interventions take place at either the local, state or federal levels and are of three types: price controls, quantity controls (or quotas), and taxes or subsidies. We illustrate these for a generic product market whose inverse demand and supply curves are given by

$$p = 24 - Q^d \quad \text{and} \quad p = 3 + 0.5Q^s. \tag{1.3}$$

Then the (unregulated) market equilibrium is $(Q^*, p^*) = (14, 10)$, the consumer surplus is \$98 and producer surplus is \$49.

1.3.1 Price ceilings

A **price ceiling** (or **price cap**) is a maximum price imposed on a particular product. For instance, in the US (and many other countries as well), the price per unit of electricity used by residential customers is capped by price regulation. For a price ceiling to be effective or binding, this level must be *below* the equilibrium market price as shown by $\hat{p} = 8$ in Figure 1.5. At this price, there is excess demand, i.e., more buyers who are willing to buy than there are sellers willing to sell. Therefore, the sellers have to engage in **rationing**. Rationing refers to a method of deciding who among the many buyers to sell to. For example, in the case of rent-controlled housing, a landlord may decide that the apartments will be rented on a first come, first served basis.

Note that some of the demand will always remain unmet, i.e., a binding price ceiling leads to a market disequilibrium. Assuming **efficient rationing**,

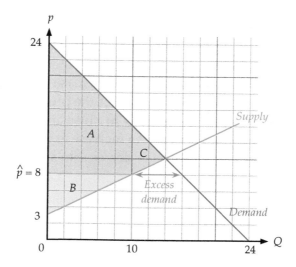

Figure 1.5 Price ceiling

buyers are allocated the good by highest willingness to pay, which results in a consumer surplus of $110 (shown by area A) in Figure 1.5 and a producer surplus of $25 (shown by area B). The aggregate gains from trade are now $135, the sum of areas A and B, which falls short of the gains from trade before the price ceiling by $12, the area C. Here area C shows the decrease in the gains from trade as a result of the ceiling and is called the **deadweight loss** of a price ceiling. A deadweight loss is an indication of **market ineffi- ciency**.

1.3.2 Price floors

A **price floor** (or **price support**) is a **minimum price** imposed on a particular product. For instance, in the US and EU countries, the price of certain agri- cultural goods cannot fall below a particular price level. For a price support to be binding, it must be set *above* the equilibrium price as shown by $\bar{p} = 14$ in Figure 1.5.

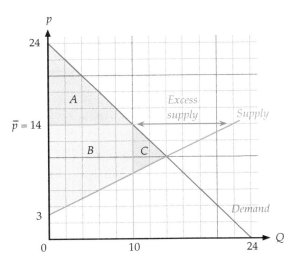

Figure 1.6 Price floor

This also results in a market disequilibrium phenomenon, that of excess supply.[4] The new consumer and producer surplus are areas A ($50) and B ($85) in Figure 1.6 and there is market inefficiency as can be inferred from the deadweight loss of area C ($12).

---

[4]With agricultural price supports, it is often the case that the government agrees to buy up the excess supply at the support price.

1.3.3   Quotas

A **quota** is a maximum quantity limit imposed on a particular product, i.e., the producers collectively cannot sell more than the quantity specified by the quota. Quotas are often imposed on imported items. In Figure 1.6, it is

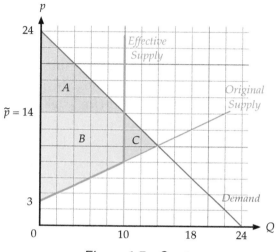

Figure 1.7   Quota

assumed that a quota of 10 units has been imposed. Effectively, the inverse supply curve for the product then becomes vertical at the quota. The new market price of $\tilde{p} = 14$ is given by the intersection of the old inverse demand and the new effective inverse supply, i.e., unlike price controls, the quota results in a new equilibrium relative to the restricted supply. The restriction in the quantity available for trade after the quota prompts the market price to increase from its previous equilibrium level of $10 to $14. As in the case of price controls, quotas also lead to market inefficiency: the new consumer is shown by area A and the new producer surplus by B, which falls short of the original surplus by the area C, the deadweight loss of the quota.

For a quota to be effective, the quantity limit has to be less than the original market equilibrium quantity. For instance, if the quota were set at 18 units, the effective supply would cross the market demand at a price of $10, so this quota would not alter the original market equilibrium.

1.3.4   Taxes

Taxes may be either **per-unit** or **ad valorem**, and imposed on either sellers or buyers. A per-unit tax is a fixed dollar amount for each unit traded to be paid by the responsible party. An ad valorem tax is a tax on the value of a sale, such as a 10 percent sales tax. We will only consider per-unit taxes.

A per-unit tax on sellers

Given the original inverse demand and supply curves in equation (1.3), suppose a tax, t, of \$6 per unit is imposed on sellers. Then, each seller will raise the minimum price she is willing to accept by the amount of this tax, thereby shifting the inverse supply curve up by \$6 at each point as shown in Figure 1.7. In other words, the new vertical intercept of the supply after the tax increases by the amount of the tax while the slope remains unchanged:

$$p_n = 9 + 0.5Q_n^s. \tag{1.4}$$

Setting this equal to the original inverse demand in (1.3), the new equilibrium price is $p_n^* = 14$ while the equilibrium quantity is $Q_n^* = 10$.

Note that a \$6 per-unit tax raised the equilibrium price from 10 to 14, not 16, i.e., the sellers were not successful in passing on the *entire* amount of the tax to consumers in terms of a higher price. The price difference of

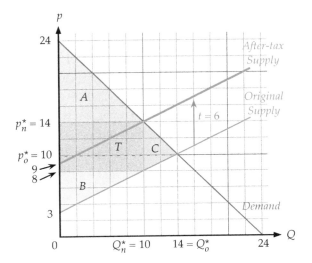

Figure 1.8   Per-unit tax on sellers

$14 - 10 = \$4$ is called the **incidence** of the tax on buyers — each buyer has to pay \$4 more than before to buy one unit of the good after the tax. Sellers earned \$10 on each unit sold previously, but now they earn $14 - 6 = \$8$ net of taxes, i.e., \$2 less than before. This \$2 is the incidence of the tax on sellers. Thus, buyers bear two-thirds of the tax of \$6, while sellers bear the remaining one-third, thereby illustrating a general principle: the incidence of a tax on buyers and sellers must add up to the tax.

Finally, notice that the consumer surplus after the tax is given by the area A in Figure 1.8. The producer surplus is based on the \$8 sellers receive after the tax is paid, shown by area B. The green rectangle labeled T is the total tax revenue, which is the per-unit tax of \$6 times the new quantity sold, $Q_n^* = 10$. Since the original gains from trade exceed the areas $A + B + T$ by the triangle C, the deadweight loss from a tax, there is market inefficiency.

A per-unit tax on buyers

Suppose the tax of \$6 had been imposed on buyers instead of sellers. What changes? Since buyers have to pay the tax after they purchase the product, each buyer will lower her maximum price by the amount of the tax, thereby shifting the demand curve *down* by \$6 at each point. Then the new vertical intercept of the demand after the tax decreases by the amount of the tax while the slope remains unchanged:

$$p_n = 18 - Q_n^d. \tag{1.5}$$

Set the new inverse demand equal to the original inverse supply in equation (1.3) to obtain the new market equilibrium quantity of $Q_n^* = 10$ (which is the same as when the tax was imposed on sellers) and the new equilibrium price is $p_n^* = 8$. This price, however, does not include the tax that buyers have to pay. Inclusive of tax, buyers have to pay $8 + 6 = \$14$ to purchase one unit of the good, while sellers receive \$8 for each unit sold. Thus the incidence of the tax on buyers is still \$4 while that on sellers is still \$2.

This example illustrates another general principle: whether a per-unit tax is imposed on buyers or sellers, the new equilibrium quantity is the same, as is the incidence of the tax on buyers and sellers.

1.3.5   Subsidies

A subsidy is a negative tax, i.e., instead of paying the government, the government pays the individual buyer or seller as the case may be. Here too, subsidies may be per-unit or ad valorem. We will only look at per-unit sub-sidies imposed on sellers.

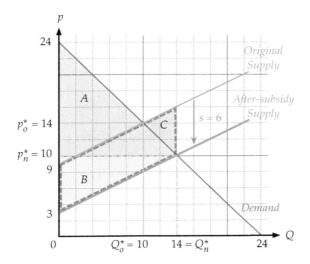

Figure 1.9 Per-unit subsidy

In Figure 1.8, the original inverse demand is $p_o = 24 - Q_o^d$ and the original inverse supply is $p_o = 9 + 0.5Q_o^s$ which result in an equilibrium quantity of $Q_o^* = 10$, an equilibrium price of $p_o^* = \$14$, and total gains from trade (i.e., consumer and producer surplus) of \$75. A \$6 per-unit subsidy moves every point on the original supply *down* vertically by this amount, resulting in a new equilibrium quantity of 14 and equilibrium price of \$10. Here the incidence of the subsidy is \$4 on buyers (they pay \$10 after the subsidy instead of \$14) and \$2 on sellers (sellers receive \$10 from each unit sold plus \$6 from the subsidy for a total of \$16, as opposed to \$14 before the subsidy).

As shown in Figure 1.9, the consumer surplus after the subsidy increases substantially to area A (\$98), while the producer surplus shown by area B (\$49) is also larger. However, this is not the aggregate gains from trade since this surplus of $A + B$ (\$147) does not include the cost of the subsidy to the government of $\$6 \times 14 = \$84$ shown by the green dashed parallelogram. Subtracting the cost of the subsidy from $A + B$ we obtain the new gains from trade after the subsidy to be equal to \$63, which is less than the original gains from trade of \$75 by \$12. In other words, the aggregate gains from trade are *smaller* than the original gains from trade by the triangle C which is the deadweight loss of the subsidy. Once again, there is market inefficiency.

1.4   Elasticities

Demand elasticities measure the responsiveness of the quantity demanded to changes in different determinants of demand, such as the price of the product, income, and prices of other goods. On the supply side, the elasticity of supply for a product measures the degree to which the quantity supplied changes with its price.

1.4.1   Price elasticity of demand

The price elasticity of demand, ε,[5] is defined as the percentage change in the quantity demanded when there is a percentage change in price. To make this more precise, let p_o denote an original price level and $D(p_o)$ the corresponding quantity demanded, while the new price is p_n and $D(p_n)$ is the new quantity demanded. Define the change in quantity demanded as $\Delta D = D(p_n) - D(p_o)$ and the corresponding change in price as $\Delta p = p_n - p_o$. Then the percentage change in quantity is $(\Delta D/D(p_o)) \times 100$ and, likewise, the percentage change in price is $(\Delta p/p_o) \times 100$. Dividing the former by the latter and simplifying, we get

$$\varepsilon = \frac{\Delta D/D(p_o)}{\Delta p/p_o} = \frac{\Delta D}{\Delta p} \cdot \frac{p_o}{D(p_o)}. \tag{1.6}$$

For infinitesimally small changes in price from p_o, $\Delta D/\Delta p$ is an approximation of the slope of the demand curve passing through the original data point. Writing the slope of the demand function at p_o as the derivative[6] $D'(p_o)$ and substituting it in (1.6), we get

$$\varepsilon = D'(p_o) \cdot \frac{p_o}{D(p_o)}. \tag{1.7}$$

Price elasticity for a linear demand

A generic linear inverse demand is written as $p = a - bQ^d$, where a indicates the vertical intercept and $-b$ is the slope. Depicting this in Figure 1.9, the vertical intercept a is given by the length of the line segment OA, while the slope is given by the ratio $-FA/FB$.

We wish to calculate the price elasticity of demand at a single point, B, where the price is OF and quantity is OE. The slope of the *demand* function,

---

[5]Or more precisely, the own-price elasticity of demand.
[6]See section A.2 in the Mathematical appendix for a review of derivatives.

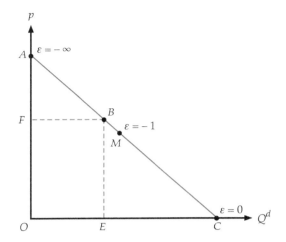

Figure 1.10 Linear demand and price elasticity

dQ^d/dp, is $-1/b = -FB/FA$. Using the formula in equation (1.7), the price elasticity at B is then

$$\varepsilon = -\frac{FB}{FA} \cdot \frac{OF}{OE}. \tag{1.8}$$

Since FB and OE have the same length, we obtain $\varepsilon = -OF/FA$. From the geometry of similar triangles, it follows that

$$\varepsilon = -\frac{OF}{FA} = -\frac{EC}{OE} = -\frac{BC}{AB}, \tag{1.9}$$

where the final ratio yields some insights into the nature of price elasticities at different points along a linear demand.

First, because the length BC is either positive (for positive prices) or equals zero (when the price is zero), the corresponding price elasticity will always be negative or zero. In particular, the price elasticity at point C can be taken to be zero, so the demand may be said to be **perfectly inelastic**. At point A, the price elasticity approaches negative infinity, so the demand can be taken to be **perfectly elastic** in the limit.

Second, $\varepsilon = -1$ at the midpoint of the demand, M, while at B (which lies above the halfway point), $|\varepsilon| > 1$. When $|\varepsilon| > 1$, we say that the demand is **elastic** or responsive to price changes because the percentage change in the quantity demanded is greater than the percentage change in price in absolute terms. Reasoning analogously, $|\varepsilon| < 1$ for any point below the halfway point and the demand is said to be **inelastic**.

Thus, different points on a linear demand have different price elasticities: from $-\infty$ at the vertical intercept, the price elasticity shrinks in absolute
value to -1 at the halfway point, to zero at the horizontal intercept.

In practice, an estimated demand function for a product might be given
by a function like

$$Q_1^d = 240 - 0.4p_1 + 0.2p_2 + 0.001m, \tag{1.10}$$

where Q_1^d is the quantity demanded of good 1, p_1 the price of this good, p_2
the price of good 2, and m the income level. Suppose we wish to calculate the
own-price elasticity of demand for good 1 (written as ε_{11}) when $p_1 = \$200$,
$p_2 = \$150$, and $m = \$100,000$. For these values of the independent variables
on the right hand side of equation (1.10), verify that $Q_1^d = 290$. Then

$$\varepsilon_{11} = \frac{\partial Q_1^d}{\partial p_1} \cdot \frac{p_1}{Q_1^d} = -0.4 \cdot \frac{200}{290} \tag{1.11}$$

which is essentially the same formula as (1.7), except the slope of the demand
is now given by the partial derivative[7] with respect to p_1. Substituting the
values, we obtain $\varepsilon_{11} = -0.28$, so the demand is inelastic.

Constant price elasticity of demand

Is it possible to have a demand function where the price elasticity of demand
does not change as one moves along the demand curve? Indeed, work out
the equation (1.7) using the demand function $Q^d = 100p^{-2}$ to verify that
it has an elasticity of –2 everywhere. In general, a demand function with a
constant price elasticity of ε will have an equation of the type

$$Q^d = Ap^\varepsilon, \tag{1.12}$$

where $A > 0$.

When $\varepsilon = 0$, we obtain $Q^d = A$, a vertical inverse demand function that is
perfectly inelastic. When $\varepsilon = -1$, we obtain $Q^d = A/p$ or $pQ^d = A$, showing
a constant expenditure by consumers of A dollars. Hence, any demand curve
that has a price elasticity of –1 throughout must consist of quantity-price
pairs such that a drop in price raises the quantity demanded by just enough
to leave the total expenditure unchanged.

---

[7]See section A.5 in the Mathematical appendix for an introduction to partial derivatives.

Total expenditure and price elasticity°

How does a change in price affect the total expenditure by consumers on this product? The answer depends on the price elasticity of demand. To see this, let $Q^d = D(p)$ be the demand function and TE denote the total expenditure by consumers, where $TE(p) = D(p) \cdot p$. Differentiate TE with respect to p using the product-of-functions rule[8] to get

$$\frac{dTE}{dp} = D(p) + D'(p)p = D(p)\left(1 + \frac{D'(p)p}{D(p)}\right).$$

Note that $D'(p)p/D(p) = \varepsilon$ from equation (1.7), so we obtain

$$\frac{dTE}{dp} = D(p)(1 + \varepsilon). \tag{1.13}$$

An elastic demand implies that $(1 + \varepsilon)$ is negative since $|\varepsilon| > 1$. Assuming that the quantity demanded at price p, $D(p)$, is positive, it follows that the right hand side of (1.13) is then negative. Therefore, for an elastic demand, an increase in p reduces TE, while a decrease in p raises TE. Conversely, when the demand is inelastic, $(1 + \varepsilon)$ is positive, so an increase in p increases TE, while a decrease in p reduces TE.

The rationale for this is that when the demand is inelastic, an increase in the price does not change the quantity demanded by as much in percentage terms. Since each purchase costs more than before, the consumers end up spending more. Likewise, when the demand is elastic, an increase in price decreases the quantity demanded drastically. So despite the higher price, the expenditure is lower.

This relationship between consumer expenditure and price-elasticity of demand is important for managers because it provides them with a rough rule of thumb: if a product is price-inelastic, raising its price slightly will raise consumer expenditures and result in higher firm revenue. For price-elastic demands, lowering the price slightly will raise consumer expenditures and hence firm revenue.

1.4.2 Other elasticities of demand

Two other elasticities of demand can be derived by replacing the price of the product, p_o, in equation (1.6) with a different determinant of demand, namely, income or the price of some other good.

---

[8] See section A.2 in the Mathematical appendix.

The income elasticity of demand, η, captures the impact of a change in the income level on the quantity demanded, keeping all other determinants, including the price of the product, fixed. Consider the estimated demand function in equation (1.10). Here the income elasticity of demand for good 1, η_1, is defined as

$$\eta_1 = \frac{\partial Q_1^d}{\partial m} \cdot \frac{m}{Q_1^d}. \tag{1.14}$$

The income elasticity when $p_1 = \$200$, $p_2 = \$150$ and $m = \$100,000$ is then

$$\eta_1 = 0.001 \cdot \frac{100,000}{290} = 0.34.$$

A normal good has a positive income elasticity which means that an increase in consumers' incomes leads to an increase in the quantity demanded. While most goods are normal goods, it is possible (though rare) that the quantity demanded *decreases* when income rises. Such goods are called inferior goods and have a negative income elasticity.

The cross-price elasticity of demand measures the impact of a change in the price of another good on the demand for a particular product. For instance, from equation (1.10), it is possible to define the cross-price elasticity of demand for good 1 when there is a change in the price of good 2 (written as ε_{12}) as follows:

$$\varepsilon_{12} = \frac{\partial Q_1^d}{\partial p_2} \cdot \frac{p_2}{Q_1^d}. \tag{1.15}$$

The cross-price elasticity when $p_1 = \$200$, $p_2 = \$150$ and $m = \$100,000$ is then

$$\varepsilon_{12} = 0.2 \cdot \frac{150}{290} = 0.1.$$

Goods are said to be substitutes if they have a positive cross-price elasticity; a larger magnitude denotes a stronger relationship. Similarly, goods are complements if they have a negative cross-price elasticity. If the cross-price elasticity is close to zero, the goods are essentially unrelated.

1.4.3   Price elasticity of supply

Finally, given a supply function $Q^s = S(p)$, we define the price elasticity of supply, ε_s, as the the degree of responsiveness of the quantity supplied to a change in the price of the product. The formula for this can be derived in an analogous manner as that for the price elasticity of demand derived in equation (1.7):

$$\varepsilon_s = S'(p_o) \cdot \frac{p_o}{S(p_o)}, \tag{1.16}$$

where $(S(p_o), p_o)$ is the quantity-price point on the supply curve at which the supply elasticity is being calculated, and $S'(p_o)$ denotes the slope of the supply function. Since the slope of the supply is generally positive or zero, the price elasticity of supply is also positive or zero.

Exercises

1.1. Suppose the demand and supply for milk in the European Union (EU) is given by

$$p = 120 - 0.7Q^d \quad \text{and} \quad p = 3 + 0.2Q^s,$$

where the quantity is in millions of liters and the price is in cents per liter. Assume that the EU does not import or export milk.

(a) Find the market equilibrium quantity, Q^*, and equilibrium price, p^*.

(b) Find the consumer and producer surplus at the market equilibrium.

(c) The European farmers successfully lobby for a price floor of $\bar{p} = 36$ cents per liter. What will be the new quantity sold in the market, $\bar{Q}$?

(d) Find the new consumer and producer surplus after the price floor.

(e) What is the deadweight loss from the price floor?

(f) If the EU authorities were to buy the surplus milk from farmers at the price floor of 36 cents per liter, how much would they spend in millions of euros? (Note: 100 cents = 1€)

1.2. The market for a product has inverse demand and supply functions given by

$$p = 120 - 0.5Q^d \quad \text{and} \quad p = 0.5Q^s,$$

where quantity is in thousands of units and the price is in dollars per unit.

(a) Find the market equilibrium quantity, Q^*, and equilibrium price, p^*.

(b) Suppose the state government levies a tax of \$20 on each unit sold, imposed on the sellers. Find the new after-tax equilibrium quantity traded in the market, Q^{**}, and the price that consumers pay on the market, p^{**}.

(c) What is the incidence of the tax on buyers?

(d) What is the incidence of the tax on sellers?

(e) What is the tax revenue?

1.3. The world inverse demand for cotton is given by $p = 150 - Q^d$ while the inverse supplies of the US and the rest of the world are given by

$$p = 30 + Q_U^s \quad \text{and} \quad p = 30 + Q_R^s,$$

where quantity is in thousands of tons and the price is in dollars per ton.

(a) Denote the world supply by $Q^s = Q_U^s + Q_R^s$. Calculate the world equilibrium quantity, Q^*, and the world equilibrium price, p^*.

(b) Suppose the US government gives a \$30 subsidy to US sellers for each ton sold. The rest of the world has the same inverse supply as before. Find the new world equilibrium quantity, Q^{**}, and the new world equilibrium price, p^{**}.

(c) What is the incidence of the subsidy on US sellers? How does the US subsidy impact sellers from the rest of the world?

(d) What is the total subsidy amount spent by the US government?

1.4. Steel is produced only in the US and the rest of the world (ROW). The inverse demand and supply in the US are

$$p = 100 - Q_U^d \quad \text{and} \quad p = 20 + Q_U^s,$$

while in the ROW, they are

$$p = 80 - Q_R^d \quad \text{and} \quad p = Q_R^s.$$

All quantities are in millions of tons and all prices are in dollars per ton. Since steel is produced more cheaply in the ROW, the US imports it from the ROW under international trade. At any price, p, the imports of the US, Q_M, is the excess demand for steel given by the difference between the quantity demanded and the quantity supplied domestically in the US: $Q_M = Q_U^d - Q_U^s$. Similarly, the exports of the ROW, Q_E, is the excess supply of steel given by the difference between how much they produce and how much they demand: $Q_E = Q_R^s - Q_R^d$.

(a) Calculate the world equilibrium price, p^*, at which the quantity exported by the ROW equals the quantity imported by the US. What is the equilibrium quantity traded, Q^*? At p^*, how many millions of tons of steel are sold in each market, in the US and the ROW?

(b) Find the consumer and producer surplus in the US at the price p^*.

(c) The US government imposes a tax of $12 per unit on the ROW's exports. Find the new world equilibrium price, p^{**}, and new world equilibrium quantity traded, Q^{**}. What are the new quantities sold in each market, in the US and the ROW?

(d) What is the tax incidence on buyers and sellers in the US? What is the tax incidence on buyers and sellers in the ROW? Explain briefly.

(e) Find the new consumer and producer surplus in the US at the price p^{**} and the tax revenue earned by the US government.

1.5. Answer the following elasticity-related questions.

(a) Given the inverse demand curve $p = 20 - 0.5Q^d$, what is the own-price elasticity of demand when the price is $15 per unit? $12 per unit?

(b) Revnol, a manufacturer of cosmetics, prices its popular pink lipstick at $8. On the basis of test-marketing, Revnol believes that women between the ages of 18 and 20 have an own-price elasticity of −1.0 and that 60 percent of them are likely to purchase the product. In the age group from 21 to 25 years, the own-price elasticity is −1.2 and 50 percent of them are likely to buy.

(i) In a market with 25,000 women aged 18 to 20, and 15,000 aged 21 to 25, how many lipsticks can the firm expect to sell at a price of $8 per unit? Show your calculations!

(ii) If Revnol were to cut prices by 10 percent, approximately how many more pink lipsticks would it expect to sell? Show your calculations!

(c) On a certain product market, 500 units are demanded at a price of $15. The own-price elasticity is –1.5. What is the equation of a linear inverse demand that passes through the point $(500, 15)$?

(d) What is the equation of a constant-elasticity demand function that has an own-price elasticity of –2 and passes through the point $(500, 10)$?

(e) The demand for good x depends on its price, p_x, the price of good y, p_y, and the average income level, m. An economist estimates the demand function to be

$$Q_x^d = 720 - 1.5p_x - 2p_y + 0.001m.$$

Suppose $p_x = \$200$ per unit, $p_y = \$100$ per unit, and $m = \$50,000$.

(i) What is the own-price elasticity for good x, ε_{xx}?

(ii) What is the cross-price elasticity of demand for good x, ε_{xy}? Are x and y complements or substitutes or unrelated goods?

(iii) What is the cross-price elasticity of demand for good x, η_x? Is good x normal or inferior?

(f) Show that any linear inverse supply that passes through the origin (i.e., an inverse supply with the functional form $p = cQ^s$ with $c > 0$) has a price elasticity of supply equal to one. Show that any linear inverse supply curve with a positive intercept (i.e., having the functional form $p = k + cQ^s$ with $c, k > 0$) must be elastic.

Chapter 2

Budgets

Traditionally, the first topic in a standard intermediate microeconomics class is neoclassical consumer choice theory. A consumer's choice behavior arises from the interaction between what she can afford and her preferences over different goods. To study this in greater detail, we introduce the idea of a budget in this chapter, the combination of all goods and services that a consumer can afford. Preferences are covered in Chapter 3, while consumer choice behavior is taken up in Chapters 4 and 5.

2.1 Commodity Space

The commodity space refers to the combination of goods and services that a consumer can potentially purchase. Since most of our economic insights can be derived by confining attention to the case of two goods, we assume that there are only two commodities (called good 1 and good 2) that a consumer can buy. The quantities of each good will be written as x_1 and x_2.

Figure 2.1 shows the commodity space with two goods. A point like $A = (4,3)$, which consists of 4 units of good 1 and 3 units of good 2, is called a commodity bundle. So the commodity space is made up of commodity bundles, different combinations of the two goods. Since goods can be consumed in positive amounts or not consumed at all, the commodity space consists of all pairs of goods (x_1, x_2) in the non-negative orthant and is denoted by X.

It is convenient to assume that these goods are divisible: they can be purchased in *any* amount, not just in whole units. So, in principle, a consumer can purchase fractional amounts of either good (e.g., half a unit of good 1),

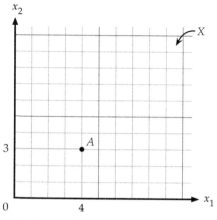

Figure 2.1   Commodity space

or even irrational amounts (e.g., $\sqrt{2}$ units of good 2). Then *any* point in X is a commodity bundle and the *entire* non-negative orthant in Figure 2.1 is the commodity space X.[1]

2.2   Competitive Budgets

Let p_1 denote the per-unit price of the first good and x_1 the quantity that the consumer purchases. Analogously, the price of one unit of good 2 is p_2 and the quantity purchased is x_2.[2] In this section, we assume that the per-unit prices of the two goods, p_1 and p_2, are fixed and given to the consumer by the market. She may buy as many units as she desires at these prices but is unable to influence p_1 or p_2 through her purchases (e.g., through discounts for bulk purchases).

Denote the consumer's income by m and assume that this too is a fixed amount. Then the consumer's **budget constraint** or **budget set** is given by

$$p_1x_1 + p_2x_2 \leq m \tag{2.1}$$

which expresses the idea that the expenditure on good 1 (p_1x_1) and the expenditure on good 2 (p_2x_2) should not exceed the consumer's income. In

---

[1]If a good is an indivisible or discrete, it can only be purchased in whole units. When both goods are discrete, the commodity space is a grid of dots where each dot is a commodity bundle with coordinates whose values are either zero or a whole number.

[2]Sometimes we will refer to the goods as x and y instead of 1 and 2. In that case, per-unit prices will be written as p_x and p_y.

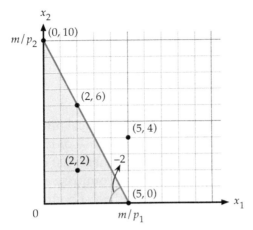

Figure 2.2 Budget line and set

other words, this combination of goods (x_1, x_2) is affordable with the consumer's income. Such a budget constraint is called a **competitive budget** because this embodies the notion of a consumer who purchases the goods in perfectly competitive markets at fixed per-unit prices.

When *all* of the consumer's disposable income is spent on these two goods, we replace the inequality in (2.1) with an equality and refer to the resulting equation

$$p_1 x_1 + p_2 x_2 = m \qquad (2.2)$$

as a **budget line**.[3] To illustrate, suppose $p_1 = \$2$, $p_2 = \$1$, and $m = \$10$. Then the budget line (shown in Figure 2.2 as a blue straight line) can be drawn simply by calculating its endpoints as follows. If the consumer were to spend all of her income of $10 on good 1, she can purchase $m/p_1 = 10/2 = 5$ units which yields the bundle $(5,0)$ on the horizontal axis; similarly if she spent all of her $10 on good 2, she can purchase $m/p_2 = 10/1 = 10$ units which yields the bundle $(0,10)$ on the vertical axis. Joining these two endpoints yields the budget line showing other combinations of x_1 and x_2 that can be purchased at the current prices while spending the consumer's entire income.

The budget constraint or budget set then consists of all bundles on the budget line or inside the shaded triangle in Figure 2.2. If a bundle lies in the interior of the budget set — say, $(2,2)$ — the consumer's income is not spent in its entirety and she has some savings. Likewise, a bundle that lies on the

---

[3]When the goods are referred to as x and y, the budget line is given by $p_x x + p_y y = m$.

budget line, such as $(2,6)$, uses up all of the consumer's income, while a bundle like $(5,4)$, which is outside the budget set, is unaffordable.

By rearranging the terms in equation (2.2), we may write

$$x_2 = \frac{m}{p_2} - \frac{p_1}{p_2}x_1,$$
(2.3)

which is the equation of a straight line with vertical intercept m/p_2 and slope $-p_1/p_2$. So a competitive budget line (in the case of two goods) will always be a straight line with a slope given by the negative of the ratio of the two prices,[4] while a competitive budget set will comprise a triangle that includes the budget line and all the points to its southwest bounded by the axes (since goods cannot be consumed in negative amounts).

2.2.1   Three goods or more

It is easy to extend the idea of a budget to three or more goods. In the case of three goods labeled as 1, 2 and 3, the budget line is

$$p_1x_1 + p_2x_2 + p_3x_3 = m,$$

where p_ix_i is the expenditure on the ith good, $i = 1, 2, 3$.

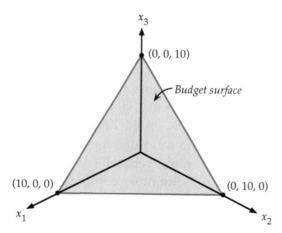

Figure 2.3   Budget surface with three goods

For instance, if $m =$ \$20 and all three goods are priced at \$2 (i.e., $p_1 = p_2 = p_3 =$ \$2) then the budget "line" is actually a *surface* shown by the

---

[4]The price of the good on the horizontal axis is always in the numerator of this ratio.

shaded triangle in Figure 2.3, while the corresponding budget set is the volume of the tetrahedron formed by the budget surface and the three axes. The three dots along the axes show consumption bundles where all the income is spent on that good; at any point on the budget surface, the consumer spends all her income on some combination of the three goods.

In general, if there are n goods where x_i denotes the ith good and p_i its price, the budget constraint is

$$p_1 x_1 + p_2 x_2 + \ldots + p_n x_n \leq m. \tag{2.4}$$

2.3   Changes in Prices or Income

By changing prices of goods or income one at a time, we can see how budgets are affected. The simplest way to see these consequences is to begin with equation (2.3) and to observe what happens to the intercept and the slope of the budget line as we change each price or income in isolation.

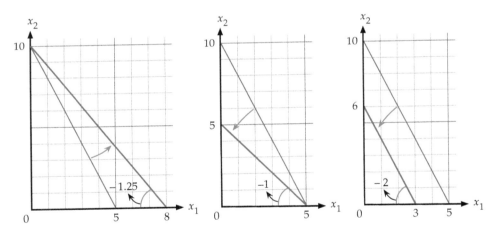

Figure 2.4   Budgets after changes in p_1, p_2 and m

Starting with the budget in Figure 2.2 where $p_1 = \$2$, $p_2 = \$1$, and $m = \$10$, consider each of the following changes. In Figure 2.4, the new positions of the budget lines after each of the changes are shown with magenta arrows.

(a) Suppose p_1 decreases to \$1.25 per unit. This leaves the vertical intercept unchanged but makes the slope of the budget –1.25, as depicted in the left panel.

(b) Suppose p_2 increases to \$2 per unit. This lowers the vertical intercept and flattens the slope of the budget from –2 to –1, as shown in the center panel.

(c) Suppose m decreases to \$6. This decreases both the horizontal and vertical intercepts but leaves the slope unchanged, as shown in the right panel.

2.3.1   Endowment budgets

Ms. i comes into the world with 4 apples and 3 bananas. We refer to this initial amount of the two goods as i's **individual endowment** and write this commodity bundle as $\omega^i = (4,3)$.[5] Suppose the price of an apple is \$1 and each banana is priced at \$2. Then we may think of the **value of an individual's endowment** as $(\$1 \times 4) + (\$2 \times 3) = \$10$ and refer to this as i's income, since this is the amount of money she would have if she sold all her apples and bananas. With this income of \$10, we can draw her budget line with slope –0.5 which is shown in Figure 2.5 with a thin blue line. If the price of an apple remains at \$1 but the price of a banana falls to \$1, then i's income becomes \$7 and the the budget line is steeper with a slope of –1, i.e., the budget line pivots around the individual endowment point as the relative price ratio changes.

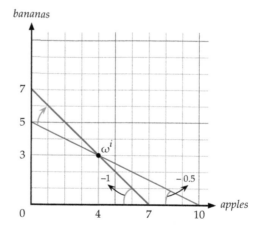

Figure 2.5   Budgets with endowments

---

[5]The Greek letter ω is read as 'omega'.

2.4 Non-Competitive Budgets

For a non-competitive budget, the price of at least one of the goods is not fixed for all units. Non-competitive budgets account for many real-world possibilities and we consider several examples below.

2.4.1 Price discounts on incremental purchases

Ms. j can buy the (divisible) goods 1 and 2 with her income of $120. The price of good 2 is fixed at $p_2 = \$6$ per unit. However, she receives a price discount for purchases in excess of 6 units of good 1: the price of good 1 is $p_1 = \$10$ per unit up to 6 units, and $6 per unit for each *subsequent* unit of good 1 or fraction thereof. This budget line is drawn in Figure 2.6. Note that it has a kink at point $A = (6, 10)$, reflecting the fact that the slope of the budget line is $-5/3$ when 6 or fewer units of good 1 are purchased, while it is -1 when more than 6 units are purchased.

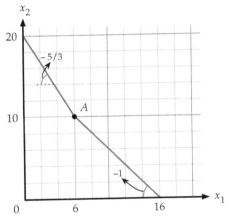

Figure 2.6 Incremental discount

2.4.2 Price discounts with bulk purchases

Suppose Ms. j's income is still $120 and p_2 remains at $6 per unit, but now p_1 is $10 per unit if she buys fewer than 6 units of good 1 and $6 per unit if she buys 6 units or more, i.e.,

$$p_1 = \begin{cases} \$10/\text{unit} & \text{if } x_1 < 6, \\ \$6/\text{unit} & \text{if } x_1 \geq 6. \end{cases}$$

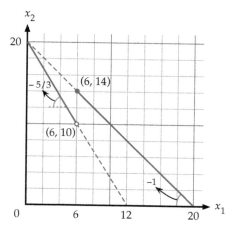

Figure 2.7   Bulk price discount

In other words, Ms. j receives a discounted per-unit price for good 1 when she buys a sufficiently large quantity, and this discount applies for *all* units of good 1 purchased.

This budget line is drawn as the two solid but broken blue lines in Figure 2.7. To figure this out, first draw what the budget would be if $p_1 = \$10$ regardless of the number of units of good 1 purchased: this is the line that goes from $(0, 20)$ to $(12, 0)$. Then draw the budget if $p_1 = \$6$ regardless of the number of units purchased, the line from $(0, 20)$ to $(20, 0)$. For fewer than 6 units of good 1 purchased, the lower budget line applies; for 6 or more units of good 1, the upper budget applies. Therefore, the budget line has a break (a jump-discontinuity) at $x_1 = 6$. Note that each linear piece has a slope given by the negative of the price ratio between the two goods that is applicable over that segment.

2.4.3   Buying and selling at different prices

Ms. k has just returned to the US from a business trip in Europe and discovers that she has €10 and $10 in her purse, so $w^k = (10, 10)$. Her foreign exchange dealer informs her that each euro has a purchase price that is different from its selling price: one euro can be purchased for $1.25 (i.e., a dollar and a quarter can be converted into one euro), but €1 can only be converted into $0.80.

The resulting budget line is then kinked at $(10, 10)$, as shown in Figure 2.8. Moving to the southeast from w^k, her budget has a slope of -1.25 when

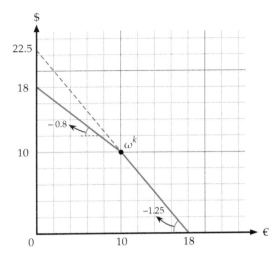

Figure 2.8 Buying and selling currencies

dollars are sold for euros. Moving northwest from ω^k along the solid blue line, Ms. k sells euros for dollars, so the budget line has a flatter slope of –0.8. If each euro could be sold for $1.25 instead, the 10 euros would be converted into $12.50, and the top kinked part would be replaced by the blue dashed line instead, resulting in a linear budget.

2.4.4   Food stamps

Suppose Ms. ℓ can purchase food (good 1) or clothing (good 2) at prices $p_1 = \$5$ and $p_2 = \$5$ per unit with her income of $m = \$100$. The government gives her an endowment of 4 food stamps where each stamp entitles her to one unit of food. We will assume that food, clothing and food stamps are divisible.

If she were to spend all her income purchasing clothing, she would be able to consume the bundle $B = (4, 20)$ thanks to the food stamps; conversely if she were to purchase only food, she would be able to afford the bundle $C = (24, 0)$ which is 4 more units of food than what she could buy with her income alone. Her budget set is then the shaded area bordered by ABC drawn in Figure 2.9, where some or all of the food stamps are unused along the line segment AB.

The presumption here is that Ms. ℓ cannot sell her food stamps. If food stamps could be sold for $5 each (i.e., at the same price as food), her budget would be the triangle bordered by $A'BC$, the bundles in the triangle

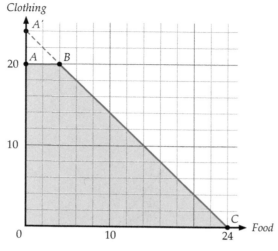

Figure 2.9   Food stamps

$A'AB$ now becoming attainable through the income derived from selling food stamps. If this were the case, then the impact of receiving food stamps is identical to an income transfer to her of $20. However, if food stamps could be sold only for a price which is less than the price of food (say, $4), then a $20 increase in income would be different from selling the 4 food stamps. We leave it to the reader to figure out the exact shape of the budget set in this case.

2.4.5   Newspaper coupons

Suppose Ms. h, who has income $m = \$10$ and normally can buy goods 1 and 2 for $1 each, cuts out a coupon from a Sunday newspaper that says: "Buy one unit of good 2 and get one free!" The fine print at the bottom of the coupon provides a clarification: "This coupon is valid for the purchase of a *single* unit of good 2." In other words, she can get at most one extra unit of good 2 by redeeming the coupon. Assuming as usual that both goods are divisible, her budget line is drawn in Figure 2.10.

To make sense of this broken budget line, suppose Ms. h spends all her $10 on good 1; in this case she will be at point A. If she spends less than a dollar on good 2, she will find herself on the segment AB since both goods are divisible. But, as soon as she spends a full dollar on good 2, she can redeem her coupon and obtain an additional unit of good 2 for free, so the bundle

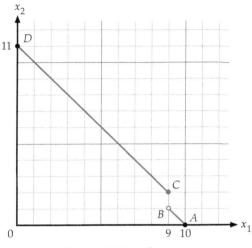

Figure 2.10   Coupons

she can afford is at $C = (9,2)$. Therefore, there is a jump-discontinuity at $B = (9,1)$. Reasoning in this manner, the rest of the budget line can be found to extend from C to D.

Exercises

2.1. Violet buys pies (x) and champagne (y) with her income of $100. The price of champagne is $p_y = 5 per bottle. Draw her budget constraints in each of the following cases assuming that both goods are divisible.

    (a) Pies cost $p_x = 5 per pie if she buys between zero and 10 pies, and $4 per pie if she buys more than 10 pies.

    (b) Pies cost $p_x = 5 per pie if she buys between zero and 10 pies; if she buys more than 10 pies, each *additional* pie or (fraction thereof) is half-price, i.e., $p_x = 2.50.

2.2. Wassilyovich wishes to spend all his weekly income of $10 on two goods x and y. Assume both goods are divisible. The price of each good is $1 per unit. Last Sunday he cut two coupons from the newspaper. One said "Buy one unit of y and get one free!" while the other said "Buy one unit of x and get one free!" Each coupon is good for the purchase of one unit of the respective good only. Draw Wassilyovich's budget constraint.

2.3. Kumar spends all his monthly income of $20 on two goods, rice ($x$) and cooking oil ($y$). The price of oil is $1 per liter. Rice can be purchased at a government-run store and also on the free market. The price of rice is $1 per kilogram at the government store but he can only buy up to 10 kgs. In the free market, the price of rice is $2 per kg. Draw Kumar's budget constraint assuming that the goods are divisible.

2.4. Harry is a stay-at-home father taking care of his two children. When he is not changing diapers or doing laundry, he can work online up to 18 hours in a day. Denote the number of hours he works by x. He receives a wage of $10 an hour up to 10 hours of work, and $15 an hour for every subsequent hour up to a maximum of 8 additional hours. He spends all the money he earns on food (y) which costs $1 per unit. Draw Harry's budget constraint assuming that x and y are divisible.

2.5. Augustin shops at a local food store where he buy chocolate bars (x) and bottles of spring water (y) *in whole units*. His income is $10; chocolate bars normally cost $2 per bar while spring water costs $1 per bottle.

(a) One day, he sees a sign at the store offering a special: "Buy one chocolate bar, get one free! No limits per customer." Draw his budget set, i.e., all combinations of x and y that Augustin can now afford.

(b) When Augustin returns to the store the next day, he finds that the store has decided to change its policy. The sign now says: "Buy one chocolate bar, get one free! Limit two per customer." Draw his budget set, i.e., all combinations of x and y that Augustin can now afford.

Chapter 3

Preferences

Preferences (or tastes) refer to a consumer's ability to compare or rank one commodity bundle over another. Because the idea of ranking one thing over another captures a relationship between two things, preferences are modeled using a mathematical concept called binary relations.[1] For example, in a gathering of family members, 'is a child of' relates any person with her or his mother or father, should they be present in the gathering. Here 'is a child of' is a binary relation that relates some family members. In the realm of numbers, 'is greater than' (the symbol '>') relates any two different numbers; in the realm of a social network such as Facebook, 'is a friend of' relates some pairs of individuals on the network but not others. In consumer theory, we will work in the realm of the commodity space, X, comparing pairs of consumption bundles.

3.1 Binary Relations

Different commodity bundles will be represented by letters A, B, C, etc. We will denote a binary relation by $\succsim$ to stand for 'is at least as good as' when comparing two bundles. So $A \succsim B$ means 'A is at least as good as B' when a consumer likes bundle A as much as bundle B. From this primitive relation, we derive two other relations:

(a) $\succ$ (read as 'is better than' or 'is preferred to'), and

(b) $\sim$ (read as 'is indifferent to').

---

[1] In the context of tastes, such a binary relation is sometimes called a preference relation.

When we write $A \succ B$ meaning that the consumer prefers A over B, it is a shorthand for writing '$A \succsim B$ *and not* $B \succsim A$'. Similarly, $C \sim D$ is a shorthand for '$C \succsim D$ *and* $D \succsim C$', meaning that the consumer is indifferent between C and D.[2] In other words, the relations of strict preference and indifference between commodity bundles are derived from the primitive idea of weak preference, $\succsim$. Henceforth, we will use the symbol $\succ$ to denote **strict prefer-ence**, $\sim$ for **indifference**, and $\succsim$ for **weak preference** (which could be either indifference or strict preference).

3.2   Properties of Binary Relations

There are five properties we would like the "at-least-as-good-as" relation $\succsim$ on a commodity space X to satisfy in order to capture a typical consumer's preferences.

3.2.1   Regular preferences

We begin with three basic properties that we expect preferences to satisfy. Any binary relation satisfying the three properties **P1–P3** below will be called **regular**.

> **P1** A binary relation $\succsim$ is **reflexive**: for any commodity bundle A in X, it must be the case that $A \succsim A$.

The property of reflexivity is something of a "sanity" requirement: for any "sane" person, it seems reasonable to require that any bundle must be at least as good as itself. This is an innocuous assumption that does not restrict a person's preferences much.

> **P2** A binary relation $\succsim$ is **total**: for any two different bundles A and B in X, it must be the case that one of the following is true:
>
> (1) $A \succsim B$, or
>
> (2) $B \succsim A$, or
>
> (3) both $A \succsim B$ and $B \succsim A$.

---

[2]The symbol $\succ$ is called the **asymmetric** part of $\succsim$, while $\sim$ is called the **symmetric** part of $\succsim$.

A total preference relation requires that any two different bundles in X can be compared. If only (1) above were to be true (so $A \succsim B$ but not the other way around), we say that $A \succ B$. If only (2) held, the reverse would be true: $B \succ A$. If (3) held, then we would say that $A \sim B$.

Therefore, to assume that **P2** holds is to claim that a consumer will be able to rank *any* two different bundles — say, a safari trip to Madagascar versus a skiing trip in the Alps — in one of these three ways, even when she has had no prior experience with either or has no basis for ranking them. This of course may be too much to expect in reality! If a person is unable to make such a ranking, we say her preference relation is partial: she may be able to compare *some* bundles and rank them, but she cannot rank *all* pairs of bundles.[3]

> **P3** A binary relation $\succsim$ is transitive: for any three different bundles A, B and C in X, whenever $A \succsim B$ and $B \succsim C$, it must be the case that $A \succsim C$ is true.

Transitivity of a preference relation lies at the heart of our intuitive notion of rationality: we expect a "rational" consumer's preferences to satisfy **P3** which requires that if one bundle is at least as good as a second, and this second bundle is at least as good as a third, then the first must be at least as good as the third. So if a person likes a serving of icecream over a popsicle, and a popsicle over a glass of Kool-Aid, then transitive preferences imply that she must like the icecream over the Kool-Aid.[4]

Note that property **P1** compares a bundle to itself, **P2** compares two different bundles, and **P3** compares three or more bundles in a pairwise fashion.

3.2.2 Monotonicity

The fourth property that we expect preferences to satisfy is fairly intuitive and captures the idea that "goods are good": more of a desirable commodity cannot make a consumer worse off.

---

[3]A binary relation is said to be complete if it is both reflexive and total. Some economists prefer to replace **P1** and **P2** with completeness instead.

[4]Whether people's preferences in reality are transitive or not is an empirical issue. While it may certainly be true that both assumptions **P2** and **P3** are unrealistic, it is standard practice to maintain these assumptions at this level — presenting consumer theory without these assumptions is possible, but beyond the scope of an intermediate-level class.

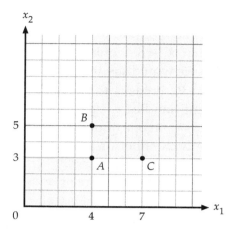

Figure 3.1   Monotonicity

P4 A binary relation $\succsim$ is **monotonic**: for any two bundles A and B in X, if A contains at least as much of each good as bundle B and more of at least one good, then **weak monotonicity** implies $A \succsim B$, whereas **strict monotonicity** implies $A \succ B$.

Weak monotonicity is the idea that having more of at least one good in bundle A as compared to B should not make the consumer worse off: either the consumer is indifferent between A and B, or she prefers A over B. On the other hand, strict monotonicity means that having more of at least one good makes the consumer strictly better off, i.e., she strictly prefers the bundle A over B.

In Figure 3.1, given bundle $A = (4, 3)$, monotonic preferences imply that any bundle to the northeast of A lying in the shaded blue area (including any bundle exactly north of A such as $B = (4, 5)$, as well as to its east such as $C = (7, 3)$) leaves the consumer as well off (in the case of weak monotonicity) or better off (in the case of strict monotonicity). So (weak) monotonicity of preferences captures the idea that more is never worse and could actually be better. Once again, this may or may not be true in real life. For example, if good 1 is icecream and good 2 is chocolate, eating too much of either good might make a consumer sick (i.e., worse off), so more is not necessarily better.[5]

---

[5] Also note that when one or both commodities is a 'bad' instead of a good — garbage, for instance — more is not better.

Monotonicity of preferences helps to determine the direction in which preferences are increasing and also the direction in which they are decreasing. For instance, in Figure 3.1, any point to the northeast of A is better (or at least not worse), while every point to the southwest of A in the pink shaded area is worse (or at least not better). So with strictly monotonic preferences, a bundle that is indifferent to A must lie either in the northwest quadrant or in the southeast quadrant from A.

3.2.3 Convexity

This assumption on preferences is *not* obvious and is somewhat technical in nature. We introduce it at this point for the sake of completeness. It will be discussed in detail in section 3.6.3.

> **P5** A binary relation $\succsim$ is **convex**: for any two bundles A and B in X where $B \succsim A$, if C is any bundle on the line segment joining bundles A and B, then $C \succsim A$.

This requirement states that if B is a bundle that is at least as good as A, then any weighted average of the commodities in bundles A and B cannot be worse than A.

3.3 Utility Representation of Preferences

Preferences as binary relations are somewhat abstract and hard to visualize. One way to make them concrete is to focus on preferences that can be represented by a **utility function**. A utility function u attaches a number to each commodity bundle so that $A \succsim B$ means that the number or 'utility' attached to bundle A is at least as large as the number attached to bundle B: $A \succsim B$ implies $u(A) \geq u(B)$, and vice versa.[6]

If there is a utility function that represents a consumer's preferences, then whenever this consumer ranks $P \succ Q$, it must be that $u(P) > u(Q)$ and vice versa; similarly, whenever $R \sim S$, it must be that $u(R) = u(S)$ and vice versa. In other words, a utility function maintains the same ranking between any two bundles as that given by the underlying preference relation: $\geq$ for $\succsim$, $>$ for $\succ$, and $=$ for $\sim$.

---

[6]You may, for now, think of the number associated with a bundle as the level of satisfaction or "utility" from that bundle measured in some mythical units called 'utils'. But as you will see in section 3.5, this interpretation is neither necessary, nor is it our preferred interpretation.

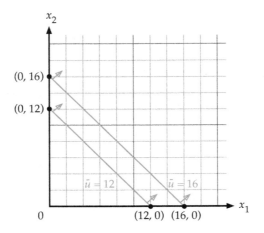

Figure 3.2 Indifference curves

To visualize what preferences look like when they can be represented by a utility function, consider the utility function $u(x_1, x_2) = x_1 + x_2$. Here good 1 is white eggs while good 2 is brown eggs and, at the risk of having a messy kitchen, we will assume as usual that they are both divisible. Since the utility of this consumer is the sum of the two goods, what the consumer cares about is not the color of the eggs but the total *number* of eggs. Suppose this consumer is baking a cake and needs a dozen eggs, i.e., her utility is fixed at $\bar{u} = 12$. Then the combinations of white and brown eggs that yield utility 12 constitute an **indifference curve** given implicitly by the equation $x_1 + x_2 = 12$ and drawn in Figure 3.2 as the line from $(0, 12)$ to $(12, 0)$.

An indifference curve joins all combinations of goods that give the consumer the same utility level. In this instance, if the consumer needs a dozen eggs to bake a cake, she does not care whether they are white or brown so long as they add up to 12. So a white egg here is a perfect $1 : 1$ substitute for one brown egg, as can be inferred from the slope of the indifference curve of −1.

Note that the indifference curve that yields $\bar{u} = 16$ lies to the right of the first one. In fact, we can draw infinitely many indifference curves (all parallel to each other in this instance and having a slope of -1) for different levels of $\bar{u}$. Indifference curves that yield a higher utility lie to the northeast of the original indifference curve; similarly, those that yield a lower utility must lie to the southwest. So we attach arrows to the indifference curves to show the direction in which utility is increasing. no two indifference curves can cross because then the bundle where the two intersect would simultaneously yield two different utility levels, which is impossible.

The family of all possible indifference curves taken together constitute the consumer's preferences. Specifically, the family of these linear indifference curves are an instance of linear preferences that we will cover in more detail in section 3.4.1.

3.3.1 Marginal rate of substitution

We refer to the magnitude (i.e., the absolute value) of the slope of an indifference curve at a point as the marginal rate of substitution of good 1 for good 2 (abbreviated as MRS_{12} or just MRS) at that point. The marginal rate of substitution shows how much x_2 a consumer is willing to give up in exchange for one unit of x_1 so as to remain on the same indifference curve. In the case of the utility function above, one brown egg can always be replaced by one white egg without affecting the utility level, so the marginal rate of substitution is a constant 1 at any point along any indifference curve.

In general, the MRS is given by the ratio of the marginal utilities:

$$MRS = \frac{MU_1}{MU_2},\tag{3.1}$$

where $MU_1 = \partial u/\partial x_1$ is the marginal utility of good 1 at a specific point on the indifference curve, and $MU_2 = \partial u/\partial x_2$ is that for good 2 at the same point. The marginal utility of good 1 shows the additional satisfaction from increasing the consumption of good 1, keeping the consumption of good 2 fixed.[7]

---

[7]Equation (3.1) can be derived using some calculus. First, fix the indifference curve of interest by setting $u(x_1, x_2) = \bar{u}$, and then take its total differential (see section A.5.2 in the Mathematical appendix):

$$d\bar{u} = \frac{\partial u}{\partial x_1}dx_1 + \frac{\partial u}{\partial x_2}dx_2.$$

Since we are moving along an indifference curve where the utility level remains the same, the change in the utility level $d\bar{u} = 0$. Substituting zero on the left hand side and rearranging we get

$$-\frac{dx_2}{dx_1} = \frac{\partial u/\partial x_1}{\partial u/\partial x_2},$$

where the left hand side is the negative of the slope of the indifference curve and the right hand side is the ratio of the marginal utilities in equation (3.1).

3.4   Types of Preferences

We introduce four types of utility functions that are commonly used in economics and which show up in many applications.

3.4.1   Linear preferences

Linear preferences can be represented by the utility function

$$u(x_1, x_2) = ax_1 + bx_2 \tag{3.2}$$

where a and b are arbitrary constants and give rise to linear indifference curves. When a and b are positive, indicating positive marginal utilities, both goods are desirable and the preferences are captured by negatively sloping linear indifference curves as shown in the left panel of Figure 3.3. Fixing the utility level at $\bar{u}$, a typical indifference curve has a vertical intercept of $\bar{u}/b$, a horizontal intercept of $\bar{u}/a$, and a slope of $-a/b$. The arrows pointing to the northeast show the direction in which utility is increasing. The marginal rate of substitution at any point on any indifference curve is a constant a/b, showing that a units of x_2 need to be substituted by b units of x_1 in order to remain on the same indifference curve. Preferences like these are therefore called **perfect substitutes**.

If both a and b are negative, both commodities are 'bads' and undesirable (such as garbage and nuclear waste), so utility increases in the southwest di-

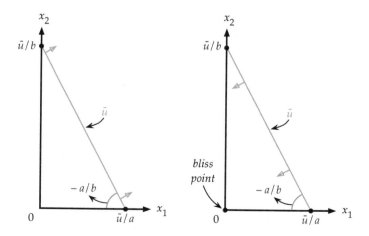

Figure 3.3   Linear preferences with goods and bads

rection, as shown by the reversed preference arrows in the right panel of Figure 3.3. The marginal rate of substitution is still a/b, so the bads are still perfect substitutes for each other. If these bads cannot be consumed in negative amounts, then the origin $(0,0)$ yields the highest utility possible. A commodity bundle that yields a maximum utility is called a **bliss point** or a point of **satiation**.

If $a > 0$ but $b = 0$ so $u(x_1, x_2) = ax_1$, then this consumer does not care about the quantity of good 2 at all. Here good 2 is called a **neutral** good and the indifference curves are vertical as shown in the left panel of Figure 3.4. Alternatively, if $a = 0$ but $b > 0$, then $u(x_1, x_2) = bx_2$ and good 1 is now the neutral good with the indifference curves being horizontal as shown in the right panel of Figure 3.4. Once again arrows indicate the direction in which utility increases.

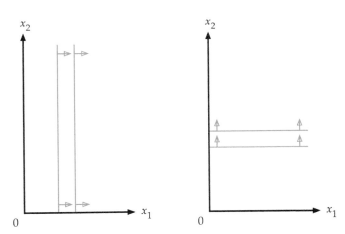

Figure 3.4   Linear preferences with neutrals

3.4.2   Leontief preferences

Leontief preferences refer to tastes when goods are **perfect complements** in consumption, i.e., they are consumed in fixed proportions, as in the case of four tires to each car, or a cup of milk to each bowl of cereal.

Suppose good 1 is cups of coffee and good 2 teaspoons of sugar. Nguyen, who is quite inflexible in how she likes her coffee, has Leontief preferences over coffee and sugar given by the utility function

$$u(x_1, x_2) = \min\{x_1, 0.5x_2\}. \tag{3.3}$$

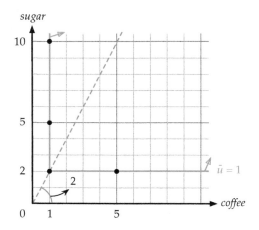

Figure 3.5   A Leontief indifference curve

If Nguyen wants to attain a utility level of $\bar{u} = 1$, she can reach this utility level from the combination $(1,2)$, which can be figured out by substituting these values into equation (3.3) and taking the minimum of the two numbers. The same utility can also be attained by the bundle $(1,5)$ or $(1,10)$: for 1 cup of coffee, any additional teaspoons of sugar beyond 2 are wasted and do not add to Nguyen's utility. Plugging $(5,2)$ into the utility function also yields a utility level of 1 because the 2 teaspoons of sugar are only adequate for 1 cup of coffee. The remaining 4 cups do not provide her with any satisfaction because they do not have adequate amounts of sugar to go with them. Therefore, all of these points — $(1,2)$, $(1,5)$, $(1,10)$, and $(5,2)$ — lie on the same indifference curve, shown in Figure 3.5.

The shape of Nguyen's indifference curve is the result of her preference to combine two teaspoons of sugar for every cup of coffee — no substitution between teaspoons of sugar and cups of coffee are possible, so the notion of marginal rate of substitution is meaningless in the case of perfect complements. As a check of your understanding, draw another indifference curve for the utility level $\bar{u} = 3$ in Figure 3.5.

A general functional form that represents such preferences is given by the utility

$$u(x_1, x_2) = \min\{ax_1, bx_2\}, \tag{3.4}$$

where a and b are positive constants. Figure 3.6 shows two generic indifference curves for such a utility function. Note that the kinks of this family of indifference curves lie on a ray through the origin with slope a/b, signifying

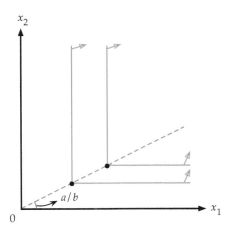

Figure 3.6 Leontief preferences

that the two goods are consumed in a proportion of b units of good 1 to a units of good 2.

There is a simple algorithm for drawing indifference curves for any 'min'-type utility function. To illustrate, suppose $u(x_1, x_2) = \min\{2x_1, 3x_2\}$ and we wish to draw the indifference curve for $\bar{u} = 6$. Follow these four steps:

1. Write $6 = \min\{2x_1, 3x_2\}$.

2. Solve each piece separately: from $6 = 2x_1$, obtain $x_1 = 3$, and from $6 = 3x_2$, obtain $x_2 = 2$.

3. Plot each piece, $x_1 = 3$ and $x_2 = 2$, as shown in Figure 3.7.

4. Take the 'outer envelope' of the lines, erasing the pieces to the south-west of $(3, 2)$, shown with the serrated lines. The line segments that remain constitute the indifference curve for $\bar{u} = 6$.

You can verify that this is indeed the desired indifference curve by plug-ging in the (x_1, x_2) coordinates from the line segments that have not been erased to check that they yield $\bar{u} = 6$. Likewise, verify that any coordinate which was crossed out, say $(0, 2)$, does not yield the desired utility level.

While the steps above are written for a specific Leontief utility function, they are easily generalized for *any* 'min'-type utility function.

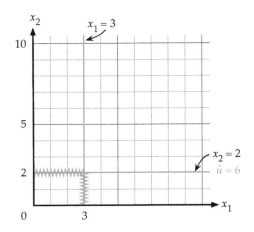

Figure 3.7   Drawing Leontief indifference curves

3.4.3   Quasilinear preferences

Suppose a utility function is of the form

$$u(x_1, x_2) = f(x_1) + x_2 \tag{3.5}$$

where the function $f(x_1)$ is strictly concave[8] in x_1 and linear in x_2, hence the name **quasilinear preferences**.

In Figure 3.8, quasilinear indifference curves are drawn for $u(x_1, x_2) = \sqrt{x_1} + x_2$ which show the possibility of substitution between x_1 and x_2. The marginal rate of substitution is $MRS = MU_1/MU_2 = 1/(2\sqrt{x_1})$ which does not depend on the level of x_2. For *any* given level of x_1, say $x_1 = 4$, the $MRS = 1/4$ regardless of the value of x_2 as shown by the slopes at A, B, C, and D. This means that all the indifference curves are 'vertically parallel': each indifference curve is essentially identical except vertically displaced. Analogously, a quasilinear utility of the form $u(x_1, x_2) = x_1 + g(x_2)$ with $g'' < 0$ has 'horizontally parallel' indifference curves. Thus the indifference curves for quasilinear preferences are either vertically or horizontally parallel.

In the case of preferences with vertically parallel indifference curves given by equation (3.5), $f'(x_1)$ decreases as x_1 increases when $f(x_1)$ is strictly concave. Since $MRS = f'(x_1)$ here, as we move from left to right along an indifference curve and the quantity of x_1 increases, there is diminishing marginal

---

[8]If the second derivative $f''(x) < 0$ for all $x > 0$, this guarantees that the function f is strictly concave in x. See section A.3 in the Mathematical appendix.

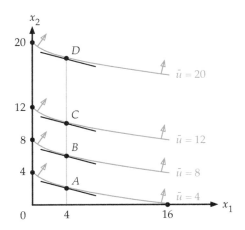

Figure 3.8   Quasilinear preferences

rates of substitution. A similar logic also holds in the case of horizontally parallel indifference curves when $u(x_1, x_2) = x_1 + g(x_2)$. Verify that the marginal rate of substitution now depends only on x_2 and is also decreasing because $g(x_2)$ is strictly concave and the quantity of x_2 decreases as we move from left to right along an indifference curve.

3.4.4 Cobb-Douglas preferences

Another type of preferences that allow for substitution possibilities are **Cobb-Douglas preferences** which are represented by the utility function of the form

$$u(x_1, x_2) = Ax_1^a x_2^b, \tag{3.6}$$

where a, b and A are positive constants. In Figure 3.9, we draw some of the indifference curves for the utility function $u(x_1, x_2) = x_1 x_2$. Note that the indifference curve for $\bar{u} = 0$ is the L-shaped indifference curve that coincides with the horizontal and vertical axes and has a kink at the origin. All indifference curves for positive levels of utility are smooth and allow continuous substitution possibilities between the two goods.

In general, $MU_1 = Aax_1^{a-1}x_2^b$ and $MU_2 = Abx_1^a x_2^{b-1}$, so the marginal rate of substitution is

$$MRS = \frac{ax_2}{bx_1}. \tag{3.7}$$

As one moves along an indifference curve, say, from A to A′ in Figure 3.9, the MRS decreases since x_2 decreases in the numerator while x_1 increases in the

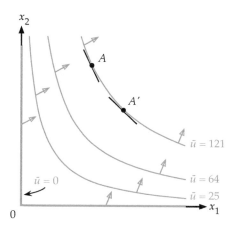

Figure 3.9   Cobb-Douglas preferences

denominator. Therefore, there is diminishing marginal rate of substitution for both quasilinear and Cobb-Douglas utilities.

3.5   The Notion of Utility

Given that a consumer's preferences can be represented by a utility function, how is one to interpret the notion of the associated 'utility level' of each consumption bundle? It turns out that the *level* of utility itself has no special significance so long as the preference ranking between any pairs of bundles is retained.

   This more subtle but important idea can be illustrated by the following example. Let u represent a consumer's preferences. We construct a new utility function v, where $v = 2u$. Suppose there are two bundles A and B such that $A \succsim B$. Then, by definition of the utility function u, it must be that $u(A) \geq u(B)$, which in turn implies that $2u(A) \geq 2u(B)$, or $v(A) \geq v(B)$. Thus v retains the same ranking over A and B as u, even though the utility *level* under the function v is twice that of the level under u. Because both u and v represent the same preferences, both u and v will generate the *same* collection of indifference curves. The only difference between them is the label attached to each bundle: if the level of utility of a particular bundle is 10 under the utility u, then under v it will be 20 (twice as much) instead. But this difference is irrelevant from the viewpoint of preferences since u and v retain the same ranking between any two bundles. Therefore, the notion of utility in economics is ordinal, not cardinal, where ordinality refers to the *ranking* (such as first, second, third, etc.) while cardinality refers to the *level* (such as 1, 2, 3, etc.).

The function $v = 2u$ is of course not the only one that preserves the ranking of the utility function, u. In general, any function $v = f(u)$ where the slope $dv/du = f' > 0$ when $u > 0$ will also be a utility representation of the same preferences. Such a function is called a positive monotonic transformation of the utility u. Verify that the following functions are all examples of positive monotonic transformations of u and thus represent the same preferences as u:

(a) $v = u^r$ for $r > 0$;

(b) $v = \ln u$;

(c) $v = au + b$ where $a > 0$;

(d) $v = e^u$.

Therefore, given the utility function $u(x_1, x_2) = x_1 + x_2$, the set of indifference curves which constitute the underlying preferences will not change if we transform this utility function to $v(x_1, x_2) = (x_1 + x_2)^2$ or $v(x_1, x_2) = \sqrt{x_1 + x_2}$; all of them generate the same family of linear indifference curves with slope -1.

Similarly, given a Cobb-Douglas utility $u(x_1, x_2) = x_1^a x_2^b$, the logarithmic transformation $v(x_1, x_2) = a \ln x_1 + b \ln x_2$ will generate the same set of indifference curves as the original utility function. Yet another common transformation of the Cobb-Douglas utility is $v = u^r$ where $r = 1/(a + b)$, i.e.,

$$v(x_1, x_2) = x_1^{\frac{a}{a+b}} x_2^{\frac{b}{a+b}} = x_1^\alpha x_2^{1-\alpha}$$

where $\alpha = a/(a + b)$. Therefore, the utility $u(x_1, x_2) = x_1^2 x_2$ generates the same indifference curves as the transformed utility $v(x_1, x_2) = x_1^{2/3} x_2^{1/3}$; they are two different ways of representing the *same* preferences.

An important point to note is that given a utility function, the marginal rate of substitution at any point on an indifference curve remains unchanged under positive monotonic transformations of the utility function. To see this, consider a utility function $u(x_1, x_2)$ and fix a commodity bundle $(\bar{x}_1, \bar{x}_2)$. At $(\bar{x}_1, \bar{x}_2)$, the marginal rate of substitution from (3.1) can be written as

$$MRS^u(\bar{x}_1, \bar{x}_2) = \frac{\partial u(\bar{x}_1, \bar{x}_2)}{\partial x_1} \bigg/ \frac{\partial u(\bar{x}_1, \bar{x}_2)}{\partial x_2}, \tag{3.8}$$

where the u-superscript on the lefthand side is a reminder that this is the MRS under the original utility u.

Now suppose $v = f(u)$ is a positive monotonic transformation of u. The marginal rate of substitution at the same bundle under the new utility v is then given by

$$MRS^v(\bar{x}_1, \bar{x}_2) = \frac{\partial v(\bar{x}_1, \bar{x}_2)}{\partial x_1} \bigg/ \frac{\partial v(\bar{x}_1, \bar{x}_2)}{\partial x_2}. \qquad (3.9)$$

But using the Chain Rule, we can write

$$\frac{\partial v(\bar{x}_1, \bar{x}_2)}{\partial x_1} = f'(u)\frac{\partial u(\bar{x}_1, \bar{x}_2)}{\partial x_1},$$

and similarly for $\partial v(\bar{x}_1, \bar{x}_2)/\partial x_2$. Therefore, equation (3.9) can be rewritten as

$$MRS^v(\bar{x}_1, \bar{x}_2) = \frac{f'(u)\partial u(\bar{x}_1, \bar{x}_2)/\partial x_1}{f'(u)\partial u(\bar{x}_1, \bar{x}_2)/\partial x_2} = MRS^u(\bar{x}_1, \bar{x}_2) \qquad (3.10)$$

because the positive $f'(u)$ term in the numerator and denominator cancel out.

3.6   Utility, Preferences and Properties

When preferences can be represented by a utility function, which of the properties **P1–P5** of preferences are satisfied in general? What specific properties do the four types of utility functions introduced in section 3.4 have? These questions are explored in this section.

3.6.1   Regularity of preferences

If a consumer's preferences can be represented by a utility function, then properties **P1–P3** hold automatically, i.e., the preferences must be regular (reflexive, total and transitive). This is always true for *any* utility function, not just the ones introduced in section 3.4.

To see this, note that for any bundle A, given a utility function u, it is trivially true that $u(A) = u(A)$, which implies that $A \succsim A$ and so the preferences must be reflexive.

For any two different bundles A and B, three cases are possible: either $u(A) > u(B)$, or $u(B) > u(A)$, or $u(A) = u(B)$. The first case implies that $A \succ B$; in the second case, $B \succ A$; and in the last case, $A \sim B$. This establishes that the preferences are total.

Finally, for any three bundles A, B, and C, if $A \succsim B$ and $B \succsim C$ is true, then by definition $u(A) \geq u(B)$ and $u(B) \geq u(C)$. Concatenating these two inequalities, it follows that $u(A) \geq u(C)$, which implies that $A \succsim C$ as transitivity requires.

3.6.2 Monotonicity of preferences

Monotonicity guarantees that more of one or both goods cannot make a consumer worse off. Strict monotonicity guarantees that more of one or both goods definitely make a consumer better off; it also rules out *thick* indifference curves. Thick indifference curves may arise, for example, from cognitive limitations since they imply that there is a range of bundles over which the consumer cannot discern a difference, for instance between a cup of coffee with 2 teaspoons of sugar on the one hand, and a cup of coffee with 2.5 teaspoons of sugar. Therefore she is indifferent between any bundle with one cup of coffee and amounts of sugar ranging from 2 to 2.5 teaspoons. Strict monotonicity rules out such preferences from consideration.

For the four types of preferences introduced in section 3.4, linear preferences with positive values for a and b are strictly monotonic — verify that ◀ ◿ more of either good leaves the consumer on a higher indifference curve. However, if one of the goods is a neutral (as in Figure 3.4), the preferences are only guaranteed to be weakly monotonic: more of just one good is no longer sufficient to leave the consumer on a higher indifference curve.

Since Leontief preferences allow for the good to be neutral along a horizontal or vertical segment of an indifference curve, it follows that these preferences too are weakly monotonic, not strictly monotonic. Quasilinear preferences are strictly monotonic. Cobb-Douglas preferences, on the other hand, are strictly monotonic so long as positive amounts of *both* goods are consumed. For example, along the horizontal axis good 2 is not consumed, so the Cobb-Douglas utility is always zero, even if more of good 1 is consumed (see Figure 3.9). A similar logic holds along the vertical axis.

3.6.3 Convexity of preferences

Recall that a set is said to be convex if the line segment joining *any* two points in that set lies within the set.[9] If this line lies strictly in the interior of the set,

---

[9]See section A.7.1 in the Mathematical appendix.

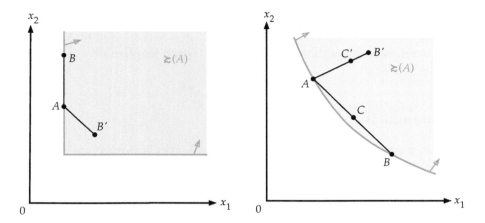

Figure 3.10   Convex and strictly convex preferences

we say that the set is strictly convex; if some part of the line overlaps with the boundary, we say the set is convex.

Now suppose a consumer with Leontief preferences picks any bundle A. In Figure 3.10, draw the indifference curve that goes through A and then shade the set of bundles that are at least as good as A. The shaded set $\succsim(A)$ is called the **weakly-better-than set** of A, i.e., the set of bundles that are at least as good as A.[10] Convex preferences then require that the set $\succsim(A)$ be a convex set. Verify that $\succsim(A)$ is a convex set by picking any point like B where $B \sim A$, or B' where $B' \succ A$. This has to be true no matter where the initial A point happens to be.

All four types of preferences introduced in section 3.4 are convex. Linear and Leontief utilities represent convex preferences since the weakly-better-than sets have linear segments as shown in the left panel of Figure 3.10 in the case of Leontief preferences.

Quasilinear and Cobb-Douglas utilities, however, represent **strictly convex preferences**: any bundle that lies in the line segment between some point A and some other point B (so long as $B \succsim A$) *must* leave the consumer on a higher indifference curve. In the right panel of Figure 3.10, this is shown when preferences are Cobb-Douglas. The bundle $B \sim A$, and any point like C that lies on the line segment joining them, must lie on a higher indifference curve, so $C \succ A$. Similarly, with bundle $B' \succ A$, a point like C' that lies on the line segment joining them is also preferred to A.

---

[10]The weakly-better-than set is also known as the **weak upper contour set**.

There are two justifications that economists give for requiring preferences to be (strictly) convex. The first is that consumers prefer 'combinations' to 'extremes'. In the right panel of Figure 3.10, suppose A is one 'extreme' bundle, consisting of 2 units of food and 6 of water, while point $B = (6, 2)$ is another 'extreme' with lots of food and little water. Then strictly convex preferences guarantee that a consumer will prefer point $C = (4, 4)$, the average of the A and B bundles, over either of the extreme bundles.

The second justification is that consumers have diminishing marginal rates of substitution. In Figure 3.11, as a consumer incrementally increases her consumption of good 1 by single units in moving from A to B to C to D to E along one indifference curve, she gives up less and less amounts of good 2 (as shown by the magenta dotted heights a, b, c, and d, where $a > b > c > d$). Thus strictly convex preferences embody diminishing marginal rates of substitution.

But why is it reasonable for a consumer to have diminishing marginal rates of substitution? The intuitive idea is that people tend to place a lower value on goods that they have in relative abundance. So at A, because she has relatively more of good 2, she is willing to give up the amount a to acquire one unit of good 1. But at B, while she *still* has relatively more of good 2, it is not as relatively abundant as before. So in moving to C, she is only willing to give up $b < a$ units of good 2.

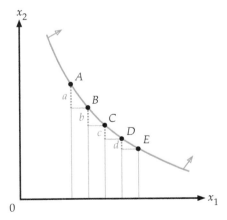

Figure 3.11 Diminishing marginal rate of substitution

3.7   Special Topics°

In this section, we present some optional material which is useful to have as a source of reference.

3.7.1   Preferences without utility representations

We began with our discussion of preferences as binary relations that satisfy **P1–P5** and then went on to introduce utility functions that represent those binary relations in order to better visualize preferences as families of indifference curves. But can *all* preference relations that satisfy properties **P1–P5** be represented by some utility function? The answer is no. While many preferences have utility representations, the notion of a preference relation is more general and there are many that cannot be so represented. One important class of such preferences is lexicographic preferences.

Lexicographic binary relations have a built-in hierarchy that dictates what a person cares about first, what she cares about second, and so on.[11] Parents who feed their children first before they feed themselves exhibit such a hierarchy where the needs of their children come first and then their own.

To illustrate, suppose a consumer's commodity space consists of bundles of food (f) and units of shelter (s) where she cares about food first and then shelter. Let $\succsim_L$ (read as 'is lexicographically at least as good as') denote her lexicographic binary relation. Then given the bundles (f_1, s_1) and (f_2, s_2), $(f_2, s_2) \succsim_L (f_1, s_1)$ means either

(a) $f_2 \geq f_1$ regardless of the values of s_1 and s_2, or

(b) $f_2 = f_1$ and $s_2 \geq s_1$.

This definition says that in comparing two bundles, this consumer first looks at the amount of food. A bundle with more food is always preferred. If two bundles have the same amount of food, then the one which provides more shelter is preferred.

In Figure 3.12, to determine whether B is lexicographically better than A, check the amount of food first. Bundle B has 6 units of food as opposed to A's 4, therefore $B \succsim_L A$. Now compare bundle C to A. Both have the same

---

[11]The psychologist Abraham Maslow's hierarchy of human needs is such an example. According to him, the primary concern of humans is meeting physiological needs (food, water, sleep etc.), followed by security needs (shelter, employment, health, etc.), social needs (family, friendship, etc.), the need for esteem, and the need for self-actualization.

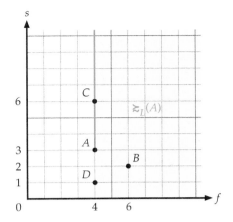

Figure 3.12   Lexicographic preferences

amount of food, so check the units of shelter. Since C has 6 units of shelter as opposed to A's 3 units, $C \succsim_L A$.

As an exercise, determine this consumer's ranking between A and D, B and D, and B and C. Verify that the only bundle that is indifferent to A is A itself; any other point is either preferred to A, or A is preferred to it. Therefore there are no indifference curves here, just indifference points.

It is instructive to derive the weakly-better-than set of A for this lexicographic preference, shaded in Figure 3.12. The weakly-better-than set $\succsim_L(A)$ includes the point A and all points with values of shelter greater than 3, and all bundles with more than 4 units of food.

3.7.2   Two more properties of preferences

We introduce two more properties of preferences that are somewhat technical: **continuity** and **homotheticity**. While all preferences encountered in subsequent chapters will be continuous, not all will be homothetic.

Continuity

In section 3.6.3, we introduced the the weakly-better-than set. Analogously, we define a **weakly-worse-than set** of A, denoted by $\precsim(A)$, to consist of all bundles that A is at least as good as. For the preferences in the right panel of Figure 3.10 which shows the weakly-better-than set of A, we now show the weakly-worse-than set of A in Figure 3.13.

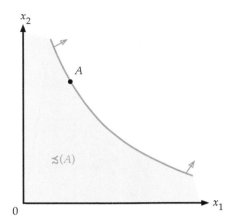

Figure 3.13   The $\precsim(A)$ set

Before defining what we mean by continuous preferences, we need another definition: a set is said to be **closed** if it contains all of its boundary points.[12]

> **P6** A binary relation $\succsim$ is **continuous**: for every bundle A in X, the sets $\succsim(A)$ and $\precsim(A)$ sets are closed.

Thus continuous preferences have closed weakly-worse-than and weakly-better-than sets. Continuity of preferences captures the notion that small changes in satisfaction can only result from small changes in consumption bundles.

Check that all the preferences that can be represented by utility functions considered in section 3.4 are continuous. However, the lexicographic preference from section 3.7.1 is not. To see this, consider the $\succsim_L(A)$ set drawn in Figure 3.12. Here the point $D = (4, 1)$ for instance is a boundary point of $\succsim_L(A)$ but is not contained in $\succsim_L(A)$. Hence, $\succsim_L(A)$ is not a closed set and therefore the lexicographic preference is not continuous.

Homotheticity

This is a property of indifference curves, i.e., the preferences must be representable by a utility function.

---

[12]This is not meant to be a precise mathematical definition, but to convey the intuition behind the definition.

P7 A binary relation $\succsim$ is **homothetic**: for every bundle $(\bar{x}_1, \bar{x}_2)$ in X, the $MRS(\bar{x}_1, \bar{x}_2) = MRS(t\bar{x}_1, t\bar{x}_2)$ for all $t > 0$.

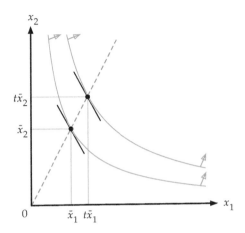

Figure 3.14 Homothetic preferences

Preferences are homothetic if the marginal rates of substitution along any ray through the origin are the same. This property is illustrated graphically in Figure 3.14 for Cobb-Douglas preferences. To derive this algebraically, recall from (3.7) that at the point $(\bar{x}_1, \bar{x}_2)$,

$$MRS(\bar{x}_1, \bar{x}_2) = \frac{a\bar{x}_2}{b\bar{x}_1}.$$

But at the point $(t\bar{x}_1, t\bar{x}_2)$ along the ray from the origin through $(\bar{x}_1, \bar{x}_2)$,

$$MRS(t\bar{x}_1, t\bar{x}_2) = \frac{at\bar{x}_2}{bt\bar{x}_1} = \frac{a\bar{x}_2}{b\bar{x}_1} = MRS(\bar{x}_1, \bar{x}_2),$$

since $t > 0$.

Linear preferences are also homothetic (the marginal rates of substitution are all the same at *any* point on *any* indifference curve, so they must be the same along any ray through the origin in particular) but quasilinear preferences are not.

Exercises

3.1. Richard is an old-fashioned Englishman who likes his tea with milk and sugar. Though he prefers more sugar to less, he cannot always distinguish between two cups unless the difference in the amount of sugar is less than a third ($< 1/3$) or more than one teaspoon (> 1). If there are two cups of tea where the difference is between a third and one teaspoon of sugar, he is indifferent ($\sim$) between them.

(a) Is Richard's strict preference relation ($\succ$) reflexive, total and transitive? Explain why or why not for each property.

(b) Is Richard's indifference relation ($\sim$) reflexive, total and transitive? Explain why or why not for each property.

(c) Is Richard's weak preference relation ($\succsim$) reflexive, total and transitive? Explain why or why not for each property.

3.2. In Sichuan province in China, 1 black cat catches 5 mice, while 1 white cat catches 10 mice. Assuming that cats are not divisible and that a consumer only cares about how many mice are caught, draw one indifference curve between black cats and white cats for catching 40 mice and one for 50 mice.

3.3. If the 'parent' binary relation $\succsim$ is transitive, what does it imply about its 'offspring', $\succ$ and $\sim$? Prove the following results.

(a) If $P \succ Q$ and $Q \succ R$, then $P \succ R$.

(b) If $P \sim Q$ and $Q \sim R$, then $P \sim R$.

(c) If $P \succ Q$ and $Q \sim R$, then $P \succ R$.

(d) If $P \sim Q$ and $Q \succ R$, then $P \succ R$.

(*Hint*: Recall that $A \succ B$ means both $A \succsim B$ and not $B \succsim A$, while $A \sim B$ means both $A \succsim B$ and $B \succsim A$. So in part (a), for example, to establish $P \succ R$, you need to show that $P \succsim R$ and not $R \succsim P$.)

3.4. Three friends, Anton, Bertil and Cecil, wish to go out for lunch together. Their choices are between a pizzeria (P), a sandwich place (S), or a Chinese restaurant (C). Each person's preference ranking over these three alternatives is regular and is given in the table below.

Anton	Bertil	Cecil
C	P	S
S	S	P
P	C	C

For example, Anton strictly prefers the Chinese restaurant over the sandwich place, the sandwich place over the pizzeria, and also the Chinese restaurant over the pizzeria (because his preferences are transitive). From these individual rankings, we want to construct an overall *social ranking* based on pairwise comparison and majority rule. For instance, since two out of three (namely, Anton and Cecil) strictly prefer S over P, we say that this 'society' of three friends strictly prefers S over P. Derive the social strict preference ranking over the alternatives C, S, and P. Is this ranking transitive? Explain!

3.5. Professor Economicus wants a grader for her class this semester. She chooses from students who have taken her class before and looks for three qualities in a grader: speed, accuracy, and sense of humor. If student A is better than student B in two of these three qualities, she will strictly prefer A to B. She is trying to rank three students based on their qualities given in the following table.

	Speed	Accuracy (%)	Humor
Evgenievich	fast	80	average
Freiherr	average	95	funny
Gustav	slow	90	hilarious

Derive Professor Economicus' preference ranking over these three students. Is ranking transitive? Explain why or why not.

3.6. For each of the following utility functions, draw indifference curves for different utility levels as indicated. Use arrows to show the direction in which utility is increasing. For parts (c)–(e), also draw the line(s) from the origin along which the kinks lie.

(a) $u(x_1, x_2) = (x_1 + 2x_2)^2$ for $\bar{u} = 4, 9$

(b) $u(x_1, x_2) = x_2 - x_1$ for $\bar{u} = 3, 4$

(c) $u(x_1, x_2) = \min\{2x_1, x_1 + x_2\}$ for $\bar{u} = 4, 6$

(d) $u(x_1, x_2) = \min\{2x_1 + x_2, x_1 + 2x_2\}$ for $\bar{u} = 3, 6, 9$

(e) $u(x_1, x_2) = \min\{x_1, x_2^2\}$ for $\bar{u} = 1, 4, 9$

(f) $u(x_1, x_2) = \begin{cases} x + y & \text{if } y < 4 \\ 4 + x & \text{if } y \geq 4 \end{cases}$ for $\bar{u} = 6, 8$

3.7. For each of the following utility functions defined over goods x and y, calculate the marginal rate of substitution for positive levels of both goods.

(a) $u(x,y) = (x + 2y)^2$

(b) $u(x,y) = 2\ln x + 3\ln y$

(c) $u(x,y) = x + 2\sqrt{y}$

3.8. Do any of the following functions qualify as a positive monotonic transformation? Explain why or why not.

(a) $f(u) = -10 + 2u$

(b) $f(u) = 10u - u^2$

(c) $f(u) = -e^{-u}$

Chapter 4

Individual Demands

Having covered budgets and preferences in Chapters 2 and 3, we are now ready to focus on consumer choice behavior. A consumer's demand for each good is found by maximizing her preferences over her budget, i.e., by finding a consumption bundle within her budget set which is strictly better or at least as good as any other affordable bundle. We find this preference-maximizing bundle graphically, deduce the necessary mathematical conditions, and apply these conditions to the preferences introduced in Chapter 3 to calculate demand functions.

4.1   Preference Maximization on Budgets

To maximize a consumer's preferences over the bundles she can afford, bring together her budget and her preferences. This is illustrated in Figure 4.1 where her budget line is drawn in blue and her preferences are represented by the orange indifference curves.While bundle A in the interior of the budget set is certainly affordable, bundle B is also affordable and lies on a higher indifference curve than A. In fact, it is easy to verify that there is no other bundle in the budget set that lies on a higher indifference curve than $\bar{u}_2$. Therefore, the quantities of the two goods $(\bar{x}_1, \bar{x}_2)$ at B maximize this consumer's preferences subject to the given budget.

The preference-maximizing bundle, $B = (\bar{x}_1, \bar{x}_2)$, is said to be an interior solution to the consumer's preference (or utility) maximization problem because $\bar{x}_1 > 0$ and $\bar{x}_2 > 0$, i.e., an interior solution is one where both goods are consumed. Here the indifference curve that passes through B is tangent to the budget line, so the slope of the indifference curve (which is the negative

61

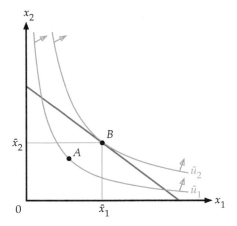

Figure 4.1 Interior preference maximization

of the *MRS*) at that point equals that of the budget constraint:

$$-MRS(\bar{x}_1, \bar{x}_2) = -\frac{p_1}{p_2},$$

or what amounts to the same thing,

$$MRS(\bar{x}_1, \bar{x}_2) = \frac{p_1}{p_2}. \tag{4.1}$$

The tangency condition given in equation (4.1) — the equality of the marginal rate of substitution to the ratio of the commodity prices — is the primary mathematical condition used to algebraically calculate individual demands in section 4.2.

Sometimes, however, the preference-maximizing bundle is a **corner solution**, meaning that either the quantity of x_1 or that of x_2 is zero. In other words, a corner solution is one where only one good is consumed. Several examples will be considered in more detail in sections 4.2.1 and 4.2.3 below in the context of linear and quasilinear preferences. As you will see, a corner solution along the horizontal axis (where $\bar{x}_1 > 0$ and $\bar{x}_2 = 0$) requires the indifference curve to be steeper than or the same slope as the budget line, i.e.,

$$-MRS(\bar{x}_1, 0) \leq -\frac{p_1}{p_2},$$

or

$$MRS(\bar{x}_1, 0) \geq \frac{p_1}{p_2}. \tag{4.2}$$

Similarly, for a corner solution along the vertical axis (where $\bar{x}_1 = 0$ and $\bar{x}_2 > 0$), the indifference curve must be as flat as or flatter than the budget line:

$$MRS(0, \bar{x}_2) \leq \frac{p_1}{p_2}. \tag{4.3}$$

In summary, at an interior utility-maximizing bundle, equation (4.1) must hold; at a corner utility-maximizing bundle, either (4.2) or (4.3) must hold.

4.2 Calculating Individual Demands

4.2.1 Demands for linear preferences

Suppose a consumer's utility is $u(x_1, x_2) = 2x_1 + x_2$ (so her indifference curves have a slope of -2) and her income is $m = \$60$. There are three possibilities, each illustrated in the panels of Figure 4.2.

In the left panel, $p_1 = \$15$ and $p_2 = \$6$, so the blue budget line has a slope of -2.5 and is steeper than the orange indifference curve. In this case the utility-maximizing bundle is at $A = (0, 10)$. Since the $MRS = 2$ and the price-ratio $p_1/p_2 = 2.5$, equation (4.3) holds with a strict inequality at A when the consumer buys no units of x_1 and spends all her income on x_2.

In the middle panel, $p_2 = \$6$ as before, but $p_1 = \$12$. The highest indifference curve the consumer can reach coincides with the budget line, so there is no *single* bundle that maximizes her preferences: *any* point on the

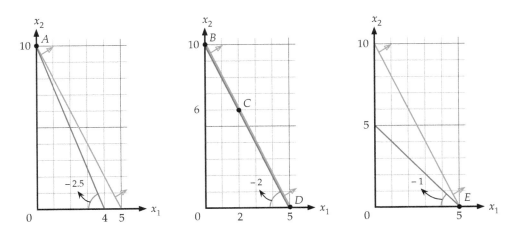

Figure 4.2 Linear preferences maximization

budget line from point B to point D inclusive maximizes her preferences. At an interior solution such as C, equation (4.1) holds. At the corner solution B where $\bar{x}_1 = 0$ and $\bar{x}_2 > 0$, (4.3) holds with an equality, while at the corner solution D where $\bar{x}_1 > 0$ and $\bar{x}_2 = 0$, (4.2) holds with an equality.

In the right panel, $p_1 = p_2 = \$12$, and the blue budget line is flatter than the orange indifference curve. Preferences are maximized at point $E = (5, 0)$ where $\bar{x}_1 > 0$ but $\bar{x}_2 = 0$. Since the $MRS = 2$ and the price-ratio $p_1/p_2 = 1$, equation (4.2) holds with a strict inequality.

Thus, which bundle is preference-maximizing depends on the slope of the budget relative to the slope of the indifference curves. Because we want to see how the preference-maximizing bundle changes with prices and incomes, we will calculate demand functions, writing the demand for x_1 as $h_1(p_1, p_2, m)$ and for x_2 as $h_2(p_1, p_2, m)$. In other words,

$$x_1 = h_1(p_1, p_2, m) \quad \text{and} \quad x_2 = h_2(p_1, p_2, m),$$

signifying that the quantity demanded of each good depends in general on p_1, p_2, and m.[1] For example, the preference-maximizing bundle in the left panel of Figure 4.2 is given by $h_1(15, 6, 60) = 0$ and $h_2(15, 6, 60) = 10$, while that in the right panel is $h_1(12, 12, 60) = 5$ and $h_2(12, 12, 60) = 0$. The demand functions for both goods together are written more compactly as

$$h(p_1, p_2, m) = (h_1(p_1, p_2, m), h_2(p_1, p_2, m)),$$

where $h(p_1, p_2, m)$ refers to the *pair* of individual demands, the demands for good 1 and good 2 listed in order.

In general then, the demand functions corresponding to the left panel in Figure 4.2 are given by

$$h_1(p_1, p_2, m) = 0 \quad \text{and} \quad h_2(p_1, p_2, m) = \frac{m}{p_2}$$

when $p_1/p_2 > 1$. When $p_1/p_2 = 1$ as in the case of the middle panel, any bundle $(\bar{x}_1, \bar{x}_2)$ that satisfies $p_1\bar{x}_1 + p_2\bar{x}_2 = m$ is preference-maximizing, so

$$h_1(p_1, p_2, m) = \bar{x}_1 \quad \text{and} \quad h_2(p_1, p_2, m) = \bar{x}_2.$$

Finally, when $p_1/p_2 < 1$ as in the right panel,

$$h_1(p_1, p_2, m) = \frac{m}{p_1} \quad \text{and} \quad h_2(p_1, p_2, m) = 0.$$

---

[1]Such demand functions are sometimes called Marshallian (after Alfred Marshall) or Walrasian (after Léon Walras) demand functions.

Summarizing these derivations, the demand for the linear utility $u(x_1, x_2) = ax_1 + bx_2$ is given by

$$h(p_1, p_2, m) = \begin{cases} \left(0, \dfrac{m}{p_2}\right) & \text{if } p_1/p_2 > a/b \\ \{(\bar{x}_1, \bar{x}_2) : p_1\bar{x}_1 + p_2\bar{x}_2 = m\} & \text{if } p_1/p_2 = a/b \\ \left(\dfrac{m}{p_1}, 0\right) & \text{if } p_1/p_2 < a/b. \end{cases} \qquad (4.4)$$

Note that even though demands depend on prices p_1, p_2, and income m in general, not all of these variables are necessarily present *simultaneously* on the right hand side; indeed, when the demand is zero, it is independent of *all* of these variables.

4.2.2 Demands for Leontief preferences

Suppose $u(x_1, x_2) = \min\{x_1, x_2\}$. Then, all the kinks in the indifference curves lie along the dashed magenta 45° ray through the origin given by $x_2 = x_1$. The highest indifference curve attainable passes through the point where this line intersects the budget line $p_1x_1 + p_2x_2 = m$ at point A in Figure 4.3.

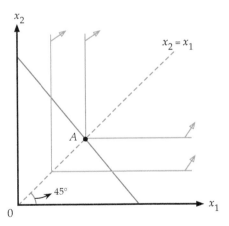

Figure 4.3   Leontief preference maximization

Replacing x_2 with x_1 in the budget and solving, we obtain the demand function for good x_1 to be

$$h_1(p_1, p_2, m) = \frac{m}{p_1 + p_2}.$$

Since $x_2 = x_1$ at the demanded bundle, $h_2(p_1, p_2, m)$ is also given by the formula above. Then, the demand functions for this Leontief utility can be written as

$$h(p_1, p_2, m) = \left(\frac{m}{p_1 + p_2}, \frac{m}{p_1 + p_2} \right). \tag{4.5}$$

In general, when $u(x_1, x_2) = \min\{ax_1, bx_2\}$, the kinks lie along the line $x_2 = ax_1/b$ and the demand functions are given by

$$h(p_1, p_2, m) = \left(\frac{bm}{bp_1 + ap_2}, \frac{am}{bp_1 + ap_2} \right). \tag{4.6}$$

Note that these demands are functions of all three variables, p_1, p_2, and m, and that the ratio of the demand for x_2 to the demand for x_1 is $a : b$.

4.2.3　Demands for quasilinear preferences

The solutions to preference maximization for quasilinear preferences may be interior or corner ones, depending on the prices and income. The following four steps provide an algorithm to find them.

1. Solve for an interior solution by using the equation $MRS = p_1/p_2$. This yields one demand function (either for good 1 or good 2 depending on the quasilinear utility function).

2. Solve for the demand for the other good by substituting the demand function obtained in step 1 into the budget equation, $p_1 x_1 + p_2 x_2 = m$.

3. For the demand derived in step 2, determine if it can be negative for certain values of p_1, p_2, and m and derive a condition for an interior solution.

4. If the demand derived in step 2 is for good 1, then the corner solution is $(0, m/p_2)$ when the condition for an interior solution does not hold. Conversely, if the demand derived in step 2 is for good 2, then the corner solution is $(m/p_1, 0)$.

Consider the case when the consumer's quasilinear preferences are represented by the utility function $u(x_1, x_2) = 2\sqrt{x_1} + x_2$. To illustrate the steps above, derive the marginal rate of substitution, $MRS = 1/\sqrt{x_1}$, and equate

▶ it to the price ratio following step 1: $1/\sqrt{x_1} = p_1/p_2$. Solving for x_1 yields the demand for good 1:

$$h_1(p_1, p_2, m) = \frac{p_2^2}{p_1^2}. \tag{4.7}$$

From step 2, substitute (4.7) in the budget equation $p_1 x_1 + p_2 x_2 = m$ and solve for x_2 to obtain the demand for good 2:

$$h_2(p_1, p_2, m) = \frac{m}{p_2} - \frac{p_2}{p_1}. \tag{4.8}$$

Note that in order to have an interior solution, h_2 must be positive. Setting the right hand side of the h_2 equation to be greater than zero, we obtain the condition $m p_1 > p_2^2$ for an interior solution. Therefore, if $m p_1 \leq p_2^2$, we no longer have an interior solution. From step 4, the demand for good 2 vanishes at a corner solution and the entire income is spent on good 1.

In summary then, the demand for this quasilinear utility function is

$$h(p_1, p_2, m) = \begin{cases} \left(\dfrac{p_2^2}{p_1^2}, \dfrac{m}{p_2} - \dfrac{p_2}{p_1} \right) & \text{if } m p_1 > p_2^2 \\ \left(\dfrac{m}{p_1}, 0 \right) & \text{if } m p_1 \leq p_2^2, \end{cases} \tag{4.9}$$

where the first case refers to the interior solution and the second, to the corner solution.

To see a numerical example and its corresponding graph, suppose $m = \$8$ and $p_1 = p_2 = \$1$. In this case, the condition for an interior solution holds, so the utility-maximizing bundle is $(1, 7)$ which is illustrated by point A in the left panel of Figure 4.4. However, if $m = \$18$, $p_1 = \$2$ and $p_2 = \$9$ instead, the condition for an interior solution no longer holds; we obtain a corner solution, as shown by point B in the right panel of Figure 4.4.

A central feature of quasilinear preferences is that the demand for one of the goods does not depend on income at an interior solution. In this specific instance, $\partial h_1 / \partial m = 0$ from equation (4.7), therefore good 1 has a zero income effect because the quasilinear indifference curves are vertically parallel (see Figure 3.8). Consequently, as long as the consumer can afford to purchase p_2^2 / p_1^2 units of good 1 with her initial income so as to be at an interior solution, the demand for good 1 will remain unchanged when m increases and all the additional income will be spent on buying more of good 2.

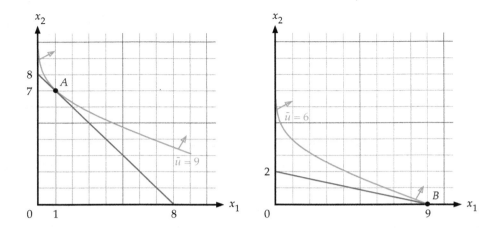

Figure 4.4   Quasilinear interior and corner solutions

4.2.4   Demands for Cobb-Douglas preferences

We solve for the demand functions for Cobb-Douglas preferences by following these steps.

1. Set $MRS = p_1/p_2$ and obtain an expression for x_2.

2. Substitute the expression from step 1 into the budget equation $p_1x_1 + p_2x_2 = m$ and solve for x_1 to derive the demand for good 1.

3. Substitute the demand derived in step 2 into the expression from step 1 (or the budget equation) to solve for the remaining demand.

To illustrate, consider the utility $u(x_1, x_2) = x_1x_2$. Then, from step 1,

$$\frac{x_2}{x_1} = \frac{p_1}{p_2},$$

and we obtain the expression $x_2 = p_1x_1/p_2$. Following step 2, we obtain $h_1(p_1, p_2, m) = m/2p_1$. Finally, from step 3, we obtain $h_2(p_1, p_2, m) = m/2p_2$. Therefore, the demands for the Cobb-Douglas utility, $u(x_1, x_2) = x_1x_2$, can be written more compactly as

$$h(p_1, p_2, m) = \left(\frac{m}{2p_1}, \frac{m}{2p_2} \right). \tag{4.10}$$

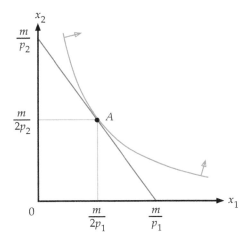

Figure 4.5   Cobb-Douglas preference maximization

Under these preferences, the consumer buys exactly half the total amount of good 1 that she could afford if she spent all her income on this good, and likewise for good 2, as shown by point A in Figure 4.5. In other words, for the Cobb-Douglas utility, $u(x_1, x_2) = x_1 x_2$, the preference-maximizing quantities will always be at the midpoint of the budget line.

For the general Cobb-Douglas utility $u(x_1, x_2) = A x_1^a x_2^b$, follow the same ◄ △ three steps to obtain the demand function

$$h(p_1, p_2, m) = \left(\frac{am}{(a+b)p_1}, \frac{bm}{(a+b)p_2} \right). \tag{4.11}$$

In general, the three-step process outlined above can be used to calculate the demand functions for any utility function that is differentiable[2] so long as the preference-maximizing bundles are interior solutions (which is most often the case).

4.2.5   Demands for lexicographic preferences°

We have been deriving demand functions from utility functions, but demand functions can be derived even when preferences cannot be represented by utility functions. As an example, consider the lexicographic preferences $\succsim_L$

---

[2]I.e., a utility function that has partial derivatives.

we introduced in section 3.7.1 over combinations of food and shelter: two bundles are related by this binary relation $(f_2, s_2) \succsim_L (f_1, s_1)$ if either

(a) $f_2 \geq f_1$ regardless of the values of s_1 and s_2, or

(b) $f_2 = f_1$ and $s_2 \geq s_1$.

Since this consumer cares about her consumption of food first, and her consumption of shelter second, this means that on a standard budget set, the bundle that maximizes her preferences is the one that has the greatest amount of food, namely, the bundle $(m/p_1, 0)$ where she spends all her income on good 1. This will be true no matter what the prices and income. Therefore, the demands for these lexicographic preferences are

$$h(p_1, p_2, m) = \left(\frac{m}{p_1}, 0\right). \tag{4.12}$$

Note that the linear utility function $u(x_1, x_2) = x_1$ whose indifference curves are vertical (see the left panel of Figure 3.4) results in the same demand function as equation (4.12)! Thus it is not possible to tell from a consumer's demand function whether the preferences she maximizes have a utility representation, or if they cannot be represented by a utility function.

4.3   Two Properties of Demand Functions

In this section, we look at two essential properties satisfied by all the demand functions you will encounter in this book.

4.3.1   Budget exhaustion

It is easy to check that when a consumer's preferences are strictly monotonic, she will always maximize her preferences on the budget line and never *inside* the budget set. This is because at any bundle that is strictly inside the budget (i.e., not on the budget line), it is possible to move slightly northwest, remain inside the budget, and yet make the consumer better off. Since most of our preferences satisfy strict monotonicity (and even for some that do not), it will be the case that the preference-maximizing bundle is on the budget line and thus exhausts (i.e., uses up) the consumer's entire income. We say that a consumer's demand satisfies **budget exhaustion** so long as

$$p_1 h_1(p_1, p_2, m) + p_2 h_2(p_1, p_2, m) = m \tag{4.13}$$

for any positive values of p_1, p_2, and m. This property is satisfied by all the demands that have been derived so far. For instance, it may be checked that the demand functions in equation (4.10) that maximize the Cobb-Douglas utility $u(x_1, x_2) = x_1 x_2$ satisfy budget exhaustion:

$$p_1 \cdot \frac{m}{2p_1} + p_2 \cdot \frac{m}{2p_2} = \frac{m}{2} + \frac{m}{2} = m.$$

4.3.2 Homogeneity of degree zero in prices and income

Review the definition of homogeneous functions from section A.7.2 of the Mathematical appendix. Then, demand functions are homogeneous of degree zero in prices and income:

$$h(tp_1, tp_2, tm) = t^0 h(p_1, p_2, m) = h(p_1, p_2, m).$$

This means that if we were to scale all prices and income by the same factor (say, $t = 4$, and so we quadruple all prices and income), the demand remains *unchanged*. This is because scaling all prices and income by the same factor leaves the budget set unchanged: $(tp_1)x_1 + (tp_2)x_2 = (tm)$ is identical to $p_1 x_1 + p_2 x_2 = m$ for $t > 0$. Since the budget set remains unchanged, the preference-maximizing bundle must be the same.

Let us verify this for the demand function for the Leontief preferences derived in equation (4.6). In the case of the demand for good 1, note that

$$h_1(tp_1, tp_2, tm) = \frac{tm}{tp_1 + tp_2} = \frac{m}{p_1 + p_2} = h_1(p_1, p_2, m).$$

Verify that all the demand functions for goods 1 and 2 derived in this chapter are homogeneous of degree zero in prices and income.

Exercises

4.1. For each of the following utility functions, calculate the demand functions for each good, $h_1(p_1, p_2, m)$ and $h_2(p_1, p_2, m)$, as functions of the prices and income.

(a) $u(x_1, x_2) = 3x_1$

(b) $u(x_1, x_2) = 2 \ln x_1 + 3 \ln x_2$

(c) $u(x_1, x_2) = x_1(x_2 - 1)$, where $x_2 > 1$

(d) $u(x_1, x_2) = [\min\{x_1, 2x_2\}]^2$

(e) $u(x_1, x_2) = x_1 + \ln x_2$

(f) $u(x_1, x_2) = \sqrt{x_1} + \sqrt{x_2}$

(g) $u(x_1, x_2) = \ln(x_1 - 1) - 2\ln(x_2 - 2)$ where $x_1 > 1$ and $0 \le x_2 \le 1.6$

4.2. Verify that the demand functions calculated in **4.1** satisfy the budget exhaustion property. For each of the demand functions, show that it is homogeneous of degree zero in prices and income.

4.3. The following utility functions are defined over *three* goods, x, y, and z. Calculate the demand functions for each good, h_j for $j = x, y, z$, as functions of the prices p_x, p_y, p_z and income m.

(a) $u(x, y, z) = xyz$

(b) $u(x, y, z) = x + \ln y + \ln z$

Show that the demand functions satisfy the budget exhaustion property in each case, i.e., $p_x h_x + p_y h_y + p_z h_z = m$.

4.4. Ali spends his income of $64 on kerosene ($x$) and food ($y$) each week. The price of food is $8 per unit. The price of kerosene is $4/liter at a government-run store and he can purchase up to 8 liters there. On the market, kerosene costs $8/liter. His utility function is Cobb-Douglas: $u(x, y) = xy^3$. How much kerosene and food does he buy given his budget constraint?

4.5. Consider Violet from problem **2.1**. Suppose her utility function over pies (x) and champagne (y) (assumed to be divisible goods) is Cobb-Douglas and given by $u(x, y) = xy$.

(a) Given Violet's budget in **2.1** part (a), calculate the quantities of pies and champagne she will consume when she maximizes her preferences.

(b) Given Violet's budget in **2.1** part (b), calculate the quantities of pies and champagne she will consume when she maximizes her preferences.

Chapter 5

Consumer Comparative Statics

Having derived demand functions by maximizing preferences on budgets, we now study what happens to the quantity demanded of any good by a consumer when there is a change in the price of a single good, or a change in income. We derive individual demand elasticities with respect to prices and income. Exploring the nature of demand further, we find that while economists generally believe that there is a 'Law of Demand' for market demand curves — a lower price increases the quantity demanded for a good — no such law is implied by a consumer's preference-maximizing behavior for *individual* demand functions.

5.1 Price and Income Consumption Curves

Individual demand functions, as we have seen in Chapter 4, generally depend on three parameters: the prices of the two goods and income. Changing any one of these at a time enables us to trace the path of preference-maximizing bundles in the commodity space. Changing one of the prices yields a price consumption curve (*PCC*) while changing income yields an income consumption curve (*ICC*). We illustrate these two concepts for specific preferences below.

5.1.1 Price consumption curves

Leontief preferences

Suppose a consumer has Leontief preferences given by the utility $u(x_1, x_2) = \min\{x_1, x_2\}$. Assume that price p_2 and income m are fixed. When the original

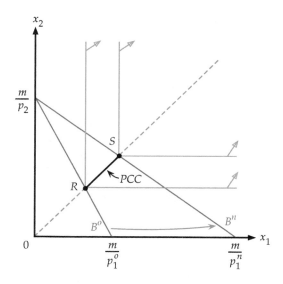

Figure 5.1   PCC for Leontief preferences

price of good 1 is p_1^o, the consumer faces the original budget B^o in Figure 5.1. Given budget B^o, her preferences are maximized at R. Now suppose that only the price of good 1 decreases, so the new price is p_1^n. Then the new budget is the flatter blue line, B^n, and preferences are now maximized at S. Joining all the preference-maximizing bundles as the price of good 1 drops continuously from p_1^o to p_1^n traces out the PCC between the original and the new budget, as shown by the solid black line RS in Figure 5.1.

It should be clear that though we considered a continuous drop in p_1 in Figure 5.1 which made the budget B^o pivot to B^n as shown by the magenta arrow, the PCC can be derived for price increases as well. For example, if we had started with budget B^n and *raised* p_1 until the budget line swiveled back to B^o, exactly the same PCC segment, RS, would be traced out in reverse.

In an analogous manner, we could keep p_1 and m fixed and change p_2 instead to trace out the PCC when only the price of good 2 changes. In either case, a positively sloping PCC indicates conformity with the 'Law of Demand': as the price of a good falls, the consumer buys more of it. A PCC with a negatively sloping segment indicates a violation of the 'Law of Demand': as the price of a good falls over this range, the consumer buys *less* of it. Such a good is called a **Giffen good**. Giffen goods are taken up in section 5.3.3 in more detail.

Cobb-Douglas preferences

Suppose a consumer has Cobb-Douglas preferences given by $u(x_1, x_2) = x_1 x_2$. In Figure 5.2, given the original budget, B^o, recall from section 4.2.4 that the midpoint of the budget line, R, is the preference-maximizing bundle. When p_1 drops to p_1^n and the budget pivots to B^n as shown by the magenta arrow, the new preference-maximizing bundle is at S, the midpoint of the new budget. Note that the quantity of good 2 at that bundle remains the same as before, $m/(2p_2)$, no matter what the budget line is between B^o and B^n. Therefore, the PCC segment is the horizontal line RS.

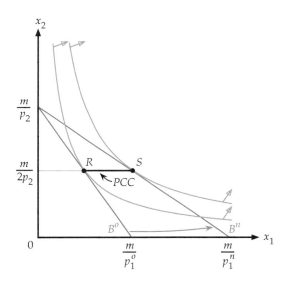

Figure 5.2   PCC for Cobb-Douglas preferences

5.1.2   Income consumption curves

Cobb-Douglas preferences

For the ICC, we keep p_1 and p_2 fixed and raise the income from m^o to m^n. In Figure 5.3, this shifts the budget line to the right from B^o to B^n in a parallel fashion. Note that because the prices are fixed, all budget lines for any income level between m^o and m^n must have the same slope, $-p_1/p_2$. For Cobb-Douglas preferences given by $u(x_1, x_2) = x_1 x_2$, the preference-maximizing bundles are at R and S, the respective midpoints of B^o and B^n. As income rises continuously from m^o to m^n, the preference-maximizing bundles will lie

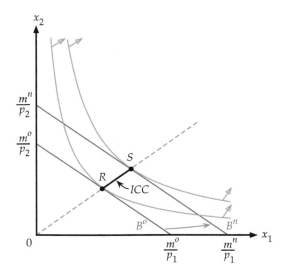

Figure 5.3   ICC for Cobb-Douglas preferences

along the line segment RS, so joining R and S gives the ICC segment.[1] This segment lies along a ray through the origin (shown by the dashed magenta line).

A positively sloping ICC denotes that both goods are normal. An ICC with a negatively sloping segment shows that the good whose purchase decreases as income increases is an inferior good over that segment. We leave it as an exercise (see question **5.3**) to show that it is not possible with only two goods for *both* to be inferior.

Quasilinear preferences

For the quasilinear preferences given by $u(x_1, x_2) = 2\sqrt{x_1} + x_2$, consider prices and income for which there is an interior solution such as the one shown at R on the original budget line, B^o, in Figure 5.4. As the consumer's income increases from the original m^o to the new m^n, the budget lines shift

---

[1]Why the preference-maximizing bundles must lie along the line segment RS is easier to grasp if you understand that Cobb-Douglas preferences are homothetic (see section 3.7.2). Homotheticity means that the marginal rates of substitution at any indifference curve along the dashed magenta ray through the origin must be the same. In particular, because the $MRS = p_1/p_2$ at R, the marginal rates of substitution along every point of the dashed ray must be p_1/p_2. Therefore, as the consumer's income rises continuously from m^o to m^n, every tangency between the budgets and the indifference curves must occur along the dashed ray.

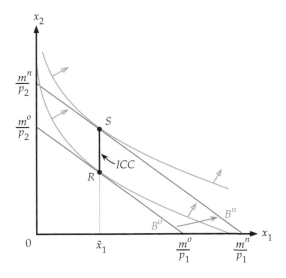

Figure 5.4   ICC for quasilinear preferences

in a parallel fashion. In section 4.2.3, we saw that because the quasilinear indifference curves are vertically parallel, there is no income effect for good 1 at an interior solution — as the income increases, the quantity of good 1 purchased remains at $\bar{x}_1$, and all the remaining income is spent on good 2. Therefore, the ICC for this income change is the vertical line segment RS.

An ICC segment that is vertical shows that the good on the horizontal axis has no income effect. Conversely, an ICC segment that is horizontal shows that the good on the vertical axis has no income effect.

5.2   Individual Elasticities of Demand

Elasticities are usually calculated for market demands, as covered earlier in section 1.4. In this section, we present the formulas for the own-price, cross-price, and income elasticities for individual demands.[2] We then calculate these elasticities for the interior quasilinear demands derived in equation (4.9) for the case when $mp_1 > p_2^2$:

$$h(p_1, p_2, m) = \left(\frac{p_2^2}{p_1^2} \frac{m}{p_2} - \frac{p_2}{p_1} \right).$$

---

[2]These mirror the elasticity formulas (1.11), (1.15) and (1.14) respectively for market-level demands seen earlier in sections 1.4.1 and 1.4.2.

5.2.1   Own-price elasticities

Define the own-price elasticity of demand for goods 1 and 2 with respect to its own price by

$$\varepsilon_{11} = \frac{\partial h_1}{\partial p_1} \cdot \frac{p_1}{h_1} \quad \text{and} \quad \varepsilon_{22} = \frac{\partial h_2}{\partial p_2} \cdot \frac{p_2}{h_2}. \tag{5.1}$$

To calculate the own-price elasticity for the quasilinear demand for good 1, note that

$$\frac{\partial h_1}{\partial p_1} = -\frac{2p_2^2}{p_1^3}.$$

Then

$$\varepsilon_{11} = -\frac{2p_2^2}{p_1^3} \cdot \frac{p_1}{p_2^2/p_1^2} = -2.$$

Therefore, the own-price elasticity for good 1 is constant (it does not depend on prices and income) and is elastic.

For good 2,

$$\frac{\partial h_2}{\partial p_2} = -\frac{m}{p_2^2} - \frac{1}{p_1} = -\frac{(mp_1 + p_2^2)}{p_1 p_2^2}.$$

Then

$$\varepsilon_{22} = -\frac{(mp_1 + p_2^2)}{p_1 p_2^2} \cdot \frac{p_2}{(mp_1 - p_2^2)/(p_1 p_2)} = -\frac{(mp_1 + p_2^2)}{(mp_1 - p_2^2)},$$

which does depend on the specific values of p_1, p_2, and m. For instance, for $p_1 = p_2 = 1$ and $m = 8$, $\varepsilon_{22} = -8/7 \approx -1.14$. However, since the numerator of ε_{22} is greater than its denominator, the own-price elasticity for good 2 is always elastic.

5.2.2   Cross-price elasticities

Define the cross-price elasticity of demand for good i with respect to price j by

$$\varepsilon_{ij} = \frac{\partial h_i}{\partial p_j} \cdot \frac{p_j}{h_i} \tag{5.2}$$

where if $i = 1$, then $j = 2$, or vice versa.

To calculate the cross-price elasticity for the quasilinear demand for good 1, first derive

$$\frac{\partial h_1}{\partial p_2} = \frac{2p_2}{p_1^2}.$$

Then

$$\varepsilon_{12} = \frac{2p_2}{p_1^2} \cdot \frac{p_2}{p_2^2/p_1^2} = 2,$$

showing that good 1 is a strong substitute for good 2 and that this elasticity does not depend on the specific values of prices and income.

Similarly, to calculate the cross-price elasticity for the quasilinear demand for good 2, first derive

$$\frac{\partial h_2}{\partial p_1} = \frac{p_2}{p_1^2}.$$

Then

$$\varepsilon_{21} = \frac{p_2}{p_1^2} \cdot \frac{p_1}{(mp_1 - p_2^2)/(p_1 p_2)} = \frac{p_2^2}{mp_1 - p_2^2},$$

which is positive, indicating that good 2 is a substitute for good 1. Its exact value depends on the parameters. For example, if $p_1 = p_2 = 1$ and $m = 8$, then $\varepsilon_{21} = 1/7 \approx 0.14$, showing that good 2 is a weak substitute.

5.2.3   Income elasticities

Define the income elasticity of demand for goods 1 and 2 by

$$\eta_1 = \frac{\partial h_1}{\partial m} \cdot \frac{m}{h_1} \quad \text{and} \quad \eta_2 = \frac{\partial h_2}{\partial m} \cdot \frac{m}{h_2}. \tag{5.3}$$

To calculate the income elasticity for the quasilinear demand for good 1, recall that

$$\frac{\partial h_1}{\partial m} = 0$$

since there is no income effect. Hence $\eta_1 = 0$ always.

Finally, to calculate the income elasticity for good 2, derive

$$\frac{\partial h_2}{\partial m} = \frac{1}{p_2}.$$

Then

$$\eta_2 = \frac{1}{p_2} \cdot \frac{m}{(mp_1 - p_2^2)/(p_1 p_2)} = \frac{mp_1}{mp_1 - p_2^2}.$$

For all prices and income for which the denominator is positive, the numerator is always greater than the denominator. Therefore, $\eta_2 > 1$ and good 2 is always a normal good.

5.3   Decomposing Price Effects

When p_1 falls while p_2 and m remain fixed, the quantity demanded of good 1 typically increases; this is called a price effect.[3] This price effect can be broken down into two constituent ones, a substitution effect and an income effect. The substitution effect refers to the consumer's desire to purchase more of the good that is relatively cheaper; the income effect refers to the consumer's desire to purchase more of the good because a reduction in p_1 increases the consumer's purchasing power. There are two ways of decomposing this price effect, one associated with Sir John Hicks and Sir Roy Allen, and the other with Evgeny (Eugen) Slutsky. For very small price changes, these two decompositions are identical.

5.3.1   The Hicks-Allen decomposition

The Hicks-Allen decomposition is found by following four steps.

1. Find the preference-maximizing bundle A at the original budget B^o which yields the utility level u^o.

2. Find the preference-maximizing bundle C at the new budget B^n which yields the utility level u^n. For the good whose price changed, the movement from A to C is the price effect.

3. Using the new price ratio, find the bundle B that barely yields the original utility level, u^o.

4. For the good whose price changed, the movement from A to B (along the original indifference curve, u^o) is the substitution effect, and the movement from B to C (from the original indifference curve, u^o, to the new indifference curve, u^n) is the income effect.

In Figure 5.5 these four steps are illustrated for generic Cobb-Douglas preferences. In step 1, suppose B^o is the original budget facing the consumer and she maximizes her preferences at A, obtaining the original utility level

---

[3]The only price effect illustrated in this section considers a decrease in p_1. The same Hicks-Allen or Slutsky procedures highlighted in sections 5.3.1 or 5.3.2 can also be used to decompose a price effect resulting from an *increase* in p_1. Similarly, the price effect resulting from a change in p_2 while keeping p_1 and m fixed can also be decomposed into its constituent effects.

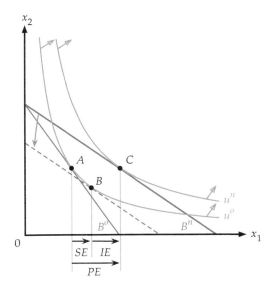

Figure 5.5   The Hicks-Allen decomposition

u^o. In step 2, when p_1 drops, her budget pivots to B^n, her new budget, where her preference-maximizing bundle is at C, yielding the new utility u^n. The increase in the quantity of x_1 purchased at C versus at A is the price effect as shown by the horizontal black arrow marked PE.

The crucial step 3 in the Hicks-Allen decomposition requires following this maxim: barely achieve the original utility level at the new price ratio. To do this, begin at point C and remove income away from the consumer in small increments so the new budget slides in the direction shown by the magenta arrow in Figure 5.5. Stop removing income at the point when taking away any further income means that the original utility level u^o can no longer be achieved. This occurs at the blue dashed budget line that is parallel to B^n and tangent to the u^o indifference curve. Label this point of tangency B. Then the increase in the quantity of x_1 in moving from A to B along the original indifference curve is called the (Hicks-Allen) substitution effect (SE). The increase in the quantity of x_1 in moving from B to C from the old utility to the new utility level is called the (Hicks-Allen) income effect (IE).

The substitution effect shows two things simultaneously: (i) how much more of x_1 the consumer wishes to buy just from the fact that good 1 is now relatively cheaper, while ensuring that (ii) the consumer is as well off as before. The cheaper relative price in (i) is shown by the flatter dashed blue budget line in Figure 5.5 at B, as opposed to the solid budget line at A; (ii) is captured by the fact that both A and B lie on the same original indifference curve, u^o.

The income effect similarly shows how much more[4] of x_1 the consumer wishes to buy based on the fact that her purchasing power has increased. This is captured by the movement from B to C between which the relative prices remain fixed (the B'' budget line has the same slope as the dashed one) but the income at C is higher than the income at B.

To see a specific numerical calculation of this decomposition, consider the Cobb-Douglas utility, $u(x_1, x_2) = x_1 x_2$, whose demands we derived in equation (4.10):

$$h(p_1, p_2, m) = \left(\frac{m}{2p_1}, \frac{m}{2p_2} \right).$$

Suppose that $m = 20$, the original price of good 1 is $p_1^o = 2$ while $p_2 = 1$, so the bundle corresponding to point A in Figure 5.5 is $(5, 10)$ and the utility level associated is $u^o = 50$. If the new price of good 1 drops to $p_1^n = 1$, the bundle corresponding to point C is $(10, 10)$, showing a price effect of 5 units for good 1. To find the intermediate bundle (x_1, x_2) corresponding to point B, note that two conditions must hold: first, $x_1 x_2 = 50$ since B lies on the indifference curve u^o in Figure 5.5, and second, the $MRS = x_2/x_1$ must equal $p_1^n/p_2 = 1$. From the latter, $x_2 = x_1$ at B; using the former, we obtain $x_1 = x_2 \approx 7.07$ approximately, so $B = (7.07, 7.07)$. Therefore, the substitution effect is the increase in good 1 due to the change in relative price of roughly 2.07 units, while the remainder of 2.93 units is the income effect.

5.3.2   The Slutsky decomposition°

An alternative decomposition of the price effect is due to Slutsky. The steps are similar to the Hicks-Allen decomposition with the exception of step 3.

1. Find the preference-maximizing bundle A at the original budget B^o which yields the utility level u^o.

2. Find the preference-maximizing bundle C at the new budget B'' which yields the utility level u''. For the good whose price changed, the movement from A to C is the price effect.

---

[4]Or possibly less if good 1 is an inferior good, as we will see in section 5.3.3.

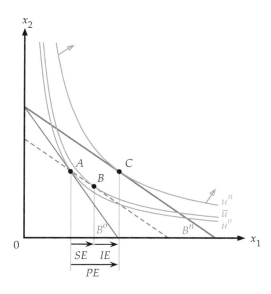

Figure 5.6 The Slutsky decomposition

3. Find the budget at the new prices that passes through A. Calculate the preference-maximizing bundle B for this budget.

4. For the good whose price changed, the movement from A to B is the substitution effect, and the movement from B to C is the income effect.

The Slutsky decomposition is shown in Figure 5.6. Here the points A and C are identical to that in Figure 5.5 under the Hicks-Allen decomposition. But, instead of trying to achieve the original *utility level* at the new price ratio, we follow the Slutsky maxim: afford the original bundle at the new price ratio. This is shown by the dashed budget line that passes through point A (the original bundle) that is parallel to B^n. The Slutsky decomposition is found by determining the utility-maximizing bundle B on this dashed budget. Then, the movement from A to B is the (Slutsky) substitution effect while the movement from B to C is the (Slutsky) income effect.

To see how this decomposition is calculated in the case of the Cobb-Douglas demands from the previous section, suppose that $m = 20$, $p_1^o = 2$ and $p_2 = 1$, so point $A = (5, 10)$ in Figure 5.6, while point $C = (10, 10)$ when the price of good 1 drops to $p_1^n = 1$. To find the intermediate bundle corresponding to point B, note that the cost of bundle A at the new set of prices is $\$1 \times 5 + \$1 \times 10 = \$15$, so this is the income corresponding to the dashed budget. Therefore, with $m = 15$ and $p_1^n = 1$ and $p_2 = 1$, the demanded bundle B is $(7.5, 7.5)$. Thus under the Slutsky decomposition, the substitution effect for good 1 is 2.5 units, while the income effect is another 2.5 units. Note that the substitution effect is slightly larger under the Slutsky decomposition as opposed to the Hicks-Allen decomposition; for infinitesimally small price changes, these two will be identical.

5.3.3 Price effects with inferior goods

In the case of positive income effects illustrated in Figure 5.5, the substitution effect is reinforced by the income effect, resulting in a larger price effect. However, with inferior goods, the income effect works in the opposite direction to the substitution effect. Depending on the magnitude of this income effect, two cases are possible.

In Figure 5.7, the Hicks-Allen decomposition is shown for preferences where the substitution effect encourages the consumer to buy more of good 1 when it is relatively cheaper (the movement from point A to B), but the negative income effect works against the positive substitution effect to dampen this desire (the movement from point B to C). Because the magnitude of the

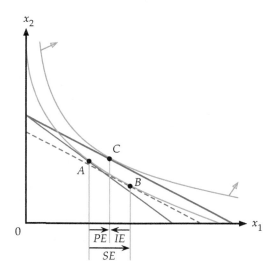

Figure 5.7 An inferior good

income effect is smaller in absolute terms than that of the substitution effect, the overall price effect still results in the consumer buying more of good 1. In other words, the 'Law of Demand' still holds: a decrease in p_1 leads to the consumer buying more of good 1.

In Figure 5.8, the Hicks-Allen decomposition is shown for a different set of preferences where the substitution effect also encourages the consumer to buy more of good 1 which has become relatively cheaper (the movement from point R to S). But in this instance, the income effect works in the opposite direction (the movement from point S to T) and is *larger* in absolute terms than the substitution effect, thereby neutralizing the substitution effect and actually causing the demand for good 1 to fall. Here, good 1 is a Giffen good for which the 'Law of Demand' is violated: for a Giffen good, there is a range of prices over which less is demanded as its price falls, so its demand function has a positive slope over this range.

We do not expect to see many instances of the *market* demand for a good to be positively sloping for certain prices. Indeed, at the level of the market, a substantial fraction of the consumers in the market would need to have positively sloping *individual* demands over the same price range in order for the market demand to be positively sloping, and this is quite unlikely. The importance of the possibility of a Giffen good lies in the fact that it stands as a counterexample to the common intuition that the 'Law of Demand' *always*

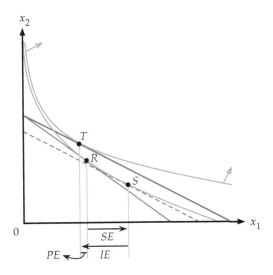

Figure 5.8 A Giffen good

holds, not only at the level of the market, but also at the level of the individual. In fact, nothing in standard consumer theory ensures that *individuals* must satisfy the 'Law of Demand'. On the contrary, individual demands which are positively sloping over some price ranges cannot be ruled out by consumer theory.

Exercises

5.1. (a) Arthur's preferences are given by the utility function $u(x_1, x_2) = \min\{x_1, x_2\}$. Suppose $p_2 = 1$ and $m = 12$. Plot this consumer's *PCC* when p_1 drops continuously 2 to 1.

(b) Bunde's preferences are given by the utility function $u(x_1, x_2) = x_1 + x_2$. Suppose $p_2 = 3$ and $m = 24$. Plot this consumer's *PCC* when p_1 drops continuously from 6 to 2.

(c) Crombie's preferences are given by the utility function

$$u(x_1, x_2) = \begin{cases} x_1 + x_2 & \text{if } x_2 < 4 \\ 4 + x_1 & \text{if } x_2 \geq 4, \end{cases}$$

i.e., the two goods are perfect substitutes when $x_2 < 4$, while good 2 is neutral whenever $x_2 \geq 4$. Suppose $p_2 = 3$ and $m = 24$. Plot this consumer's *PCC* when p_1 drops continuously from 12 to 2.

(d) Damaso's preferences are given by the utility function $u(x_1, x_2) = x_1 + \ln x_2$. Suppose $p_2 = 1$ and $m = 10$. Calculate an equation of the form $x_2 = g(x_1)$ for this consumer's *PCC*.

5.2. For each consumer in question **5.1** above, calculate the *ICC* for the following prices and income changes.

(a) Arthur: $p_1 = p_2 = 1$ and m increases from 8 to 12

(b) Bunde: $p_1 = 6$, $p_2 = 3$, and m increases from 24 to 30

(c) Crombie: $p_1 = 4$, $p_2 = 2$, and m increases from 12 to 24

(d) Damaso: $p_1 = 2$, $p_2 = 1$, and m increases from 10 to 20

5.3. Given that $p_1 = p_2 = 1$ and $m = 5$, draw a consumer's budget constraint and preference-maximizing bundle $(3, 2)$. On the same graph, draw the consumer's budget constraint when prices are unchanged but $m = 8$. Assuming that preferences are strictly convex, establish graphically that it is not possible for both x_1 and x_2 to be inferior goods.

5.4. Consider two consumers, one whose preferences are Leontief and given by the utility function $u = \min\{x_1, x_2\}$, and another whose preferences are Cobb-Douglas and given by the utility $u = x_1 x_2$. Their demands are given by equations (4.5) and (4.10):

$$h(p_1, p_2, m) = \left(\frac{m}{p_1 + p_2}, \frac{m}{p_1 + p_2}\right) \quad \text{and} \quad h(p_1, p_2, m) = \left(\frac{m}{2p_1}, \frac{m}{2p_2}\right).$$

For each consumer, calculate the price elasticities $\varepsilon_{11}, \varepsilon_{12}, \varepsilon_{21}$, and ε_{22}, and income elasticities η_1 and η_2 as functions of p_1, p_2, and m.

5.5. Find the demand functions for George whose preferences are given by the utility function $u = x_1 - 1/x_2$ and calculate the price elasticities $\varepsilon_{11}, \varepsilon_{12}, \varepsilon_{21}$, and ε_{22}, and income elasticities η_1 and η_2 as functions of p_1, p_2, and m.

5.6. Bunde's preferences are given by the utility function $u(x_1, x_2) = x_1 + x_2$. For each of the following cases, decompose the price effects into the substitution and income effects using either the Hicks-Allen or Slutsky decompositions.

    (a) Suppose $m = 120$, $p_1 = 12$, and $p_2 = 20$. The price p_1 then falls to 5, keeping p_2 and m fixed.

    (b) Suppose $m = 100$, $p_1 = 20$, and $p_2 = 10$. The price p_1 then falls to 5, keeping p_2 and m fixed.

5.7. Douglas' preferences are given by the utility function

$$u(x_1, x_2) = \min\{2x_1 + x_2, x_1 + 2x_2\}.$$

Suppose $m = 120$, and $p_1 = p_2 = 12$. The price p_1 then falls to 4, keeping p_2 and m fixed. Decompose the price effect into its substitution and income effects using either the Hicks-Allen or Slutsky decompositions.

5.8. Elliot's preferences are given by the utility function $u(x_1, x_2) = x_1 + 2\sqrt{x_2}$. Suppose $m = 10$, $p_1 = 2$, and $p_2 = 1$. The price p_1 then falls to to 1, keeping p_2 and m fixed. Decompose the price effect into its substitution and income effects using either the Hicks-Allen or Slutsky decompositions.

Chapter 6

Exchange Economies

One of the significant advances in economic theory in the 20th century has been the development of **general equilibrium** analysis which explores the possibility of simultaneous equilibrium in multiple markets, as opposed to the older **partial equilibrium** analysis of Alfred Marshall which studies the possibility of equilibrium in a single market in isolation. Today, much of modern macroeconomic theory is developed in a general equilibrium framework. In this chapter, we take up the simplest possible general equilibrium model with two consumers and two goods. Because there is no production, the consumers may only choose to trade the available supplies of the goods; ergo, such an economic environment is called a **pure exchange economy**.

6.1 The Edgeworth Box

Suppose there are only two consumers, a and b, and two goods, 1 and 2. We will use the superscript i to refer to either individual, and the subscript j to refer to either good. Each consumer i has a **characteristic** e^i which consists of two pieces of information specific to her, namely, her preferences and her individual endowment. Her preferences are represented by a utility function, u^i, over the two goods; her individual endowment, ω^i, is a commodity bundle which shows the total amounts of the two goods that she possesses initially, i.e., $\omega^i = (\omega_1^i, \omega_2^i)$. Then i's characteristic is written as

$$e^i = (u^i, \omega^i) \tag{6.1}$$

which summarizes all the relevant information about this consumer. Finally, an **economy**, e, is a list of the characteristics of all consumers:

$$e = (e^a, e^b) = ((u^a, \omega^a), (u^b, \omega^b)).\qquad(6.2)$$

This economy e is our prototype of a two-person private goods pure exchange economy.[1]

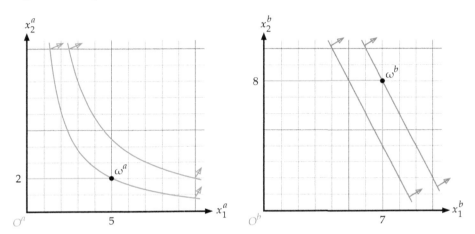

Figure 6.1   Characteristics of consumers a and b

To make things more concrete, suppose consumer a's characteristic e^a is given by a Cobb-Douglas utility $u^a = x_1^a x_2^a$ and an endowment $\omega^a = (5,2)$, while e^b is given by a linear utility $u^b = 2x_1^b + x_2^b$ and $\omega^b = (7,8)$. The left panel of Figure 6.1 shows consumer a's origin, O^a, a couple of her orange indifference curves and her endowment bundle, ω^a. The right panel of Figure 6.1 shows b's origin, O^b, a couple of her linear green indifference curves and her endowment bundle, ω^b. By adding the endowment of each consumer, we obtain the **aggregate endowment**, Ω (read as 'capital omega'), which shows the total supply of all goods in the economy:

$$\Omega = \omega^a + \omega^b = (5,2) + (7,8) = (12,10).$$

Any list of consumption bundles (x^a, x^b) for the two consumers is called an **allocation**. Suppose the total supplies of both goods are divided between

---

[1] A good is said to be **private** if one person's consumption of a good precludes it being consumed by someone else, and if others can be excluded from consuming it. See Chapter 16 for more details.

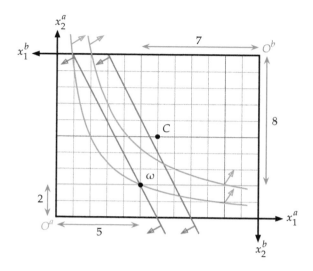

Figure 6.2   The Edgeworth box

the two consumers so that a receives the bundle $\bar{x}^a = (4,7)$ while b receives the remainder, $\bar{x}^b = (8,3)$. Then we say that the pair of consumption bundles $(\bar{x}^a, \bar{x}^b) = ((4,7),(8,3))$ is a **feasible allocation**, meaning that this allocation is actually possible given the total supply of the goods. In fact any pair (x^a, x^b) is a feasible allocation so long as $x^a + x^b \leq \Omega$.

In order to better understand allocations, take the right panel of Figure 6.1, rotate it counterclockwise by $180°$, and place it over the left panel so that the bundles ω^a and ω^b coincide as shown by the point ω in Figure 6.2. The rectangle contained between the origins O^a and O^b is known as an **Edgeworth box** named after Francis Edgeworth.[2]

Any point inside this box represents a feasible allocation, where the consumption bundle for individual a is read from her origin, O^a, while that of b is read (upside down!) from the perspective of b's origin, O^b. For example, the point $\omega = (\omega^a, \omega^b)$ is the allocation $((5,2),(7,8))$. This is called the **initial endowment** for this Edgeworth box economy; it shows the consumption bundle each person starts out with before any trade takes place. The allocation corresponding to O^b is $((12,10),(0,0))$ where individual a gets everything while b gets nothing. Conversely, the allocation corresponding to O^a is $((0,0),(12,10))$.

---

[2]It is also known as an Edgeworth-Bowley box, after the English statistician and economist Arthur Bowley who popularized it.

The length of an Edgeworth box shows the total supply of good 1, while the height shows the total supply of good 2. Given the Edgeworth box and the initial endowment, any exchange of goods between the consumers entails a movement to another allocation inside the box. Starting from any allocation inside the Edgeworth box — say, the center, $C = ((6,5),(6,5))$ — to an allocation to its northeast makes consumer a better off and b worse off because both consumers' preferences are strictly monotonic. Conversely, any allocation to the southwest of the box makes b better off and a worse off.

6.2 Properties of Allocations

Given the preferences of the individuals and the initial endowment, we can now discuss properties of allocations. Some allocations may be more desirable than others. We explore two different notions of desirability.

6.2.1 Individually rational allocations

Individual rationality embodies the idea that if two people trade voluntarily, that trade must leave each person at least as well off as before they trade; if trade hurts either consumer, they will have no incentive to engage in such an exchange of goods.

We define an allocation (x^a, x^b) to be individually rational if

$$u^a(x^a) \geq u^a(\omega^a) \quad \text{and} \quad u^b(x^b) \geq u^b(\omega^b), \tag{6.3}$$

i.e., each person's utility at her consumption bundle x^i is at least as great as her utility from her endowment ω^i, where $i = a, b$. Thus, the movement from the endowment bundle ω^a to the bundle x^a leaves consumer a no worse off than initially, and similarly for consumer b.

In Figure 6.3, the individually rational allocations lie in the blue lens-shaped area (labeled IR) between the indifference curves of each consumer that pass through the initial endowment. For example, in moving from ω to A, both consumers are better off than initially because A lies on a higher indifference curve for each consumer. At an allocation such as B, consumer a remains on her initial indifference curve and so remains as well off, but consumer b is on a higher indifference curve. You can verify this by drawing b's indifference curve through point B. At C, consumer b is as well off as initially but a is better off.

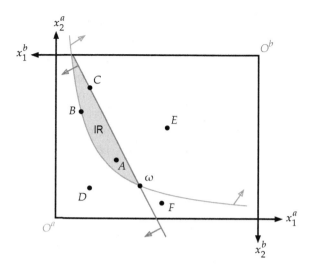

Figure 6.3   Individually rational allocations

Note that any allocation inside the Edgeworth box but outside of the IR area places at least one consumer behind her indifference curve, signifying that she is worse off than at ω. For example, at D, consumer a is worse off; at E, b is worse off, and at F, both consumers are worse off. If we expect the consumers to barter and trade with each other starting at ω, the only allocations that they would agree to move to voluntarily must lie within the IR area since neither is made worse off by such a move; indeed, it is quite possible for one or even both of them to be better off.

Individually rational allocations inside the Edgeworth box can be found by following the three steps summarized below.

1. Identify the initial endowment, ω, in the Edgeworth box.

2. Draw an indifference curve for consumer a that passes through ω, using arrows to show the direction in which her utility is increasing. Do the same for consumer b.

3. The area between the indifference curve for consumer a and that for consumer b (including the indifference curves themselves) is the set of individually rational allocations.

6.2.2 Pareto efficient allocations

Pareto efficiency (or more traditionally, Pareto optimality) embodies the idea of non-wastefulness in allocating the total supply of goods at our disposal among consumers.[3] Given an allocation, if it is possible to reallocate the goods so as to make at least one person happier and no one worse off, then the original allocation is wasteful in the sense that there is scope for improving on it. At a Pareto efficient allocation, it is not possible to reallocate the goods so as to make one consumer better off without hurting someone else, so it is non-wasteful.

To illustrate this idea simply, suppose we have an apple and a banana to allocate between two persons. Consumer a is indifferent between an apple and a banana, but consumer b has an aversion to bananas and strictly prefers apples over bananas. Then the allocation that gives a the apple and b the banana is wasteful because it is possible to make at least one person better off without hurting the other. Simply give the banana to consumer a and the apple to b; then a is as well off, but b is better off. Giving the banana to a and the apple to b is a Pareto efficient allocation because it is not possible to reallocate the goods and make at least one person happier without hurting the other.

Before we can define what a Pareto efficient allocation is formally, we need another definition. Starting from an allocation (x^a, x^b), the allocation $(\bar{x}^a, \bar{x}^b)$ is said to be Pareto superior to (or a Pareto improvement over) (x^a, x^b) if nobody is worse off at $(\bar{x}^a, \bar{x}^b)$ and at least one person is better off. In other words, if we started with the initial allocation (x^a, x^b) and moved to $(\bar{x}^a, \bar{x}^b)$, then that would constitute an improvement because nobody is hurt and someone is happier. An allocation $(\hat{x}^a, \hat{x}^b)$ is Pareto efficient if there is no other allocation that is Pareto superior to $(\hat{x}^a, \hat{x}^b)$. In other words, at a Pareto efficient allocation, it is not possible to make at least one person happier without hurting anyone else — any reallocation of goods either hurts somebody, or leaves everyone as well off.

Graphical representation

Typically an Edgeworth box will have many Pareto efficient allocations. These Pareto efficient allocations can be found by following this algorithm.

---

[3] Pareto efficiency is named after Vilfredo Pareto, an influential economist and sociologist. The phrase "non-wastefulness" was coined by Leonid Hurwicz.

1. Fix the utility of one consumer, say individual b, at some arbitrary level $\bar{u}^b$ inside the Edgeworth box.

2. Maximize the utility of consumer a while keeping b on the indifference curve $\bar{u}^b$. Then the allocation reached is a Pareto efficient allocation.

3. To find other Pareto efficient allocations, repeat the process by picking a different utility level for b in step 1.

To find one Pareto efficient allocation and understand how this algorithm works, arbitrarily fix b's utility at $\bar{u}^b$ shown by the green $\bar{u}^b$ indifference curve in Figure 6.4. Maximize a's preferences while keeping b on her green indifference curve, yielding the allocation A. Then A is a Pareto efficient allocation. To check this, consider the different regions of the Edgeworth box where an

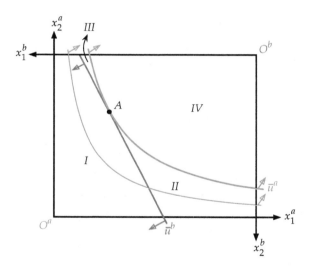

Figure 6.4 A Pareto efficient allocation

alternative allocation could be picked. Any allocation in region I (which lies to the southwest of the green indifference curve) makes consumer a worse off. In regions II and III, both a and b are worse off as they are behind their indifference curves $\bar{u}^a$ and $\bar{u}^b$. In region IV (which lies to the northeast of the orange indifference curve $\bar{u}^a$), b is worse off. Therefore, beginning with A, there is no Pareto superior allocation in the Edgeworth box, and hence A is Pareto efficient.

Two remarks are in order. First, the fact that we fix the utility of b in step 1 is totally arbitrary. In other words, the same set of Pareto efficient allocations can be found by reversing the roles of a and b, namely, fixing the utility of a instead in step 1, and maximizing b's utility while keeping a at this utility in step 2.

Second, unlike individually rational allocations, Pareto efficient allocations do not depend on the initial endowment as a reference point. They only depend on the consumers' preference and the aggregate supplies of the goods, Ω. In other words, given the consumers' preferences and the dimensions of the Edgeworth box, the set of Pareto efficient allocations would remain unchanged if the initial endowment were to be some other point inside the Edgeworth box.

Algebraic derivation

The algorithm to find the Pareto efficient allocations graphically is tedious since there are infinitely many utility levels that could be picked in the first step. The alternative algebraic method presented here holds the promise of finding many, if not all, the Pareto efficient allocations in the interior of the Edgeworth box at once.

The algebraic derivation is motivated by Figure 6.4 which suggests that at an interior Pareto efficient allocation, the tangency of the consumers' indifference curves is a necessary condition, i.e., if $(\bar{x}^a, \bar{x}^b)$ is Pareto efficient, then $MRS^a(\bar{x}^a) = MRS^b(\bar{x}^b)$. When preferences are strictly monotonic and convex, the tangency of the indifference curves is also sufficient to guarantee Pareto efficiency, i.e., if $MRS^a(\bar{x}^a) = MRS^b(\bar{x}^b)$, then $(\bar{x}^a, \bar{x}^b)$ is Pareto efficient. Therefore, the tangency of the indifference curves is often a way to find (interior) Pareto efficient allocations algebraically, or to verify whether a given allocation in the interior of the Edgeworth box is Pareto efficient.

To find the interior Pareto efficient allocations algebraically for the economy in section 6.1, set the marginal rate of substitution for a equal to that for b to obtain

$$MRS^a = x_2^a / x_1^a = MRS^b = 2.$$

Then $x_2^a = 2x_1^a$, which means that when the two consumers' indifference curves are tangent, person a consumes twice as much of good 2 as good 1. Plot the equation $x_2^a = 2x_1^a$ in Figure 6.5 beginning from O^a, joining interior Pareto efficient allocations such as R and S where the consumers' indifference curves are tangent as shown.

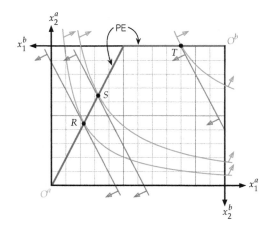

Figure 6.5   The Pareto set or contract curve

However, there are other Pareto efficient allocations in addition to the allocations that lie along the line $x_2^a = 2x_1^a$. For instance, verify by inspection that a point like $T = ((9,10),(3,0))$ which is on the edge (and not the interior) of the Edgeworth box is also Pareto efficient. Generally, the tangency condition will not hold at Pareto efficient allocations along the edges of the Edgeworth box. For instance, at T, $MRS^a(9,10) = 0.9$ while $MRS^b(3,0) = 2.$[4] The set of all Pareto efficient allocations (often called the contract curve) for this economy is labeled PE.

When the contract curve consists of allocations in the interior of the Edgeworth box, it is possible to find an equation for it by following these three steps.

1. Set $MRS^a = MRS^b$.

2. From the supply constraints for the two goods, $x_1^a + x_1^b = \Omega_1$ and $x_2^a + x_2^b = \Omega_2$, derive $x_1^b = \Omega_1 - x_1^a$ and $x_2^b = \Omega_2 - x_2^a$. Use these to eliminate x_1^b and x_2^b in the equation from step 1.

3. Solve the equation from step 2 to write x_2^a as a function of x_1^a. Then this is the equation for the contract curve with O^a as the origin.

---

[4]In general, at a Pareto efficient allocation that lies on the left hand or top edge of the Edgeworth box, it will be the case that $MRS^a \leq MRS^b$; the inequality will be reversed for a Pareto efficient allocation that lies on the right hand or bottom edge of the Edgeworth box.

To illustrate, suppose both consumers have Cobb-Douglas preferences, where a's utility function is $u^a(x_1^a, x_2^a) = x_1^a x_2^a$ while b's utility is $u^b(x_1^b, x_2^b) = (x_1^b)^2 x_2^b$. Suppose that there are 10 units of each good in this economy, i.e., $\Omega = (10, 10)$. Then from step 1, we get

$$\frac{x_2^a}{x_1^a} = \frac{2x_2^b}{x_1^b}.$$

From step 2, $x_1^b = 10 - x_1^a$ and $x_2^b = 10 - x_2^a$. Substituting these into the equation above and solving, we get the contract curve

$$x_2^a = \frac{20x_1^a}{10 + x_1^a},$$

where $0 \leq x_1^a \leq 10$.

Finally, to end this section on Pareto efficiency, note that in moving from one Pareto efficient allocation to another, there will typically be a change in the distribution of the goods that makes one person better off at the expense of another. In other words, no Pareto efficient allocation can be Pareto superior to another Pareto efficient allocation. For example, the extreme situation where consumer a gets the aggregate endowment (at the point O^b) or its polar opposite where consumer b gets everything (at the point O^a) are both Pareto efficient. Thus, the notion of Pareto efficiency is insensitive to distributional concerns.

6.3 Walras Equilibrium

We will now consider the possibility of the two consumers trading goods 1 and 2 in markets at a per-unit price of p_1 and p_2. Even though there are only two consumers for now, we will assume that each takes the market prices as given and outside of their control.[5] Given these prices, each consumer decides how much she wishes to buy or sell of each good. The markets are said to clear if the quantity demanded of good 1 by both consumers equals its supply, and likewise for good 2. Then the question that Léon Walras asked in the 1870s in the context of our Edgeworth box economy is: does there exist a price pair $(\hat{p}_1, \hat{p}_2)$ for which both markets clear? We explore this question graphically to uncover the basic insights and then fill in the more technical details.

---

[5]This assumption would of course be more plausible if there were a very large number of consumers.

6.3.1   Graphical representation

We begin with a definition. A **Walras equilibrium** (or a **competitive equilibrium**) consists of prices $(\hat{p}_1, \hat{p}_2)$ and an allocation $(\hat{x}^a, \hat{x}^b) = ((\hat{x}_1^a, \hat{x}_2^a), (\hat{x}_1^b, \hat{x}_2^b))$ such that:

(a) the consumption bundle $\hat{x}^a$ maximizes u^a subject to the budget constraint $\hat{p}_1 x_1^a + \hat{p}_2 x_2^a \le \hat{p}_1 w_1^a + \hat{p}_2 w_2^a$;

(b) the consumption bundle $\hat{x}^b$ maximizes u^b subject to the budget constraint $\hat{p}_1 x_1^b + \hat{p}_2 x_2^b \le \hat{p}_1 w_1^b + \hat{p}_2 w_2^b$; and

(c) the markets for goods 1 and 2 clear:

$$\hat{x}_1^a + \hat{x}_1^b = w_1^a + w_1^b \text{ and } \hat{x}_2^a + \hat{x}_2^b = w_2^a + w_2^b.$$

Therefore a Walras equilibrium is a pair of prices and a pair of consumption bundles at which each consumer maximizes her utility given her budget constraint, and the total demand for each good equals its supply.

Note that the right hand side of consumer i's budget constraint in (a) and (b) above represent her income which is merely the value of i's endowment at the equilibrium prices, i.e.,

$$\hat{m}^i = \hat{p}_1 w_1^i + \hat{p}_2 w_2^i.$$

Therefore (a) and (b) are an alternative way of saying that $\hat{x}^i$ is the bundle demanded by consumer i when the prices are the equilibrium ones and her income is $\hat{m}^i$:

$$\hat{x}^i = h^i(\hat{p}_1, \hat{p}_2, \hat{m}^i).$$

Before we see what happens in equilibrium, consider an arbitrary pair of prices $(\bar{p}_1, \bar{p}_2)$ set by a mythical **Walrasian auctioneer** whose job is to find the equilibrium prices. In Figure 6.6, the blue budget line with slope $-\bar{p}_1/\bar{p}_2$ is shown passing through the initial endowment, w. Viewed from origin O^a, this is the endowment budget[6] for consumer a, while the same line is the endowment budget for consumer b when viewed from origin O^b. Note that the slope of this budget line is $-\bar{p}_1/\bar{p}_2$ irrespective of whether you view it using O^a as your origin, or whether you turn the page upside down and view it with O^b as your origin.

---

[6]See section 2.3.1 and Figure 2.5.

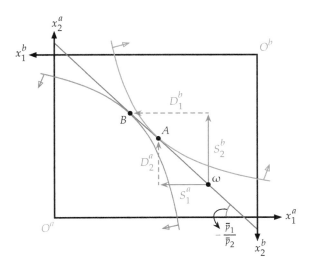

Figure 6.6 Demand and supply at $(\bar{p}_1, \bar{p}_2)$

Given this budget, consumer a demands the bundle at point A. In other words, starting from ω, she is willing to supply S_1^a units of good 1 (shown by the solid magenta arrow) in exchange for D_2^a units of good 2 (shown by the dashed magenta arrow) to move to the bundle at A. Likewise, consumer b would like to move from ω to point B, supplying S_2^b units of good 2 in exchange for D_1^b units of good 1. But the market for good 1 does not clear at these prices: consumer a would like to supply S_1^a units but consumer b demands more, D_1^b. Similarly, the market for good 2 does not clear either as the demand for good 2, D_2^a, is less than its supply, S_2^b.

Assume now that the Walrasian auctioneer raises p_1 which makes consumer a wish to supply more and consumer b to demand less of good 1, and/or lowers p_2 which makes consumer a demand more of good 2 and consumer b supply less of it. In other words, beginning with the initial dotted blue budget line in Figure 6.7, the auctioneer can raise the *relative* price ratio, p_1/p_2, to find a set of prices $(\hat{p}_1, \hat{p}_2)$ shown by the steeper, solid blue budget line. Note that this new budget pivots around the endowment ω as the relative price ratio increases, and equates $S_1^a = D_1^b$ for good 1, and $S_2^b = D_2^a$ for good 2. Then, $(\hat{p}_1, \hat{p}_2)$ are the **Walras prices**, the prices at which the consumers attain the **Walras allocation**, $E = (\hat{x}^a, \hat{x}^b)$, where each person is maximizing her utility given her budget (at the Walras prices) and the demand for each good equals its supply.

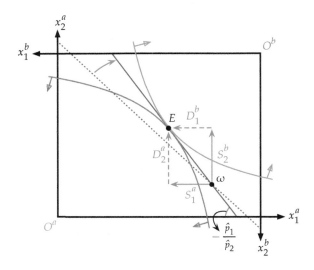

Figure 6.7   Walras equilibrium

There are three insights regarding Walras equilibria that can be gleaned from Figure 6.7:

(1) whenever the market for one good is in equilibrium, the other must also be in equilibrium;

(2) what matters for bringing about equilibrium is the *relative* price ratio, not the absolute price levels; and

(3) the Walras allocation is both individually rational and Pareto efficient.

Insight (1) follows from the fact that in moving from the initial endowment ω to the Walras allocation E in Figure 6.7, the quantities that each consumer wants to buy and sell are opposite sides of a rectangle (shown with the solid and dashed magenta arrows). It is not possible, for example, for the market for good 1 to clear but not that of good 2. Mathematically, this follows from **Walras' Law**[7] which states that the value of everyone's consumption expenditures must always add up to the value of the aggregate endowment. A consequence of Walras' Law is that if there are ℓ goods with prices $\hat{p}_1, \hat{p}_2, \ldots, \hat{p}_\ell$ so that every market but one is in equilibrium, then that remaining market must also be in equilibrium. Since here there are two goods ($\ell = 2$), this corollary to Walras' Law guarantees that finding prices

---

[7]Section 6.5.1 below presents a formal statement and proof.

to bring about equilibrium in one market ensures that the other market is automatically in equilibrium.

Insight (2) follows from the fact that in going from the initial prices of $(\bar{p}_1, \bar{p}_2)$ to the Walras equilibrium prices of $(\hat{p}_1, \hat{p}_2)$, what equilibrates the two markets is the steeper *slope* of the latter budget. If the slope of the budget at the Walras prices is -2 for example, there are infinitely many price combinations that give rise to this slope. Therefore, the absolute levels of the prices is indeterminate at a Walras equilibrium. To peg the level of the Walras prices, we normalize the price of one good to $1; this good is then called the **numéraire** good and the prices of all other goods are measured in terms of this numéraire. For instance, if a pack of chewing gum is the numéraire, then the price of a shirt worth $30 would be priced at 30 packs of gum — packs of gum are the unit of account.

Finally, regarding insight (3), individual rationality holds since each consumer is on a higher indifference curve at E as compared to ω. Indeed, since trade is voluntary, neither consumer would wish to move to the Walras allocation from ω unless they are at least as well off as initially. Pareto efficiency of the Walras allocation follows from the tangency of the consumers' indifference curves at E. This result, known as the **First Welfare Theorem**, is one of the key insights of microeconomic theory and is a precise modern restatement of the idea attributed to Adam Smith that the greatest social good arises when individuals follow their self-interest in free markets.

6.3.2   Algebraic derivation

Consider a two-person economy where the utilities are Cobb-Douglas and given by

$$u^a = x_1^a x_2^a \text{ and } u^b = (x_1^b)^2 x_2^b$$

and endowments are

$$\omega^a = (6, 4) \text{ and } \omega^b = (2, 8).$$

Then the demand functions for each consumer (using the formulas in equation (4.11)) are

$$h^a(p_1, p_2, m^a) = \left(\frac{m^a}{2p_1}, \frac{m^a}{2p_2} \right) \text{ and } h^b(p_1, p_2, m^b) = \left(\frac{2m^b}{3p_1}, \frac{m^b}{3p_2} \right),$$

where $m^a = 6p_1 + 4p_2$ and $m^b = 2p_1 + 8p_2$ are the values of each consumer's endowment.

Solving for the Walras equilibrium for this economy requires four steps.

1. Normalize one of the prices to 1.

2. Invoke the corollary to Walras' Law to ignore one market. Since there are two goods, select any one.

3. Set the total demand for the selected good equal to its supply and solve for the price.

4. Substitute the Walras prices into the demand functions to obtain the Walras allocation.

Following these steps, suppose we first set $p_2 = 1$. In step 2, ignore the first good, i.e., pick the market for good 2.[8] In step 3, equate the total market demand to the supply of good 2:

$$\frac{m^a}{2} + \frac{m^b}{3} = \frac{6p_1 + 4}{2} + \frac{2p_1 + 8}{3} = 4 + 8.$$

Solve for p_1 to obtain $\hat{p}_1 = 2$. So the Walras prices are $(\hat{p}_1, \hat{p}_2) = (2, 1)$. Finally, substitute these in the demand functions to obtain the Walras allocation, $(\hat{x}^a, \hat{x}^b) = ((4, 8), (4, 4))$.

We can directly verify that the First Welfare Theorem holds at the Walras allocation. Since $u^a(\hat{x}^a) = 32 > u^a(\omega^a) = 24$ and $u^b(\hat{x}^b) = 64 > u^b(\omega^b) = 32$, the Walras allocation is individually rational. Next check the marginal rates of substitution: $MRS^a(\hat{x}^a) = 8/4 = 2$ and $MRS^b(\hat{x}^b) = 8/4 = 2$. Since these are the same and the preferences are strictly monotonic, it follows that the Walras allocation is Pareto efficient.

6.4   Allowing for More Goods or Consumers

In this section we explore how the above results generalize when there are more than two goods and/or more than two people.

Consider first the case of two consumers and three goods. In solving for the Walras equilibrium, we essentially follow the same steps as before with appropriate modifications. In step 1, normalize one of the prices, say

[8]As an exercise, ignore the second good and pick the market for good 1 instead. Verify that the Walras equilibrium is the same.

$p_3 = 1$. Then there are two prices, p_1 and p_2, that need to be calculated so as to ensure that all three markets clear. Next, in step 2, invoke the corollary to Walras' Law to eliminate one of the three markets, say market 1. Then in step 3, set the demand for good 2 equal to its supply, and similarly for good 3. This results in two equations in two unknowns, p_1 and p_2. Solving these simultaneously yields the Walras prices, $\hat{p}_1$ and $\hat{p}_2$. Finally, substitute these prices into the consumers' demand functions to calculate the Walras allocation.

The First Welfare Theorem will hold here as well. While individual ratio-nality is straightforward to verify, the condition for Pareto efficiency has to be modified. With three goods, there are three marginal rates of substitution for each consumer i: between good 1 and 2, between 1 and 3, and between 2 and 3 which we write as MRS^i_{12}, MRS^i_{13}, and MRS^i_{23}. Then interior Pareto efficient allocations require that each of the marginal rates of substitution for one person equals the corresponding marginal rates of substitution of the other:

$$MRS^a_{12} = MRS^b_{12}, \quad MRS^a_{13} = MRS^b_{13}, \quad MRS^a_{23} = MRS^b_{23}.$$

Now consider what happens when there are more than two individuals. The only new wrinkle this introduces is in step 3: the good 2 demand func-tions for *all* individuals need to be added and set equal to its supply, and likewise for the good 3 demand functions. All other steps are unchanged. Finally, the necessary condition for Pareto efficiency in the general case with n persons and ℓ goods is that the marginal rate of substitution between *any* two different goods be the same across all individuals. Indexing the individ-uals by $1, 2, \ldots, n$, this means that

$$MRS^1_{jk} = MRS^2_{jk} = \ldots = MRS^n_{jk}$$

for all goods j and k $(j, k = 1, 2, \ldots, \ell, j \neq k)$.

6.5   Walras' Law and the Welfare Theorems°

In this section, we provide formal proofs for Walras' Law, and the First Wel-fare Theorem in the special case of the two-person Edgeworth box economies when preferences are strictly monotonic.[9] We also state and briefly discuss the Second Welfare Theorem.

---

[9]The assumption of strict monotonicity of preferences is sufficient but not necessary; it can be weakened. However, doing so would take us beyond the scope of this text.

6.5.1   Walras' Law

Proposition. *When consumers have strictly monotonic preferences, the value of the goods demanded must equal the value of all goods supplied at any set of prices.*

Proof. Suppose there are ℓ goods and $(\bar{p}_1, \bar{p}_2, \ldots, \bar{p}_\ell)$ is any set of prices. Let $(\bar{x}^a, \bar{x}^b)$ denote the allocation where $\bar{x}^i$ is consumer i's utility-maximizing bundle over her budget. Then consumer a's budget constraint must hold at $\bar{x}^a$, i.e.,

$$\bar{p}_1 \bar{x}_1^a + \ldots + \bar{p}_\ell \bar{x}_\ell^a \leq \bar{p}_1 \omega_1^a + \ldots + \bar{p}_\ell \omega_\ell^a,$$

where ω_j^i shows the endowment of the jth good held by consumer i. However, if this constraint holds with a strict inequality, then the income left over after buying $\bar{x}^a$ can be used to buy more of some good which would leave a better off than at bundle $\bar{x}^a$ because preferences are strictly monotonic, contradicting the premise that $\bar{x}^a$ is utility-maximizing over a's budget. Therefore, consumer a's budget constraint must hold with a strict equality:

$$\bar{p}_1 \bar{x}_1^a + \ldots + \bar{p}_\ell \bar{x}_\ell^a = \bar{p}_1 \omega_1^a + \ldots + \bar{p}_\ell \omega_\ell^a. \tag{6.4}$$

Similarly, for consumer b,

$$\bar{p}_1 \bar{x}_1^b + \ldots + \bar{p}_\ell \bar{x}_\ell^b = \bar{p}_1 \omega_1^b + \ldots + \bar{p}_\ell \omega_\ell^b. \tag{6.5}$$

Denote the total supply of good $j = 1, \ldots, \ell$ by Ω_j. Then adding (6.4) and (6.5) together and grouping terms yields

$$\begin{aligned}
\bar{p}_1(\bar{x}_1^a + \bar{x}_1^b) + \ldots + \bar{p}_\ell(\bar{x}_\ell^a + \bar{x}_\ell^b) &= \bar{p}_1(\omega_1^a + \omega_1^b) + \ldots + \bar{p}_\ell(\omega_\ell^a + \omega_\ell^b) \\
&= \bar{p}_1 \Omega_1 + \ldots + \bar{p}_\ell \Omega_\ell.
\end{aligned}$$

Then the left hand side is the sum of the value of the goods demanded by a and b while the right hand side is the value of all goods supplied. ∎

Corollary. *If $(\hat{p}_1, \ldots, \hat{p}_\ell)$ are prices at which $\ell - 1$ markets out of ℓ are in equilibrium, then the remaining market must also be in equilibrium.*

Proof. Suppose that $(\hat{x}^a, \hat{x}^b)$ are the demands corresponding to the prices $(\hat{p}_1, \ldots, \hat{p}_\ell)$. Without loss of generality, assume that markets 2 through ℓ are in equilibrium. We need to show that the market for good 1 must be in equilibrium.

From Walras' Law, it follows that

$$\hat{p}_1(\hat{x}_1^a + \hat{x}_1^b) + \hat{p}_2(\hat{x}_2^a + \hat{x}_2^b) \ldots + \hat{p}_\ell(\hat{x}_\ell^a + \hat{x}_\ell^b) = \hat{p}_1 \Omega_1 + \hat{p}_2 \Omega_2 \ldots + \hat{p}_\ell \Omega_\ell.$$

Since markets 2 through ℓ clear by assumption, it follows that $\hat{x}_j^a + \hat{x}_j^b = \Omega_j$ for all goods $j = 2, \ldots, \ell$. Canceling the last $\ell - 1$ terms on each side of the equality, we obtain

$$\hat{p}_1(\hat{x}_1^a + \hat{x}_1^b) = \hat{p}_1\Omega_1,$$

from which it follows that $\hat{x}_1^a + \hat{x}_1^b = \Omega_1$: the market for good 1 clears. ∎

6.5.2   First Welfare Theorem

Proposition. *Let* $(\hat{p}_1, \hat{p}_2)$ *and* $(\hat{x}^a, \hat{x}^b)$ *be a Walras equilibrium and the consumers' preferences be strictly monotonic. Then the Walras allocation is individually rational and Pareto efficient.*

Proof. To show individual rationality, note that for each individual, $\hat{x}^i = h_i(\hat{p}_1, \hat{p}_2, \hat{m}^i)$, i.e., the consumption bundle for each person is utility maximizing given the Walras prices. Since $\hat{m}^i = \hat{p}_1\omega_1^i + \hat{p}_2\omega_2^i$ (each consumer's income equals the value of her individual endowment), both ω^i and $\hat{x}^i$ are available in i's budget set. Because $\hat{x}^i$ maximizes i's utility on her budget, it follows that $u^i(\hat{x}^i) \geq u^i(\omega^i)$.

To show Pareto efficiency, we first establish that any consumption bundle that is strictly better than $\hat{x}^i$ for consumer i must be unaffordable at the Walras prices. By way of contradiction, suppose that there is a bundle $\bar{x}^i$ which is as good as $\hat{x}^i$ but cheaper, i.e., $u^i(\bar{x}^i) \geq u^i(\hat{x}^i)$ and $\hat{p}_1\bar{x}_1^i + \hat{p}_2\bar{x}_2^i < \hat{m}^i$. Since $\bar{x}^i$ lies in the interior of the budget set and i's preferences are strictly monotonic, there is some bundle $\tilde{x}^i$ to the northeast of $\bar{x}^i$ which is better and affordable, i.e., $u^i(\tilde{x}^i) > u^i(\bar{x}^i)$, and

$$\hat{p}_1\tilde{x}_1^i + \hat{p}_2\tilde{x}_2^i \leq \hat{m}^i.$$

From $u^i(\tilde{x}^i) > u^i(\bar{x}^i)$ and $u^i(\bar{x}^i) \geq u^i(\hat{x}^i)$, it follows that $u^i(\tilde{x}^i) > u^i(\hat{x}^i)$, contradicting that $\hat{x}^i$ maximizes i's preferences on the Walras budget. This establishes that given a preference-maximizing $\hat{x}^i$, anything that is strictly preferred must be unaffordable.

Now suppose that $(\hat{x}^a, \hat{x}^b)$ is not Pareto efficient. Then there is some other allocation $(\tilde{x}^a, \tilde{x}^b)$ which is feasible (i.e., $\tilde{x}_1^a + \tilde{x}_1^b = \Omega_1$ and $\tilde{x}_2^a + \tilde{x}_2^b = \Omega_2$), and where neither consumer is hurt when compared to $(\hat{x}^a, \hat{x}^b)$ and at least one is better off. Without loss of generality, suppose a is the person better off and b the person who is not hurt, i.e., $u^a(\tilde{x}^a) > u^a(\hat{x}^a)$ and $u^b(\tilde{x}^b) \geq u^b(\hat{x}^b)$. Then, as established in the previous paragraph, $\tilde{x}^a$ must lie outside of a's Walras budget and is unaffordable:

$$\hat{p}_1\tilde{x}_1^a + \hat{p}_2\tilde{x}_2^a > \hat{p}_1\omega_1^a + \hat{p}_2\omega_2^a. \tag{6.6}$$

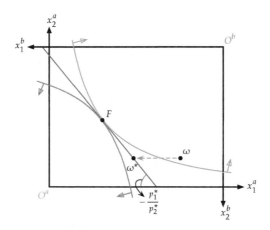

Figure 6.8   The Second Welfare Theorem

Since $u^b(\tilde{x}^b) \geq u^b(\hat{x}^b)$ for b, it follows that

$$\hat{p}_1 \tilde{x}_1^b + \hat{p}_2 \tilde{x}_2^b \geq \hat{p}_1 \omega_1^b + \hat{p}_2 \omega_2^b. \tag{6.7}$$

Adding (6.6) and (6.7) and grouping terms, we get

$$\hat{p}_1(\tilde{x}_1^a + \tilde{x}_1^b) + \hat{p}_2(\tilde{x}_2^a + \tilde{x}_2^b) > \hat{p}_1(\omega_1^a + \omega_1^b) + \hat{p}_2(\omega_2^a + \omega_2^b),$$

or

$$\hat{p}_1 \Omega_1 + \hat{p}_2 \Omega_2 > \hat{p}_1 \Omega_1 + \hat{p}_2 \Omega_2,$$

a contradiction. Therefore $(\hat{x}^a, \hat{x}^b)$ is Pareto efficient. ■

6.5.3   Second Welfare Theorem

Proposition. *Let (x^{a*}, x^{b*}) be any interior Pareto efficient allocation where consumers' preferences are strictly monotonic and convex. Then there is an endowment ω^* and prices (p_1^*, p_2^*) for which (x^{a*}, x^{b*}) is the Walras allocation. The endowment ω^* may be attained from the initial endowment ω through appropriate lump-sum taxes and transfers.*

The Second Welfare Theorem shows that distributional issues may be addressed through the market mechanism: any interior Pareto efficient allocation can be attained via competitive markets as a Walras allocation from a suitable endowment point.

To see this, suppose the interior Pareto efficient allocation F in Figure 6.8 is the allocation where the distribution of the two goods is regarded as desirable from society's point of view. Starting from the initial endowment w, this allocation can be attained with a two-step process. In the first step, use a lump-sum tax and transfer to move the participants from the initial endowment w to, say, w^* as shown: this requires consumer a to pay a tax in terms of good 1 equal to the length of the magenta arrow to the government, and then transferring that amount to consumer b. Then, in the second step, let the consumers participate in Walras markets starting from the post-tax-and-transfer endowment, w^*. The desired allocation F can be attained as a Walras allocation via trade along the blue Walras budget line. Note that there is nothing unique about the post-tax-and-transfer endowment w^* above. A tax-and-transfer scheme that moves the initial endowment w to any other point along the blue Walras budget line will result in the the the same Walras equilibrium.

The major weakness of this theorem is that the first step involving taxes and transfers will typically not be individually rational, so not all of the participants will voluntarily want to take part in this tax-and-transfer scheme; neither will the final allocation reached be individually rational in general (relative to the initial endowment, w). Another criticism is that if the government (presumably) has the ability to modify the initial endowment through taxes and transfers, then it can bypass the Walras mechanism altogether and just use taxes and transfers to move from the initial endowment w directly to the final allocation F without the use of markets.

The importance of this theorem lies therefore not in its plausibility, but whether Pareto efficient allocations can in principle be attained as outcomes of Walras markets. This kind of reasoning becomes important in a different context, say, in the presence of externalities (see Chapter 14) or asymmetric information (see Chapter 15) or market imperfections, when a Walras allocation is no longer guaranteed to be Pareto efficient. In that case, it is important to know whether Pareto efficient outcomes can be achieved in principle using markets, perhaps in conjunction with appropriate governmental interventions.

Exercises

6.1. For each economy (e^a, e^b), draw an Edgeworth box showing the individually rational allocations, and another showing the Pareto efficient allocations.

(a) $e^a = (\min\{x^a, y^a\}, (2,3))$ and $e^b = (x^b + y^b, (4,1))$

(b) $e^a = (\min\{x^a, y^a\}, (3,2))$ and $e^b = (\min\{x^b, y^b\}, (3,2))$

(c) $e^a = (\min\{2x^a + y^a, x^a + 2y^a\}, (4,0))$ and $e^b = (2x^b + y^b, (2,4))$

6.2. For the following two-person two-commodity pure exchange economy, the price of good y is normalized to \$1. The table below gives the utility functions, endowments, and demands for goods x and y, where m^i denotes the value of consumer i's endowment, $i = a, b$.

Person i	u^i	ω^i	x^i	y^i
a	$x^a + \ln y^a$	$(1,4)$	$(m^a/p_x) - 1$	p_x/p_y
b	$x^b + 2\ln y^b$	$(3,2)$	$(m^b/p_x) - 2$	$2p_x/p_y$

(a) Draw the set of interior Pareto efficient allocations in an Edgeworth box for this economy.

(b) Calculate the Walras equilibrium price $\hat{p}_x$ and Walras allocation $((\hat{x}^a, \hat{y}^a), (\hat{x}^b, \hat{y}^b))$. Check that the Walras allocation is Pareto efficient graphically and algebraically.

6.3. Two individuals, a and b, consume goods x and y. Their endowments are $\omega^a = (2,5)$ and $\omega^b = (10,1)$. Both have identical Cobb-Douglas utility functions $u^i(x^i, y^i) = x^i y^i$ where $i = a, b$. The price p_y is normalized to 1; for simplicity we write p_x as just p. Then consumer i's demand for each good is

$$x^i = \frac{m^i}{2p} \quad \text{and} \quad y^i = \frac{m^i}{2},$$

where m^i refers to the value of consumer i's endowment.

(a) Draw the set of interior Pareto efficient allocations in an Edgeworth box for this economy.

(b) Calculate the Walras equilibrium price $\hat{p}$ and Walras allocation $((\hat{x}^a, \hat{y}^a), (\hat{x}^b, \hat{y}^b))$. Check that the Walras allocation is Pareto efficient graphically and algebraically.

6.4. For the following three-person two-commodity pure exchange economy, the price of good y is normalized to $1 and p_x is written as p. The
table below gives the utility functions, endowments, and demands for
goods x and y, where m^i denotes the value of consumer i's endowment.
Calculate the Walras equilibrium price of good x, $\hat{p}$, and the Walras al-
location, $((\hat{x}^a, \hat{y}^a), (\hat{x}^b, \hat{y}^b), (\hat{x}^c, \hat{y}^c))$. Check that the Walras allocation is
Pareto efficient.

Person i	u^i	ω^i	x^i	y^i
a	$x^a y^a$	$(2,0)$	$m^a/(2p)$	$m^a/2$
b	$(x^b)^3 y^b$	$(0,12)$	$3m^b/(4p)$	$m^b/4$
c	$x^c(y^c)^2$	$(12,0)$	$m^c/(3p)$	$2m^c/3$

6.5. For the following two-person three-commodity pure exchange economy, the price of good z is normalized to $1. Calculate the Walras
equilibrium prices, $(\hat{p}_x, \hat{p}_y)$, as well as the Walras allocation for this
economy, $((\hat{x}^a, \hat{y}^a, \hat{z}^a), (\hat{x}^b, \hat{y}^b, \hat{z}^b))$. Check that the Walras allocation is
Pareto efficient.

Person i	u^i	ω^i	x^i	y^i	z^i
a	$x^a y^a z^a$	$(4,2,0)$	$m^a/(3p_x)$	$m^a/(3p_y)$	$m^a/(3p_z)$
b	$(x^b)^2 y^b z^b$	$(8,0,4)$	$m^b/(2p_x)$	$m^b/(4p_y)$	$m^b/(4p_z)$

6.6. An economy consists of two types of people, males (indexed by M) and
females (indexed by F). There are four males, all identical to each other,
while there are eight females who are identical to each other. There are
two goods, x and y. The price of y is normalized to $1; the price of x is
p. The table below shows the type, utility, endowment, and demands
for x and y for each type of person.

Type i	u^i	ω^i	x^i	y^i
M	$x^M y^M$	$(4,0)$	$m^M/(2p)$	$m^M/2$
F	$x^F(y^F)^3$	$(0,12)$	$m^F/(4p)$	$3m^F/4$

At a Walras allocation, each male will consume the same bundle, while
each female will consume a different bundle. Calculate the Walras
equilibrium price $\hat{p}$ and Walras consumption bundle $(\hat{x}^M, \hat{y}^M)$ for a
male, and the bundle $(\hat{x}^F, \hat{y}^F)$ for a female. Check that the Walras allocation is Pareto efficient.

Chapter 7

Technology

Firms produce goods and services using other goods and services as inputs. In an economist's way of looking at the production process, a **technology** (or synonymously, a **production function**) is a black box into which inputs go in and are converted to output. Just as preferences are essential to study consumer behavior, technologies are the counterpart in studying producer theory. Indeed, this parallel is exploited in the next two sections explicitly: just as a utility function determines the utility level from consumption bundles, a production function analogously determines an output level from input bundles.

7.1 Production Functions and Productivity

A production function is a function written as

$$q = f(x_1, x_2, \ldots, x_n)$$

where $\mathbf{q} = (q_1, q_2, \ldots, q_k)$ denotes k different outputs produced using the input levels $(x_1, x_2, \ldots, x_n)$. These inputs will typically include various types of skilled and unskilled labor, machines, raw materials, energy use, managerial supervision, and infrastructure: land, warehouses, factories, telephone and internet services — in short, including anything that goes into a production process. We will restrict attention to the case when there is no joint production, i.e., we assume that only a single output is produced which will be denoted by q.

The **short run** is defined to be a period of time over which some inputs are **fixed** and others are **variable**. Examples of fixed inputs include machines, managerial labor, phone lines, or warehouse space whose availability or use cannot be changed from day to day. The amount of variable inputs used, such as raw materials, electricity, and unskilled labor, can be changed in the short run and will depend on how much is being produced. The **long run** is taken to be a time period over which *all* inputs are variable. What constitutes the short run or the long run will vary from one production activity to another.

Consider a production function that uses a single variable input, $q = f(x)$.[1] The **marginal product of input** x is defined to be

$$MP_x = \frac{dq}{dx} = f'(x)$$

and shows how much additional output can be produced with an incremental use of the input. Often it is assumed that there is **diminishing marginal productivity**, i.e., $dMP_x/dx < 0$, which amounts to assuming that $f''(x) < 0$. The **average product of input** x is defined to be

$$AP_x = \frac{q}{x} = \frac{f(x)}{x}.$$

Similarly, for a production function $q = f(x_1, x_2, \dots, x_n)$ that has more than one variable input, the marginal product of any input x_i is given by the partial derivative,

$$MP_i = \frac{\partial q}{\partial x_i} = \frac{\partial f}{\partial x_i}(x_1, x_2, \dots, x_n) = f_i(x_1, x_2, \dots, x_n),$$

and its average product is

$$AP_i = \frac{q}{x_i} = \frac{f(x_1, x_2, \dots, x_n)}{x_i}.$$

In the following section, we present some common production functions of the form $q = f(x_1, x_2)$ when there are two variable inputs.

---

[1] This of course is not very realistic since nothing can be produced using a single input by itself. So typically there are additional inputs that are used in the production process but their use is fixed at some level. So if x refers to fertilizer use and q to tons of corn, the use of land, tractors, labor, and other inputs are taken to be fixed and the production function then captures the relationship between fertilizer use and the output of corn.

7.2   Types of Technologies

For a consumer, an indifference curve shows combinations of the consumption goods that give the same level of satisfaction. The corresponding notion for a producer is an isoquant. An isoquant shows all combinations of the inputs that can be used to produce a fixed level of output. While the rate at which one good can be substituted for another and yet leave a consumer on the same indifference curve is called the marginal rate of substitution and is given by the ratio of the marginal utilities (recall equation (3.1)), the rate at which one input can be substituted for another along an isoquant is called the technical rate of substitution, TRS. It is given by the ratio of the marginal productivities:

$$TRS = \frac{MP_1}{MP_2} = \frac{\partial f / \partial x_1}{\partial f / \partial x_2}. \tag{7.1}$$

We now consider several technologies, some of which are the production counterparts of preferences familiar to us from Chapter 3 in the context of consumption.

7.2.1   Linear technologies

A production function of the form

$$f(x_1, x_2) = a x_1 + b x_2 \tag{7.2}$$

where a and b are marginal products of inputs x_1 and x_2 respectively results in linear isoquants so long as at least one marginal product is strictly positive. When both are positive, the TRS is a/b analogous to the indifference curves depicted in the left panel of Figure 3.3. When $a > 0$ but $b = 0$, the isoquants look like the indifference curves in the left panel of Figure 3.4, while for $a = 0$ and $b > 0$, the isoquants are like the indifference curves in the right panel.

7.2.2   Leontief technologies

A production function of the form

$$f(x_1, x_2) = \min\{a x_1, b x_2\} \tag{7.3}$$

(where a and b are non-negative and at least one is strictly positive) generates L-shaped isoquants with kinks along the ray from the origin with slope a/b,

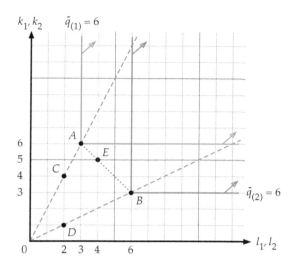

Figure 7.1   Two Leontief technologies

analogous to the indifference curves depicted in Figure 3.5. Here, of course, there are no substitution possibilities between the inputs — they are comple- ments in that the two inputs are always used in fixed proportions according to the ratio $b : a$.[2]

However, if a firm has access to two *different* Leontief technologies, e.g., two plants for producing the *same* good where the inputs are combined in different fixed proportions, then input substitution possibilities arise. To see this, let the inputs be labor ℓ and capital k, and (ℓ_1, k_1) and (ℓ_2, k_2) denote the levels of these inputs used in plant 1 and plant 2 respectively. Now suppose the production functions for the plants are

$$q_{(1)} = \min\{2\ell_1, k_1\} \text{ and } q_{(2)} = \min\{\ell_2, 2k_2\},$$

where $q_{(j)}$ is the level of output produced in plant j. In the former, one unit of labor is used for every two units of capital, while in the latter, two units of labor are used with every unit of capital. Then the firm's overall production function is

$$q = q_{(1)} + q_{(2)} = \min\{2\ell_1, k_1\} + \min\{\ell_2, 2k_2\}.$$

---

[2]Wassily Leontief was a Russian-American economist whose work on input-output anal- ysis assumes fixed proportions technologies in production. He won the Nobel Prize in Eco- nomics in 1973.

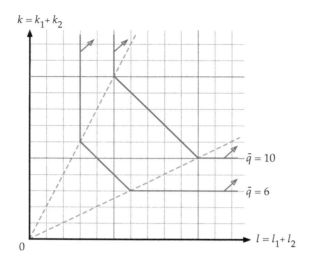

Figure 7.2   Multiplant isoquants

In Figure 7.1, the isoquants for each plant are shown: the orange isoquant is for plant 1 and the green one for plant 2 when the level of production in each plant is 6. The least amount of the inputs needed to produce 6 units in either plant uses the input combination $A = (3,6)$ in the first plant, or $B = (6,3)$ in the second.

But an output level of 6 can also be split up between the two production processes. For instance, the input combination $C = (2,4)$ can be used in the first plant to generate 4 units of output, and $D = (2,1)$ in the second for the remaining 2 units. Thus the input bundle $E = (4,5)$ — the sum of input combinations C and D — also produces 6 units of output when appropriately apportioned between the two Leontief technologies. Other input combinations on the blue dotted line segment between A and B in Figure 7.1 will also generate an output of 6. Figure 7.2 shows what the isoquants for this multiplant firm look like when it can operate two different Leontief technologies, each by itself or both simultaneously. Even though each technology by itself does not allow for any substitution possibilities between capital and labor, operating each technology in different proportions gives rise to substitution possibilities. Each isoquant for this multiplant firm inherits kinks along the same dashed magenta diagonals as the individual technologies, but between the two dashed lines, there is now a substitution possibility of one unit of labor for one unit of capital.

7.2.3 Cobb-Douglas technologies

A technology that allows for continuous substitution possibilities is given by a Cobb-Douglas production function written as

$$f(x_1, x_2) = A x_1^a x_2^b, \tag{7.4}$$

where a, b, and A are positive constants. Here the $TRS = a x_2 / b x_1$ and the isoquants are analogous to the indifference curves shown in Figure 3.9.[3]

7.2.4 CES technologies°

A more general production function that also allows for smooth substitution possibilities is the **constant elasticity of substitution** (CES) technology

$$f(x_1, x_2) = A(a x_1^s + b x_2^s)^{1/s} \tag{7.5}$$

where a, b, and A are positive constants and $-\infty < s < 1$. Its $TRS = a x_2^{1-s} / b x_1^{1-s}$.

The **elasticity of substitution**, given by $1/(1-s)$, shows the percentage change in the **input intensity**, the x_1/x_2 ratio, when there is a percentage change in the technical rate of substitution along an isoquant. The input intensity indicates whether an input bundle favors input 1 over 2. For instance, if the first input is labor, ℓ, and the second is capital, k, then the input bundle with a larger ℓ/k ratio is said to be more labor-intensive. With a CES technology, as we move along any isoquant from one input combination to another, the elasticity of substitution remains unchanged, i.e., the percentage change in input intensity changes by a constant multiple of the percentage change in the TRS.

When $s = 1$, the CES production function becomes a linear production function which has an infinite elasticity of substitution. It can be shown that as s approaches $-\infty$, we obtain a Leontief technology which has a zero elasticity of substitution. When s approaches zero, we obtain a Cobb-Douglas technology which has an elasticity of substitution equal to 1. Thus the CES technology is a general functional form that subsumes the other types of technologies as special cases.

---

[3]Though named after Charles Cobb and Paul Douglas who used this functional form to fit data on labor and capital in 1928, it had been used by Vilfredo Pareto in the context of utility in 1892 and by Knut Wicksell in the context of production in 1901.

7.3   Returns to Scale

Returns to scale refers to the overall behavior of the production function, providing some insight as to how much the output increases when all inputs are scaled up. Let $q_o = f(\bar{x}_1, \bar{x}_2)$ denote the original output level at the input bundle $(\bar{x}_1, \bar{x}_2)$. Suppose both inputs are scaled up by a factor of $t > 1$ to $(t\bar{x}_1, t\bar{x}_2)$; for example, all inputs are doubled when $t = 2$, or tripled if $t = 3$. Returns to scale relates the new output level $q_n = f(t\bar{x}_1, t\bar{x}_2)$ to the old $q_o = f(\bar{x}_1, \bar{x}_2)$.

We say that there is **constant returns to scale** (CRS) if scaling the original input levels t times increases the output level by the same factor t, i.e.,

$$q_n = tq_o.$$

There is **decreasing returns to scale** (DRS) if

$$q_n < tq_o;$$

finally, there is **increasing returns to scale** (IRS) if

$$q_n > tq_o.$$

7.3.1   Graphical representation

Consider the linear technology $q = x_1 + x_2$ which is an example of a CRS technology. In the left panel of Figure 7.3, fix the isoquant for $\bar{q} = 3$ and pick the input bundle $(1, 2)$. When inputs are doubled from $(1, 2)$ to $(2, 4)$ — moving twice as far from the origin as from the origin to $(1, 2)$ — the output doubles to 6. When inputs are tripled to $(3, 6)$, the output triples to 9.

In the right panel of Figure 7.3, we replicate the analogous situation for the linear production function $q = (x_1 + x_2)^2$ which is IRS. Here the same three isoquants have different output labels: 9, 36, and 81. In other words, doubling the inputs from $(1, 2)$ to $(2, 4)$ more than doubles the output, and tripling the inputs to $(3, 6)$ more than triples the output. This is true along any ray through the origin: moving northeast by the same fixed distance increases the input bundle by a factor of 2, 3, 4, etc., but the output from those bundles more than doubles, triples, quadruples and so on. By analogy, for a DRS technology, as we move northeast along any ray from the origin, moving by a fixed distance leads to output levels that are less than double, less than triple and so on. This provides an intuitive graphical check to verify the returns to scale for any technology.

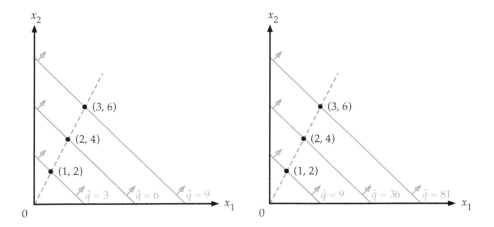

Figure 7.3   A CRS and IRS technology

7.3.2   Algebraic derivation

For production functions that are homogeneous[4] of degree r, it will be the case that

$$q_n = f(t\bar{x}_1, t\bar{x}_2) = t^r f(\bar{x}_1, \bar{x}_2) = t^r q_o.$$

Therefore, if $r = 1$, we have $q_n = tq_o$, so the production function is CRS. If $r < 1$, we have $q_n < tq_o$ since $t > 1$, a DRS production function. Analogously, if $r > 1$, we have $q_n > tq_o$ since $t > 1$, an IRS production function. Thus the degree of homogeneity, r, is an index of the returns to scale in the case of homogeneous production functions.

For the linear technology $q = x_1 + x_2$, for example, fix any input bundle $(\bar{x}_1, \bar{x}_2)$, so $q_o = \bar{x}_1 + \bar{x}_2$. Then

$$q_n = (t\bar{x}_1) + (t\bar{x}_2) = t(\bar{x}_1 + \bar{x}_2) = tq_o,$$

so this is CRS.

For the Cobb-Douglas production function, $q = x_1 x_2$, fix any input pair $(\bar{x}_1, \bar{x}_2)$ so $q_o = \bar{x}_1 \bar{x}_2$. Scaling the inputs by a factor t, we obtain

$$q_n = (t\bar{x}_1)(t\bar{x}_2) = t^2 \bar{x}_1 \bar{x}_2 = t^2 q_o.$$

Therefore this Cobb-Douglas production function is IRS. This means that if we double the inputs ($t = 2$), this will *quadruple* the output; tripling the inputs ($t = 3$) will increase the output ninefold. In general, for a Cobb-Douglas

---

[4]See section A.7.2 in the Mathematical appendix.

production function of the form $q = Ax_1^a x_2^b$, its degree of homogeneity is $a + b$ and so its returns to scale depends on whether the exponents of the inputs add up to a number less than, equal to, or greater than 1.

While the examples considered so far have a specific returns to scale for *any* input combination, there are production functions whose returns to scale differ across different ranges of output. For instance, a production function which has IRS for low output levels, CRS for an intermediate range, and DRS for high levels of output may be considered to be typical of manufacturing production processes. Such production functions are not homogeneous of any degree.

If a technology is homogeneous of some degree, then we can say something about its returns to scale. However, the opposite is not true: a non-homogeneous production function may display increasing or decreasing returns to scale throughout. For instance, the quasilinear production function $q = x_1 + \sqrt{x_2}$ is not homogeneous of any degree but displays decreasing returns so long as both inputs are used. For such production functions, we will see in Chapter 8 that the returns to scale may be deduced from its cost function.

7.4   Production Possibility Frontiers

Given the aggregate endowment of inputs available in an economy and the technologies for producing different goods using those inputs, we can derive a **production possibility frontier** (PPF) or **transformation frontier** which shows the maximum combinations of the goods that may be produced. In this section, we derive PPFs in the case of a single input as well as two inputs.

7.4.1   Deriving PPFs when technologies use one input

When the production of each output uses a single input, say labor, the PPF can be found by following these three steps.

1. Invert each technology to express the labor required for a given level of output.

2. Replace for the labor requirements in the resource constraint.

3. Express the transformation frontier implicitly.

To illustrate, suppose two goods can be produced using only labor, ℓ, according to the production functions $q_1 = \ell_1/5$ and $q_2 = \sqrt{\ell_2}$. The total amount of labor available is $\ell_1 + \ell_2 = 100$. Then from the first step, invert the production functions to obtain $\ell_1 = 5q_1$, and $\ell_2 = q_2^2$. In the second step, substitute these into the resource equation to obtain $5q_1 + q_2^2 = 100$. In the final step, the transformation frontier can be written as

$$T(q_1, q_2) = 5q_1 + q_2^2 - 100, \tag{7.6}$$

by taking all terms from the resource equation to the left hand side. Then, the implicit function, $T(q_1, q_2) = 0$, plotted in Figure 7.4 provides the maximum possible combinations of goods 1 and 2 given the technologies and the resource constraint.

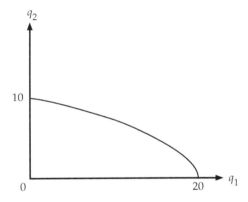

Figure 7.4   A concave PPF

The PPF captures the trade-off or **opportunity cost** between the two outputs. More precisely, the opportunity cost of good 1 is given by the absolute value of the slope of the PPF, $|dq_2/dq_1|$, and is called the **marginal rate of transformation**, *MRT*. The *MRT* shows how many units of good 2 need to be given up in order to obtain an additional unit of good 1 when all inputs are allocated between the production processes. Since the PPF gets steeper in Figure 7.4 as we move from left to right, the opportunity cost of obtaining good 1 increases.

The marginal rate of transformation is calculated as the ratio of the two partial derivatives of the transformation frontier:

$$MRT = \frac{\partial T/\partial q_1}{\partial T/\partial q_2}. \tag{7.7}$$

To see where this formula comes from, take the total differential of the implicit transformation frontier, $T(q_1, q_2) = 0$:

$$\frac{\partial T}{\partial q_1} dq_1 + \frac{\partial T}{\partial q_2} dq_2 = 0.$$

✎▶ Rearrange the terms to get

$$\left| \frac{dq_2}{dq_1} \right| = \frac{\partial T / \partial q_1}{\partial T / \partial q_2},$$

where the left hand side is the *MRT*.

✎▶ Therefore, for the transformation frontier given by (7.6), $MRT = 5/2q_2$. It is then apparent that as q_2 decreases, the *MRT* increases. In general, a concave (bowed out) PPF signifies increasing opportunity cost. A linear PPF signifies constant opportunity cost, while a convex (bowed in) one implies decreasing opportunity cost.

7.4.2   Deriving PPFs when technologies use two inputs

When there are two inputs, we have to reduce the problem to that of a single input, after which the three steps outlined in section 7.4.1 can be used to find the transformation frontier. We illustrate with an example.

Suppose there are two inputs, labor and capital, denoted by ℓ and k. There are two goods, 1 and 2, whose production functions are Cobb-Douglas and linear respectively:

$$q_1 = \sqrt{\ell_1 k_1} \quad \text{and} \quad q_2 = \frac{4\ell_2}{9} + k_2.$$

The resource constraints are $\ell_1 + \ell_2 = 9$ and $k_1 + k_2 = 4$. We can now draw an **input Edgeworth box** as shown in Figure 7.5 where the origin O_1 refers to good 1 and O_2 to good 2. The dimension of this input Edgeworth box is $(9, 4)$, given that there are 9 units of labor and 4 units of capital to be allocated across the two technologies.

Production efficiency or **Lerner efficiency** (named after Abba Lerner) requires that keeping the output of good 2 at the level indicated by a green isoquant, we maximize the production of good 1, i.e., find the highest orange isoquant that we can attain.[5] An input allocation $((\ell_1, k_1), (\ell_2, k_2))$ is Lerner efficient if there is no other allocation in the input Edgeworth box

---

[5]This mimics exactly the steps for finding a Pareto efficient allocation from section 6.2.2.

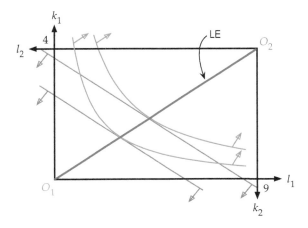

Figure 7.5 An input Edgeworth box

that yields a higher output for one good without reducing the output of the other. Then, just as in the case of Pareto efficient allocations for consumers, Lerner efficient input allocations are found at the points where the isoquants from each technology are tangent. To find these points of tangency (i.e., the input contract curve), set $TRS_1 = TRS_2$. Then $k_1/\ell_1 = 4/9$, from where we deduce that $k_1 = 4\ell_1/9$ along the input contract curve from the perspective of origin O_1, labeled LE in Figure 7.5.

We can now reduce our two-input technologies into a single-input technology by substituting for the Lerner efficient level of capital in the technology: put $k_1 = 4\ell_1/9$ into the technology for good 1 to obtain $q_1 = 2\ell_1/3$. For the second technology, turn the page upside down and verify that along the input contract curve from the perspective of origin O_2 in Figure 7.5, it is also true that $k_2 = 4\ell_2/9$.[6] Substituting this into the second technology, we get $q_2 = 8\ell_2/9$. Now follow the three steps from section 7.4.1 to obtain the PPF in Figure 7.6:

$$q_2 = 8 - \frac{4}{3}q_1.$$

Since this is a linear PPF, the *MRT* of 4/3 shows a constant opportunity

---

[6] Alternatively, use the resource constraints, $\ell_1 + \ell_2 = 9$ and $k_1 + k_2 = 4$, to eliminate k_1 and ℓ_1 in the input contract curve equation, $k_1 = 4\ell_1/9$. Since $k_1 = 4 - k_2$ and $\ell_1 = 9 - \ell_2$, we have

$$4 - k_2 = \frac{4(9 - \ell_2)}{9},$$

which upon simplification yields $k_2 = 4\ell_2/9$.

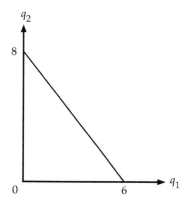

Figure 7.6 A linear PPF

cost. This is a consequence of the fact that both technologies in this example are CRS and that all the Lerner efficient input allocations involve a constant capital-to-labor ratio, as shown by the blue diagonal in Figure 7.5.

In conclusion, we summarize below the steps to reduce the two-input case to a single input case to find the PPF.

1. Calculate an equation for the input contract curve from the origin O_1.

2. Use this equation to eliminate one input (either labor or capital) from the first technology.

3. From step 1 and using the resource constraints if necessary, calculate an equation for the input contract curve from the origin O_2.

4. Use the equation from step 3 to eliminate the same input (either labor or capital) from the second technology.

5. Follow the three steps from section 7.4.1 to derive the PPF.

Exercises

7.1. Draw two representative isoquants for the following production functions and indicated output levels.

    (a) $q = (x_1 + x_2)^2$ for $q = 4$ and 9

(b) $q = x_1 + \min\{x_1, x_2\}$ for $q = 4$ and 6

(c) $q = \min\{x_1, x_2^2\}$ for $q = 9$ and 16

(d) $q = \min\{2x_1, 0.5x_1 + 0.5x_2, x_2\}$ for $q = 4$ and 6

(e) $q = \min\{2x_1 + x_2, x_1 + 2x_2\}$ for $q = 12$ and 15

7.2. Find the returns to scale for the following production functions where q denotes output, and x_1, x_2, and x_3 are inputs.

(a) $q = x_1^{\frac{1}{3}} x_2^{\frac{1}{3}}$

(b) $q = 4x_1 x_2 x_3$

(c) $q = (2x_1 + 3x_2)^{\frac{1}{2}}$

(d) $q = [0.3\sqrt{x_1} + 0.7\sqrt{x_2}]^2$

(e) $q = [\min\{x_1, 2x_2\}]^2$

7.3. Two goods can be produced using labor. For each of the pairs of production functions below, derive the transformation frontier $T(q_1, q_2)$ when the total amount of labor is $\ell_1 + \ell_2 = 12$ and find an expression for the marginal rate of transformation, MRT.

(a) $q_1 = 2\ell_1$ and $q_2 = 3\ell_2$

(b) $q_1 = 2\sqrt{\ell_1}$ and $q_2 = \sqrt{\ell_2}$

(c) $q_1 = \sqrt{\ell_1}$ and $q_2 = \ell_2^2$

7.4. Three goods can be produced using labor according to the following production functions: $q_1 = 2\ell_1$, $q_2 = 3\ell_2$, and $q_3 = \ell_3$. The total amount of labor is $\ell_1 + \ell_2 + \ell_3 = 12$. Derive the transformation frontier $T(q_1, q_2, q_3)$ and calculate the marginal rates of transformation between the different pairs of goods, MRT_{12}, MRT_{13}, and MRT_{23}. Here $MRT_{jk} = \frac{\partial T}{\partial q_j} / \frac{\partial T}{\partial q_k}$ shows how much of good k has to be given up for a unit of good j.

7.5. Two goods can be produced using labor (ℓ) and capital (k). For each of the technologies and resources below, derive the transformation frontier $T(q_1, q_2)$ and find an expression for the marginal rate of transformation, MRT.

(a) $q_1 = \ell_1 + k_1$, $q_2 = \ell_2 k_2$, $\ell_1 + \ell_2 = 10$ and $k_1 + k_2 = 10$

(b) $q_1 = \ell_1 k_1$, $q_2 = \sqrt{\ell_2 k_2}$, $\ell_1 + \ell_2 = 40$ and $k_1 + k_2 = 10$

Chapter 8

Costs

Production activity requires costly inputs, both fixed and variable. Variable inputs such as labor and raw materials generate variable costs (also known as operating expenses) while fixed inputs that do not change with the level of output such as the number of telephone lines and salaried managers generate fixed costs (sometimes called overhead). It is in the interest of a profit-maximizing firm to produce a given level of output in the cheapest way possible. In this chapter we will study how this can be accomplished in principle.

8.1 Deriving Cost Functions from Technologies

A cost function encapsulates the expenses of operating a technology, the least cost of producing any output level given the prices of all inputs. We begin with the case of a single variable input and then consider the various two-input technologies introduced in the previous chapter.

8.1.1 Costs with one variable input

Suppose that $q = Ax^a$ is a production function with constants $A, a > 0$. The reader can check that the returns to scale for this production function depends on the value of parameter a. It has DRS if $0 < a < 1$, CRS if $a = 1$, and IRS for $a > 1$.[1]

---

[1]In this single input case, DRS also coincides with diminishing marginal productivity with respect to the input x, CRS with constant marginal productivity, and IRS with increasing marginal productivity.

To produce any specific output level q, the input level required (i.e., the input demanded) is found by inverting the production function and solving for x:

$$x(q) = (q/A)^{1/a}.$$

When the price of the input is fixed at $\$w$ per unit, the total variable cost of purchasing this input level is $wx(q) = w(q/A)^{1/a}$. Since there are no fixed costs, this is also the cost function. Therefore, $c(w,q) = w(q/A)^{1/a}$.

A special case of a single variable input arises when the underlying technology uses multiple inputs but all inputs are fixed except for one. For instance, take the case of a Cobb-Douglas technology $q = \sqrt{x_1 x_2}$ which uses two inputs, x_1 (labor) which is variable, and x_2 (machines) which is fixed at 4 units. This may be viewed as a short-run situation when the number of machines is fixed at 4 and cannot be changed, but the level of labor use can be altered as desired. Substituting $x_2 = 4$, the production function simplifies to $q = 2\sqrt{x_1}$. Then the input demand for labor is $x_1(q) = q^2/4$; the input demand for machines is fixed, so $x_2(q) = 4$. Denoting the price per unit of labor by w_1 and that of machines by w_2, the cost function is the sum of the expenditures on each input:

$$c(w_1, w_2, q) \equiv w_1 x_1(q) + w_2 x_2(q) = \frac{w_1 q^2}{4} + 4w_2.$$

To summarize, the cost function for a single variable input technology can be calculated using this two-step procedure.

1. Invert the production function to find the input demanded as a function of the output level, q. Note any other inputs whose levels are fixed.

2. Multiply each input by its per-unit price and add them to obtain the cost function.

8.1.2   Costs with two variable inputs

The procedure for deriving cost functions differ for technologies which have smooth, bowed isoquants as opposed to linear or Leontief technologies.

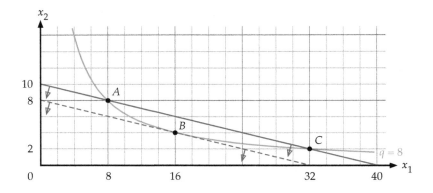

Figure 8.1   Minimizing costs for a Cobb-Douglas technology

Cost function for a Cobb-Douglas technology

Consider the two-input Cobb-Douglas technology $q = \sqrt{x_1 x_2}$ when both inputs are variable as would be the case in the long run. Before we show how to calculate the cost function for this technology, i.e., the minimum cost of producing *any* level of output q, it is helpful to consider the case where a producer wishes to produce a specific level of output at specific input prices, say, when $q = 8$ and $(w_1, w_2) = (1, 4)$.

In Figure 8.1, the isoquant for $q = 8$ is drawn in orange and this shows the input bundles that the producer has to choose from in minimizing its cost. If the producer spends $40 on both inputs for example, we can draw the combination of inputs she can purchase by plotting the line $w_1 x_1 + w_2 x_2 = x_1 + 4x_2 = 40$ drawn in solid blue. This line is analogous to a consumer's budget from Chapter 2 except it shows affordable *input* combinations and is called an **isocost** line and its slope is given by the input price ratio $-w_1/w_2$. The arrows indicate the direction in which costs are *decreasing*: lower levels of cost outlay result in parallel isocosts that lie to the southeast. The objective is to minimize the cost given that 8 units of output are to be produced, i.e., find the lowest isocost line that barely touches the isoquant for $q = 8$.

For instance, the output level of 8 can be produced by the combination $A = (8, 8)$ for a cost outlay of $1 \times 8 + $4 \times 8 = $40, or by the combination $C = (32, 2)$ which also costs $40. But the same output can be achieved at $B = (16, 4)$ for the smaller cost of $1 \times 16 + $4 \times 4 = $32. In fact there is no other input combination that costs less and still yields the output of 8, as can be inferred from the blue dashed isocost that is tangent to the isoquant at B.

Thus the cost-minimizing input combination for any given level of output is one where the isoquant is tangent to the isocost, i.e., where the slope of the isoquant $(-TRS)$ equals the slope of the isocost $(-w_1/w_2)$. In other words, cost minimization requires that $TRS = w_1/w_2$.

We derive a cost function for the given Cobb-Douglas technology in a series of steps. In step 1, set $TRS = w_1/w_2$ to obtain

$$\frac{x_2}{x_1} = \frac{w_1}{w_2}, \tag{8.1}$$

from where we can derive an expression for input 2:

$$x_2 = \frac{w_1 x_1}{w_2}. \tag{8.2}$$

To obtain the least-cost input combination, we want the quantity of the inputs demanded given the input prices, w_1 and w_2, and the output level, q. These **conditional input demand functions** are written as $g_1(w_1, w_2, q)$ and $g_2(w_1, w_2, q)$, i.e.,

$$x_1 = g_1(w_1, w_2, q) \quad \text{and} \quad x_2 = g_2(w_1, w_2, q).$$

In step 2, substitute equation (8.2) for x_2 in the production function $q = $ ◀ ⬛
$\sqrt{x_1 x_2}$ and solve for x_1 to obtain the conditional input demand for input 1:

$$g_1(w_1, w_2, q) = \frac{\sqrt{w_2} q}{\sqrt{w_1}}. \tag{8.3}$$

Then $g_1(w_1, w_2, q)$ shows the cost-minimizing level of this input demanded for any input prices w_1 and w_2, and any output level q.

In step 3, substitute equation (8.3) into (8.2) and derive the conditional input demand for input 2, ◀ ⬛

$$g_2(w_1, w_2, q) = \frac{\sqrt{w_1} q}{\sqrt{w_2}}. \tag{8.4}$$

Finally, in step 4, the cost function is found by calculating the expenditure associated with the conditional input demands in equations (8.3) and (8.4): ◀ ⬛

$$c(w_1, w_2, q) \equiv w_1 g_1(w_1, w_2, q) + w_2 g_2(w_1, w_2, q) \tag{8.5}$$
$$= 2q\sqrt{w_1 w_2}. \tag{8.6}$$

Thus this procedure for calculating cost functions can be summarized as follows.

1. Set the $TRS = w_1/w_2$ and find an expression for one of the inputs.

2. Substitute for this input in the production function and solve for the conditional demand for the other input.

3. Substitute the conditional demand from step 2 into the expression in step 1 to get the remaining conditional demand.

4. Substitute the conditional input demands into the cost function definition given by equation (8.5).

This four-step procedure to derive cost functions works for *any* two-input technology that has smooth, bowed isoquants, not just for Cobb-Douglas production functions. However, it cannot be used for Leontief or linear technologies in general, so these are considered separately below.

Cost function for a Leontief technology

In the case of a Leontief technology, the sufficient condition for cost minimization involving the tangency of the isoquant and isocost is no longer possible because the slope of a Leontief isoquant at its kink is not defined. Nevertheless, as illustrated in Figure 8.2, for a general two-input Leontief

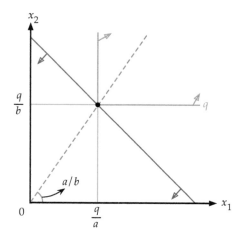

Figure 8.2   Minimizing costs for a Leontief technology

technology $q = \min\{ax_1, bx_2\}$, the minimum quantity of inputs necessary to produce any arbitrary output level q will always be the kink point of the isoquant for this output level regardless of the slope of the isocost line. Thus the conditional input demands are

$$g_1(w_1, w_2, q) = \frac{q}{a} \quad \text{and} \quad g_2(w_1, w_2, q) = \frac{q}{b}. \tag{8.7}$$

Using equation (8.5) we obtain

$$c(w_1, w_2, q) = w_1 \frac{q}{a} + w_2 \frac{q}{b} = \left(\frac{w_1}{a} + \frac{w_2}{b} \right) q. \tag{8.8}$$

Thus the steps to finding a cost function for Leontief technologies are:

1. Calculate the input bundle at the kink point only.

2. The cost function is the cost of the kink point.

These steps are illustrated in equations (8.7) and (8.8).

Cost function for a linear technology

In the case of a general linear technology $q = ax_1 + bx_2$, there are three possible cases illustrated in Figure 8.3. In all three panels, the objective is to produce a fixed level of output q shown by the orange isoquant. The isocosts, however, are different in each panel and shown by blue lines.

In the left panel, when $w_1/w_2 < a/b$ — i.e., the blue isocost is flatter than the orange isoquant — the cost-minimizing bundle is given by point A where only input x_1 is employed to produce the output, so the conditional input demand is

$$g(w_1, w_2, q) = \left(\frac{q}{a}, 0 \right).$$

In the middle panel, the isoquant and isocost happen to have the same slope so *any* input combination on the isoquant minimizes costs, including the corner solutions of points B or D or any point in between such as C. Lastly, in the right panel, when $w_1/w_2 > a/b$, the blue isocost is steeper than the orange isoquant and costs are minimized at point E where

$$g(w_1, w_2, q) = \left(0, \frac{q}{b} \right).$$

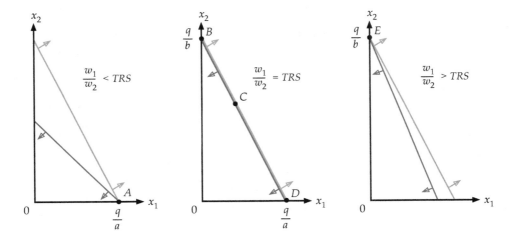

Figure 8.3   Minimizing costs for a linear technology

We may summarize these conditional input demands as

$$g(w_1, w_2, q) = \begin{cases} \left(\dfrac{q}{a}, 0\right) & \text{if } \dfrac{w_1}{w_2} < \dfrac{a}{b} \\ (x_1, x_2) \text{ where } ax_1 + bx_2 = q & \text{if } \dfrac{w_1}{w_2} = \dfrac{a}{b} \\ \left(0, \dfrac{q}{b}\right) & \text{if } \dfrac{w_1}{w_2} > \dfrac{a}{b}. \end{cases} \tag{8.9}$$

Therefore, the cost function for the linear technology is either the cost of purchasing the input bundle A (given by $w_2 q / b$) in the left panel, or the cost of purchasing the input bundle B (given by $w_2 q / b$) in the middle panel,[2] or the cost of purchasing input bundle E (given by $w_1 q / a$) in the right panel, depending on which cost is the smallest. A compact way to write this cost function is then

$$c(w_1, w_2, q) = \min\left\{\frac{w_1 q}{a}, \frac{w_2 q}{b}\right\} = q \min\left\{\frac{w_1}{a}, \frac{w_2}{b}\right\}. \tag{8.10}$$

Equation (8.10) means that the lowest cost of producing any given level of output when the technology is linear is to utilize either input 1 or input 2 exclusively, depending on which is cheaper. We can then summarize the two steps for calculating the cost function for a linear technology:

---

[2]Since all cost-minimizing input combinations cost the same in the middle panel of Figure 8.3, we may assume without loss of generality that the firm chooses the corner solution B in this case.

1. Calculate the cost-minimizing input bundle by looking at the corner solutions only.

2. The cost function is the minimum cost of the corner input bundles.

8.2 Cost Concepts

Earlier, we had alluded to two types of costs that production activity entails, namely, fixed and variable costs. Given a cost function (sometimes called a total cost function), we can explore these two types of costs and several interrelated subsidiary cost concepts more explicitly. The taxonomy and definitions of these concepts and the important relationships between them are explored next.

8.2.1 Types of costs

To simplify the presentation, we provide a taxonomy of the different cost concepts derived from a cost function $c(w,q)$ when the output q is produced by a single input whose price is w.

(i) The total fixed cost (TFC) is the cost incurred even when nothing is produced: $TFC = c(w,0)$.

(ii) The total variable cost (TVC) is the part of the cost function not including the fixed costs: $TVC = c(w,q) - c(w,0)$.

(iii) The average cost (AC) is the cost of producing each unit of output when q units are produced: $AC = c(w,q)/q$.

(iv) The average fixed cost (AFC) is the average expenditure on overhead when q units are produced: $AFC = c(w,0)/q$.

(v) The average variable cost (AVC) is the average expenditure on operating expenses when q units are produced:

$$AVC = \frac{TVC}{q} = \frac{c(w,q) - c(w,0)}{q} = AC - AFC.$$

(vi) The marginal cost (MC) is the cost of producing an additional unit of output: $MC = \partial c / \partial q$.

To illustrate each of these cost concepts, consider the single-input technology $q = Ax^a$ from section 8.1.1 with $A = 2$ and $a = 0.5$, and where the input is priced at $w = \$8$ per unit. Then the production function is $q = 2\sqrt{x}$ shown in the left panel of Figure 8.4. That this technology displays decreasing returns to scale can be deduced from its concavity: as output doubles from q_1 to q_2, the corresponding input use more than doubles from x_1 to x_2.

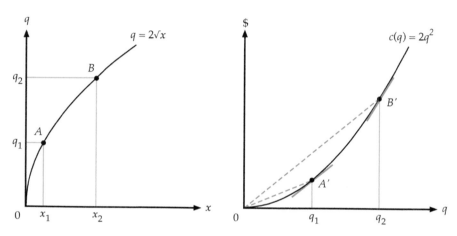

Figure 8.4   DRS technology and cost

The cost function corresponding to this production function is $c(q) = 2q^2$ and is a convex function as shown in the right panel of Figure 8.4. The two panels capture a fundamental dual relationship between production and costs: the returns to scale in production is reflected in the shape of the cost function, and vice versa. In particular, when production is characterized by DRS, the cost function is convex (total costs are increasing at an increasing rate), and vice versa.

Using the definition of the average cost, we find that $AC = 2q$ and so the AC increases with the level of output, q.[3] To see this graphically, pick the two output levels q_1 and q_2 in the right panel of Figure 8.4. Then the vertical height associated with point A' is the total cost of producing q_1, and the slope of the dashed line $0A'$ (which is the ratio of the total cost of producing q_1 divided by q_1) is the AC for this level of output. Likewise, the slope of dashed line $0B'$ is the AC at q_2, and since $0B'$ is steeper, the AC increases with production.

---

[3]We know from (v) on the previous page that $AC = AFC + AVC$. Because $c(0) = 0$ here, $TFC = 0$, and hence $AFC = 0$. Therefore, $AC = AVC$, and the AVC is also increasing in q.

The marginal cost here is $MC = 4q$. At q_1, for example, the MC is the slope of the tangent at point A' in the right panel of Figure 8.4, while at q_2, it is the slope of the tangent at B'. By comparing the AC and the MC, two facts can be deduced from this graph: (a) both the AC and the MC are increasing with the output level, and (b) the $MC > AC$ for any positive output level.

It is instructive to calculate the corresponding cost functions for a CRS production function (e.g., when $a = 1$ in the technology $q = Ax^a$) as well as an IRS case (e.g., when $a = 2$) and compare the shape of the production function to its cost, as well as explore the graphical shapes of the AC and MC in each case.

The cost concepts defined above generalize in a straightforward manner to the case of two or more inputs. For example, in the case of the cost function $c(w_1, w_2, q) = w_1 q^2/4 + 4w_2$ corresponding to the two-input Cobb-Douglas case from section 8.1.1 where input 1 was variable and input 2 was fixed, the $TFC = 4w_2$ and the $TVC = w_1 q^2/4$. The $AVC = w_1 q/4$, $AC = w_1 q/4 + 4w_2/q$, and $MC = w_1 q/2$.

Similarly, for the cost function $c(w_1, w_2, q) = 2q\sqrt{w_1 w_2}$ corresponding to the Cobb-Douglas technology from section 8.1.2 with two variable inputs, $TFC = 0$ and $AVC = AC = MC = 2\sqrt{w_1 w_2}$.

8.2.2 Relationship between averages and marginals

Let $c(q)$ be a cost function with $c(q) = v(q) + F$ where the function $v(q)$ stands for variable costs (TVC), and F for fixed costs (TFC) which is assumed to be positive. From the definitions in section 8.2.1, we can derive the average variable cost as $AVC = v(q)/q$, and the marginal cost as $MC = c'(q) = v'(q)$ (since $dF/dq = 0$; fixed costs do not change with the level of production). Then the AVC and MC are mathematically related in a relationship that can be summarized as follows.

> When the average is increasing/decreasing/constant, the marginal must be more/less/the same as the average.

Most students have an intuitive understanding of this relationship from their experience with their grade point average (GPA). For example, when a student with a 'B' average wishes to *raise* her GPA, she will have to score *higher* than a 'B' in the next (i.e., 'marginal') class that she takes. Scoring less than a 'B' would lower her GPA, while scoring a 'B' would leave her GPA unchanged. Therefore, to increase the average, the marginal score must be more than the average.

To derive the relationship between averages and marginals mathematically, take the derivative of $AVC = v(q)/q$ with respect to q to obtain the slope of the AVC curve. Using the quotient rule of calculus,[4] we obtain

$$\frac{dAVC}{dq} = \frac{d(v(q)/q)}{dq} = \frac{qv'(q) - v(q) \cdot 1}{q^2}$$

at any positive output level. If the slope of the AVC is positive, then it must be that the numerator satisfies

$$qv'(q) - v(q) > 0$$

or

$$v'(q) > \frac{v(q)}{q},$$

signifying that the $MC > AVC$. Similarly, if the slope is negative, then by the same logic $MC < AVC$. Note that if the AVC has a zero slope for some production level, the MC and AVC are equal at that point.

To see this relationship in a specific instance, consider the cost function

$$c(q) = \frac{q^3}{480} - \frac{q^2}{2} + 50q + 2500.$$

Figure 8.5 depicts the AC, AVC, and MC curves for this cost function; their derivation are left to the reader. Note that when the AVC is falling between 0 and 120 units of output, the MC lies below the AVC; at $q = 120$, the AVC has a zero slope and the $MC = AVC$ at that point; for output levels above 120, the AVC is rising and the MC curve lies above the AVC. That the $MC = AVC$ at the minimum point of the AVC curve is a general property.[5]

Note that the same relationship holds between the MC and the AC curves: the MC lies below the AC for output levels from zero to 147.56, is equal to the AC at its minimum value of 38.52 for $q = 147.56$, and goes above the AC for output levels above 147.56.

---

[4]See section A.2 in the Mathematical appendix.
[5]It is also always true that $AVC = MC$ at $q = 0$. This can be derived from:

$$\lim_{q \to 0} \frac{v(q)}{q} = \lim_{q \to 0} \frac{v'(q)}{1} = v'(0),$$

where the second ratio follows from L'Hôpital's rule.

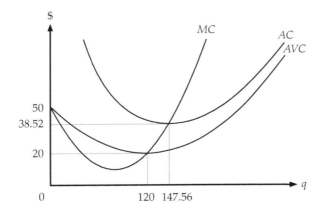

Figure 8.5 Relationships between AC, AVC and MC

8.3 Returns to Scale Revisited

We saw in section 8.2.1 that the returns to scale in production for a single input technology is reflected in the shape of the cost function. More precisely, the returns to scale for a production function is reflected in the shape of its AC curve. An increasing AC curve reflects DRS in production, a decreasing AC shows IRS, and a constant AC shows CRS. This relationship is true for a technology with *any* number of inputs.

To get an intuitive understanding of this relationship, suppose that $q = f(x_1, x_2)$ is a CRS production function and q_o is the original output level. Let $c(w_1, w_2, q)$ be the cost function for this technology, where the input prices w_1 and w_2 are given. Then there is some conditional input bundle (x_1^*, x_2^*) that minimizes costs, i.e., $c(w_1, w_2, q_o) = w_1 x_1^* + w_2 x_2^*$. When we scale this input bundle by $t > 1$, the new input bundle (tx_1^*, tx_2^*) produces a new output level q_n. But because the technology is CRS, it follows that

$$q_n = f(tx_1^*, tx_2^*) = tf(x_1^*, x_2^*) = tq_o.$$

It can be shown that the input bundle (tx_1^*, tx_2^*) also minimizes the cost of producing the new output level q_n, i.e.,

$$c(w_1, w_2, q_n) = w_1(tx_1^*) + w_2(tx_2^*) = t(w_1 x_1^* + w_2 x_2^*) = tc(w_1, w_2, q_o).$$

In other words, the cheapest cost of producing q_n, $c(w_1, w_2, q_n)$, equals t times $c(w_1, w_2, q_o)$, the cheapest cost of producing q_o. Dividing both sides of this relationship by q_n, and using the fact that $q_n = tq_o$ on account of the CRS technology, we get

$$\frac{c(w_1, w_2, q_n)}{q_n} = \frac{tc(w_1, w_2, q_o)}{q_n} = \frac{tc(w_1, w_2, q_o)}{tq_o} = \frac{c(w_1, w_2, q_o)}{q_o}.$$

Then the extreme left hand ratio is AC_n and equals the extreme right hand ratio, AC_o, i.e., the average cost is constant as output increases from q_o to q_n. Hence, we conclude that a cost function corresponding to a CRS technology has constant AC.

Using an analogous reasoning, it is possible to show that a DRS technology implies an increasing AC and vice versa, while an IRS technology has a decreasing AC and conversely.

This relationship between returns to scale in production and the slope of the AC is handy when it is not possible to directly conclude a technology's returns to scale. For instance, the production function $q = x_1 + \sqrt{x_2}$ is not homogenous of any degree when both inputs are used in positive amounts, so its returns to scale is not immediately apparent. However, its cost function can be calculated to be

$$c(w_1, w_2, q) = w_1 q - \frac{w_1^2}{4w_2},$$

where we assume that $q > w_1/(4w_2)$ so that costs are positive. Then

$$AC = w_1 - \frac{w_1^2}{4w_2 q}.$$

It is now easy to show that $\partial AC/\partial q > 0$, implying that the technology is DRS.

8.4   Cost Functions with Multiple Technologies°

Suppose a firm has access to two or more technologies for producing the *same* product. An example of this would be a company that manufactures paper using different processes, possibly with different inputs in different plants. For each technology, one can of course calculate a cost function as described in section 8.1. But when the firm can operate all the technologies simultaneously, we can derive its overall cost function which we will call the **joint total cost** (*JTC*) function.[6]

---

[6]We assume that the firm incurs no fixed costs of operating each plant. Alternatively, we may assume that the firm must pay the associated fixed costs even if it shuts down a plant.

Consider first a firm that has two identical plants indexed by j whose cost functions are given by $c_j(q_j) = \frac{1}{2}q_j^2$, where q_j is the quantity produced in plant $j = 1, 2$. If the firm wishes to produce a total quantity $Q = 100$, it may assign that to one plant, say plant 1, for a total cost of $5000. But a little reflection reveals that if this total quantity were to be split equally between the plants so that $q_1 = q_2 = 50$, then the overall total cost is considerably less:

$$\frac{1}{2}(50)^2 + \frac{1}{2}(50)^2 = \$2500.$$

The rationale for splitting the total quantity in this manner arises from the fact that the marginal cost in each plant is $MC_j = q_j$ which is increasing in the quantity produced in that plant. So when all 100 units are produced in the first plant, the marginal cost of the last unit of output is $100. If this unit were produced in the second plant instead, its marginal cost would only be a dollar. Similarly, producing the 99th unit (which has a marginal cost of production of $99) in plant 2 instead would incur a marginal cost of only $2. Reasoning in this manner, a firm should assign quantities to each plant until the marginal cost from the last unit produced in each plant is equalized, which in this instance means that $q_1 = q_2 = Q/2$. Therefore, the joint total cost when both technologies are used in this manner is

$$JTC(Q) \equiv c_1(q_1) + c_2(q_2) = \frac{1}{2}\left(\frac{Q}{2}\right)^2 + \frac{1}{2}\left(\frac{Q}{2}\right)^2 = \frac{Q^2}{4}.$$

Then the **joint average cost** (i.e., the lowest average cost of producing Q units of output using both technologies) is $JAC = JTC/Q = Q/4$ while the **joint marginal cost** is $JMC = dJTC/dQ = Q/2$. Note that both the JAC and JMC are much lower for any output level with two plants in operation than with one.

Now suppose that a firm has two non-identical plants whose cost functions are $c_1(q_1) = \frac{1}{2}q_1^2$ while $c_2(q_2) = q_2^2$, i.e., the second plant is twice as expensive as the first. Any level of output to be produced, Q, has to be split between the two plants so that the marginal cost of producing the last unit in either plant is the same, i.e., set $MC_1 = MC_2$ to obtain

$$q_1 = 2q_2. \tag{8.11}$$

Since $Q = q_1 + q_2$, substitute $q_2 = Q - q_1$ into equation (8.11) and solve to obtain $q_1 = 2Q/3$ and $q_2 = Q/3$. Hence, the joint total cost is the cost of

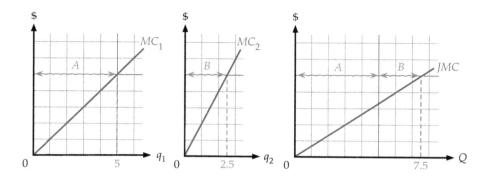

Figure 8.6   Deriving the JMC graphically

producing two-thirds of Q in plant 1 and one-third of Q in plant 2:

$$JTC(Q) = \frac{1}{2}\left(\frac{2Q}{3}\right)^2 + \left(\frac{Q}{3}\right)^2 = \frac{Q^2}{3}.$$

Here the joint average cost is $JAC = Q/3$ while the joint marginal cost is $JMC = 2Q/3$.

From studying these two examples, it can be seen that the JMC curve is the horizontal sum of the individual MC_j curves, as shown in Figure 8.6 for the case of non-identical plants. The rationale follows from the fact that the total quantity to be produced, Q, is split between the plants in a two-to-one ratio so as to equalize the marginal cost of producing the last unit in each plant. Figure 8.6 illustrates this by showing that when $Q = 7.5$ for instance, then $MC_1 = MC_2$ when 5 units are produced in plant 1 and 2.5 units in plant 2.

To summarize, here are the steps for calculating the JTC function when a firm has two plants with increasing marginal costs.

1. Write the total production as the sum of what is produced in each plant, i.e., $Q = q_1 + q_2$.

2. Set the marginal costs of each plant equal to the other: $MC_1 = MC_2$ which results in one equation in q_1 and q_2.

3. The equations in steps 1 and 2 provide two equations in the two unknown variables, q_1 and q_2, so it is possible to solve for each as a func-

tion of the total production, Q. Call these solutions $q_1^* = f_1(Q)$ and $q_2^* = f_2(Q)$ which show what fraction of Q is produced in each plant.

4. Substitute the solutions from step 3 into the cost functions of each plant. Add those costs to obtain the *JTC* as a function of Q.

These steps can be modified in a straightforward manner to allow for more than two plants. For example, with three plants, step 1 would set $Q = q_1 + q_2 + q_3$ while step 2 would set $MC_1 = MC_2$ and $MC_2 = MC_3$. This provides three equations in three unknowns which can be solved for the fractions produced in each plant.

8.5 Deriving Technologies Underlying Cost Functions°

Just as cost functions can be derived from production functions, the reverse is also possible: for a given cost function, it is possible to recover a technology whose cost function is exactly the one we started with.[7]

The main result that is used in going from cost functions to technologies is **Shephard's lemma** which states that the partial derivative of the cost function with respect to w_i is the ith conditional input demand function.

Shephard's Lemma. *Given a cost function* $c(w_1, w_2, q)$,

$$\frac{\partial c}{\partial w_1} = g_1(w_1, w_2, q) \text{ and } \frac{\partial c}{\partial w_2} = g_2(w_1, w_2, q).$$

Proof. Fix an output level $\bar{q}$ and input prices $(\bar{w}_1, \bar{w}_2)$ and suppose that the input bundle $(\bar{x}_1, \bar{x}_2)$ minimizes costs, i.e.,

$$\bar{x}_1 = g_1(\bar{w}_1, \bar{w}_2, \bar{q}) \text{ and } \bar{x}_2 = g_2(\bar{w}_1, \bar{w}_2, \bar{q}),$$

so $c(\bar{w}_1, \bar{w}_2, \bar{q}) = \bar{w}_1 \bar{x}_1 + \bar{w}_2 \bar{x}_2$. Now define a function

$$z(w_1) = w_1 \bar{x}_1 + \bar{w}_2 \bar{x}_2 - c(w_1, \bar{w}_2, \bar{q}).$$

---

[7]For a function to be a legitimate cost function, it must satisfy some properties whose exploration would take us too far afield. So to make sense of this section, it is convenient to imagine that an absent-minded economist calculated a cost function but then forgot which technology that cost function was supposed to be for.

Note that the function z depends only on w_1 and attains a value of zero when $w_1 = \bar{w}_1$, while for other values of w_1 it must be the case that $z(w_1) \geq 0$ since $\bar{x}_1$ will not in general be a cost-minimizing conditional input demand for input 1. Therefore, the function z attains a minimum when $w_1 = \bar{w}_1$. From the first-order necessary condition for a minimum, it must be that $z'(\bar{w}_1) = 0$. But since

$$z'(w_1) = \bar{x}_1 - \frac{\partial c}{\partial w_1}(w_1, \bar{w}_2, \bar{q}),$$

it follows that at $\bar{w}_1$,

$$z'(\bar{w}_1) = \bar{x}_1 - \frac{\partial c}{\partial w_1}(\bar{w}_1, \bar{w}_2, \bar{q}) = 0$$

or

$$\frac{\partial c}{\partial w_1}(\bar{w}_1, \bar{w}_2, \bar{q}) = \bar{x}_1 \equiv g_1(\bar{w}_1, \bar{w}_2, \bar{q}).$$

Since the choice of input prices $(\bar{w}_1, \bar{w}_2)$ and $\bar{q}$ was arbitrary, it follows that

$$\frac{\partial c}{\partial w_1}(w_1, w_2, q) = g_1(w_1, w_2, q)$$

for any (w_1, w_2) and q. Similarly, it is straightforward to show that the partial derivative of the cost function with respect to w_2 yields the conditional input demand $g_2(w_1, w_2, q)$. ∎

To see how Shephard's Lemma is used to derive a production function from a cost function, suppose we have a cost function

$$c(w_1, w_2, q) = q\sqrt{w_1 w_2}.$$

Then from Shephard's Lemma

$$\frac{\partial c}{\partial w_1} = \frac{q\sqrt{w_2}}{2\sqrt{w_1}} = g_1(w_1, w_2, q) = x_1, \qquad (8.12)$$

$$\frac{\partial c}{\partial w_2} = \frac{q\sqrt{w_1}}{2\sqrt{w_2}} = g_2(w_1, w_2, q) = x_2. \qquad (8.13)$$

Rearrange equation (8.12) to obtain

$$\frac{\sqrt{w_1}}{\sqrt{w_2}} = \frac{q}{2x_1}. \qquad (8.14)$$

Substitute from equation (8.14) into (8.13) to obtain

$$\frac{q}{2} \cdot \frac{q}{2x_1} = x_2,$$

from where we obtain the production function, $q = 2\sqrt{x_1 x_2}$, corresponding to the cost function we started with.

Exercises

8.1. For each of the production functions below, calculate the least cost of producing one unit of output for the given input prices. Explain your reasoning.

(a) $q = x_1 + 2x_2$; $(w_1, w_2) = (1, 4)$

(b) $q = \min\{2x_1 + x_2, x_3\}$; $(w_1, w_2, w_3) = (4, 1, 2)$

(c) $q = \min\{x_1, x_2\} + x_3$; $(w_1, w_2, w_3) = (1, 4, 2)$

(d) $q = \min\{x_1, x_2\} + \min\{x_2, x_3\}$; $(w_1, w_2, w_3) = (1, 4, 2)$

8.2. For each of the two-input production functions below, calculate the corresponding cost function, $c(w_1, w_2, q)$.

(a) $q = x_1^{\frac{1}{2}} x_2^{\frac{1}{2}}$

(b) $q = \dfrac{x_1}{2} + \sqrt{x_2}$

(c) $q = x_1(x_2 - 8)$

(d) $q = [\min\{x_1, 3x_2\}]^{\frac{1}{2}}$

(e) $q = x_1 - \dfrac{1}{x_2}$

8.3. For each of the two-input production functions below, draw a representative isoquant for $q = 12$ and use it to calculate the corresponding cost function, $c(w_1, w_2, q)$.

(*Hint*: Note that in each case, the technologies are a combination of Leontief and linear production functions. Therefore, all conditional input demands will either be at kink points and/or corner solutions of isoquants.)

(a) $q = \min\{2x_1 + x_2, x_1 + 2x_2\}$

(b) $q = \min\{2x_1, 2(x_1 + x_2)/3, 2x_2\}$

8.4. For each of the two-input cost functions below, calculate the corresponding production function, $q = f(x_1, x_2)$. Use the cost function to determine the returns to scale of the production function.

(a) $c(w_1, w_2, q) = w_1 q + \sqrt{w_1 w_2}$

(b) $c(w_1, w_2, q) = w_2 q^2 + w_1 q + 4w_1$

(c) $c(w_1, w_2, q) = \dfrac{w_1 w_2}{w_1 + w_2} q$

8.5. For each of the following cases, a multiplant firm wishes to produce a total level of output $Q = \Sigma q_j$ where quantity q_j is produced in plant j. Find the joint total cost (JTC) from operating all plants and the joint marginal cost (JMC) as functions of Q.

(a) $c_1(q_1) = q_1^2$ and $c_2(q_2) = 3q_2^2$

(b) $c_1(q_1) = 4q_1 + 0.5q_1^2$ and $c_2(q_2) = 4q_2 + q_2^2$

(c) $c_1(q_1) = 0.5q_1^2$, $c_2(q_2) = q_2^2$, and $c_3(q_3) = 2q_3^2$

Chapter 9

Competitive Firms

In this chapter, we analyze how firms behave in the short and the long run in a single market under **perfect competition**. Perfect competition is an idealized market structure characterized by many potential sellers for an identical product that has many potential buyers. While it does not correspond *exactly* to any particular market, arguably the market for agricultural commodities such as a particular type of soy beans, or for certain financial assets that are traded in stock exchanges come close. Perhaps more importantly, it provides a benchmark against which to compare various forms of imperfect competition.

The primary behavioral assumption on the part of all traders (whether consumers or producers) under perfect competition is that each economic agent considers herself to be a **price-taker**, i.e., she behaves as if she is unable to influence the current market price through her consumption or production behavior. Whether the inability to affect the price is real (e.g., when each consumer or producer is one of many, so a single agent's consumption or production is a tiny fraction of the total quantity traded in the market) or not (as would be the case in a two-person Edgeworth box economy where a single agent is responsible for a large fraction of the quantity traded), what is important is that each agent behaves as if she were unable to influence the market price.

Additionally, there are no market frictions: all changes are instantaneous and all relevant information permeates through the economy without agents having to incur any cost in gathering them. In particular, there are no exclusive technology or patents that confer an advantage to any firm. The best technology and business practices are commonly known. Thus any variation in costs across producers are generally small and mainly due to managerial efficiencies or differing opportunity costs of the entrepreneurs.

Finally, there is complete mobility of firms. Existing firms may leave the industry in the medium to long run if they find that to be advantageous, or new entrepreneurs may enter the market. We assume that there are no substantial costs or difficulties in making entry or exit decisions.

9.1   Defining Profits

The profit of a firm, π, is defined as the difference between total revenue (TR) which is the earnings from sales, and total cost (TC):

$$\pi = TR - TC.$$

Since $TR = p \times q$ where q units of output are sold at a per-unit price of p, and $TC = c(q)$ is the firm's cost function, the firm's profit π is a function of the output q, and may be written as

$$\pi(q) = pq - c(q).$$

We will assume that the cost function includes a normal profit margin which is the smallest compensation that an entrepreneur needs in order to remain in business, i.e., the entrepreneur's opportunity cost. With this included in the TC, it follows that if $\pi = 0$, then the revenues earned are *just enough* to pay for the operating expenses (the cost of variable inputs such as labor and raw materials), the overhead (cost of fixed inputs, such as salaries of managers, the cost of hosting the firm's website, the firm's property taxes, etc.) as well as the entrepreneur's compensation. Therefore when $\pi = 0$, we will say that the firm makes normal profits; if $\pi > 0$, we say that the firm makes supernormal profits, while $\pi < 0$ signifies losses.

For future reference, note that when a firm makes normal profits, $TR = TC$ and so

$$pq = c(q).$$

Dividing both sides by q, we get $p = c(q)/q$, i.e., when a firm's profits are zero, the price of output must equal the average cost of producing that output. Therefore if $p > AC$, the firm earns supernormal profits while if $p < AC$, it must make losses.

9.2   Short-Run Profit Maximization

9.2.1   The case of a single input

Suppose a firm purchases a quantity of an input x in a competitive market at a fixed price of w per unit. It produces output q using a DRS production function $q = f(x)$, and sells the output at the current market price of p per unit. Then the firm's profit level, π, is given by

$$\pi = pq - wx \tag{9.1}$$

where the term pq refers to the total revenue, while wx is the cost of purchasing x units of the input. Assuming that there are no other costs aside from the cost of this single input, wx is also the total cost. Fixing the level of profit at some arbitrary $\bar{\pi} > 0$, we can then rearrange (9.1) as

$$q = \frac{\bar{\pi}}{p} + \frac{w}{p}x. \tag{9.2}$$

Then (9.2) is the equation of an **isoprofit line** which shows all possible combinations of input x and output q that yield the profit level $\bar{\pi}$ as shown by the solid blue line in Figure 9.1; since the isoprofit equation is linear, its vertical intercept is $\bar{\pi}/p$ and its slope is w/p. The arrows indicate the direction in which the profit level is increasing.

It follows that an increase in $\bar{\pi}$ increases the isoprofit's intercept while keeping its slope unchanged. Then we may maximize this firm's profit by picking the highest isoprofit attainable while being on the technology frontier, $f(x)$. This occurs at point A: the input-output level (x^*, q^*) generates a

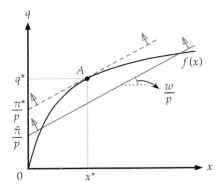

Figure 9.1   Profit maximization

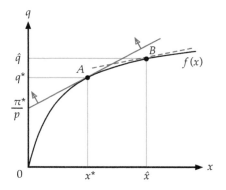

Figure 9.2   Decrease in w

maximum profit of π^* at the prices (p, w). Note that at $x^* > 0$ (an interior maximizer), the production function is tangent to the isoprofit:

$$f'(x^*) = w/p,\qquad(9.3)$$

i.e., the marginal product at the profit-maximizing input level must equal the relative price of the input to the output.[1]

This profit maximization condition can also be derived using calculus. Suppose that input level x^* maximizes the profit function derived from (9.1) after substituting $q = f(x)$ when prices (p, w) are fixed:

$$\pi(x) = pf(x) - wx.$$

Then by a first-order necessary condition for a maximum,[2] it follows that $\pi'(x^*) = 0$, i.e., the slope of the profit function at the maximum point is zero. Therefore, $pf'(x^*) - w = 0$, from which it follows that $f'(x^*) = w/p$.

In Figure 9.2, the comparative static effect of a decrease in w is shown. Such a decrease lowers the ratio w/p, flattening the slope of the isoprofit as shown by the dashed blue line. Then the profit-maximizing input-output level is $(\hat{x}, \hat{q})$ at point B. Thus a fall in the input price leads to higher input use and therefore a higher output level. What happens to the isoprofit and the consequent input use when p changes is left up to the reader to discover.

Profit maximization is possible only with DRS production functions. To see why, consider a CRS technology instead given by the linear technology

---

[1] Another way to state the same condition is to write it as $pf'(x^*) = w$ whose interpretation is that the value of the marginal product, $pf'(x^*)$, must equal the input price, w.

[2] See section A.4 in the Mathematical appendix.

$q = 10x$ and fixed prices (p, w). From equation (9.3), it follows that at an interior maximizer, the slope of the production function of 10 must equal w/p. Even if the values of w and p were such that this were true, the highest isoprofit line would be tangent along the entire technology frontier, rendering the maximizing input level indeterminate. If the value of $w/p > 10$, then the isoprofit is steeper than the technology frontier so the profit-maximizing input level is zero. Conversely, if $w/p < 10$ the isoprofit is flatter and the firm can make infinite profit by using infinite amounts of the input. Similarly with ◀⏎ an IRS technology, either zero will be produced or infinite amounts.

9.2.2 A general case

An alternative way to formulate the problem of profit maximization utilizes a cost function. The firm's cost function $c(q)$ embodies the cheapest cost of manufacturing any given level of output. Therefore, the profit function can simply be written as

$$\pi(q) = pq - c(q). \tag{9.4}$$

Assuming that there is a unique q^* that maximizes the profit function given p, the first-order necessary condition for a maximum is that $\pi'(q^*) = 0$, from where we obtain that

$$p = c'(q^*). \tag{9.5}$$

Equation (9.5) is **Rule 1**: a competitive firm's profits are maximized when it produces where the price equals the marginal cost.

A second-order sufficient condition for a maximum is that $\pi''(q^*) < 0$. To derive the implication of this condition, differentiate (9.4) twice and set ◀⏎ $q = q^*$ to obtain $-c''(q^*) < 0$ which can be rewritten as

$$c''(q^*) > 0. \tag{9.6}$$

Equation (9.6) is **Rule 2**: a competitive firm's profits are maximized when it produces at a point where the marginal cost is rising.

Figure 9.3 illustrates Rules 1 and 2 in the specific instance of the cost function we encountered in section 8.2:

$$c(q) = \frac{q^3}{480} - \frac{q^2}{2} + 50q + 2500.$$

If the prevailing market price is $35, this is the competitive firm's marginal revenue as shown by the line labeled MR. The marginal revenue shows

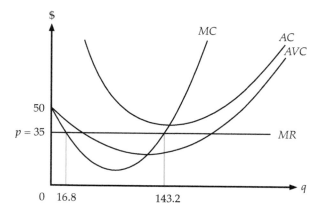

Figure 9.3   Producing in the short run

how much each sale brings in, in this case $35. Using Rule 1, set $p = c'(q)$
and solve for q to obtain (using the quadratic formula) 16.8 or 143.2 approximately. Since Rule 2 specifies that production should take place at the point
where the MC is rising, the firm should produce at $q^* = 143.2$.

However, at $q^* = 143.2$, this firm's total revenue is $35 \times 143.2 = \$5012$
while $c(143.2) \simeq 5525$, so the firm is running at a loss of approximately
$513. Should it continue to produce in the short run in the hope that the
price might go up in the future and restore profitability, or should it shut
down (i.e., cease production temporarily)? If it shuts down, the firm will
still incur the fixed cost of $2500 while avoiding any operating expenses;
however, because it brings in no revenue, its losses will now be much higher
at $2500! Therefore, in the short run, it is better for the firm to produce (in
accordance with Rules 1 and 2) and incur a loss of $513 than to shut down
and lose $2500.

The logic of the decision to shut down or not depends on whether the
revenues generated from sales cover the operating expenses or not. Denote
the total variable cost by

$$v(q) = \frac{q^3}{480} - \frac{q^2}{2} + 50q,$$

so the cost function can be written as $c(q) = v(q) + 2500$. Any revenue
in excess of the operating expenses can be used to cover overhead costs of
$2500, at least in part. In the example above, at $q^* = 143.2$, the TVC is
$v(143.2) = 3025$ approximately. Since the TR of $5012 exceeds the TVC of

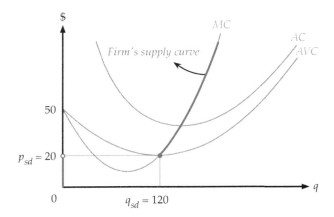

Figure 9.4   Individual firm's supply curve

$3025, the excess of $1987 can be applied towards the total fixed cost of $2500 to minimize losses.

Thus we obtain **Rule 3**: a competitive firm should produce in the short run so long as TR equals or exceeds TVC:

$$pq \geq v(q). \tag{9.7}$$

Dividing both sides of (9.7) by q we obtain an alternative, more useful, statement of Rule 3:

$$p \geq \frac{v(q)}{q} \equiv AVC, \tag{9.8}$$

i.e., a competitive firm should produce in accordance with Rules 1 and 2 so long as the market price exceeds the AVC.

9.2.3   Deriving a firm's supply curve

Applying the rules to Figure 9.3, we graphically derive a **firm's supply curve** in Figure 9.4. When $0 \leq p < 20$, p is less than the minimum AVC of 20 and Rule 3 no longer goes through. Therefore, the quantity supplied will be zero at these prices, as indicated by the vertical blue line segment at $q = 0$.

At $p = 20$, the firm is indifferent between producing and not producing in the short run: in either case, its loss amounts to $2500. We will assume that when the firm is indifferent between producing and not producing, it chooses to produce.

For prices above $20, all three rules apply and so production takes place where the MR line would cross the MC line (as at $q = 143.2$ in Figure 9.3), i.e., along the rising portion of the MC curve above the minimum AVC point. Hence, an individual competitive firm's supply curve is given by the heavy blue line with the break at $20. This liminal price, the minimum AVC, is denoted by p_{sd} and called the **shutdown price** since the firm shuts down production when the market price falls below this level. We will refer to the corresponding quantity as the **shutdown quantity** and denote it by q_{sd}.

To calculate this shutdown price, follow these two steps that exploit the fact that the MC passes through the minimum AVC.

1. Set the MC equal to the AVC and derive the shutdown quantity, q_{sd}.

2. Substitute q_{sd} into either the MC (or the AVC) to derive the shutdown price, p_{sd}.

As an example, we derive the shutdown price and the firm's supply curve for the cost function from the previous subsection,

$$c(q) = \frac{q^3}{480} - \frac{q^2}{2} + 50q + 2500.$$

Following step 1, set the $MC = AVC$ to get the shutdown quantity:

$$\frac{q_{sd}^2}{160} - q_{sd} + 50 = \frac{q_{sd}^2}{480} - \frac{q_{sd}}{2} + 50.$$

Solving, we obtain $q_{sd} = 120$. Substitute this into the MC (or AVC) to obtain $p_{sd} = 20$ as shown in Figure 9.4.

The firm's supply curve is found in two steps.

1. A competitive firm chooses to produce according to **Rule 1**, so setting p equal to the MC gives us the firm's inverse supply curve.

2. The firm's supply curve is the inverse of the equation from step 1.

From step 1, set $p = q^2/160 - q + 50$. Taking p to the right hand side and using the quadratic formula, we get

$$q = 80 + \sqrt{160(p - 10)},$$

which is the equation for the upward sloping part of the supply curve for $p \geq p_{sd} = 20$. Thus the firm's supply curve is

$$q^s(p) = \begin{cases} 80 + \sqrt{160(p - 10)} & \text{if } p \geq 20 \\ 0 & \text{if } 0 \leq p < 20. \end{cases}$$

A market supply curve, $Q^s(p)$, is the sum of the firms' supply curves, so mathematically $Q^s(p) = \sum_{j=1}^{n} q_j^s(p)$ if there are n firms indexed by j. Graphically, the market supply is found by horizontally adding all the individual firm supply curves.

9.3   Shifts in a Firm's Supply

In Chapter 1, we briefly alluded to the factors that shift the market supply curve: a change in productivity, a change in input prices, as well as taxes or subsidies. In this section, we examine the impact of the same factors on a firm's supply curve.

9.3.1   Changes in productivity

An increase in productivity ought to shift a firm's inverse supply curve down at each output level, i.e., it should make the cost of producing any level of output cheaper, leading the firm to be willing to sell more at the same price. To see how this works, consider the single-input technology from section 8.1.1, $q = Ax^a$, whose associated cost function is $c(w, q) = w(q/A)^{1/a}$. Suppose that $a = 1/2$, $A = 1$, and $w = 12$. Then the cost function is $c(w, q) = 12q^2$, so the marginal cost is $c'(q) = 24q$. Verify that $p = 24q$ is ◀ ⬀ the inverse firm supply.

Suppose there is a technological innovation that increases productivity which we capture by changing the parameter $A = 2$. You may verify that this implies that the marginal productivity of x has now doubled. The new cost function is then $c(w, q) = 3q^2$, resulting in the new inverse firm supply, ◀ ⬀ $p = 6q$. Comparing the new and old inverse supplies, the new one lies entirely below the old, meaning that at any price, more will be supplied by this firm than before.

9.3.2   Changes in input prices

A decrease in the price of an input ought to have the same impact on a firm's inverse supply as an increase in productivity. To see this, consider a decreasing returns Cobb-Douglas technology $q = (x_1 x_2)^{1/4}$ whose cost function is $c(w_1, w_2, q) = q^2 \sqrt{w_1 w_2}$. Let the initial input prices be $w_1 = \$4$ and $w_2 = \$9$. Then $c(4, 9, q) = 6q^2$, so the inverse supply is $p = 12q$. Now if the price of input 1 falls to $\$1$ keeping the technology and the price of input 2 fixed, the new cost function $c(1, 9, q) = 3q^2$, so the new inverse supply $p = 6q$ lies below the old one.

9.3.3   The impact of a tax or subsidy

We illustrate the impact of a per-unit subsidy given to a firm on its cost curves. Suppose a firm's original cost function is

$$c_o(q) = \frac{q^2}{2} + 2q + 72.$$

Then its cost curves are

$$AC_o = \frac{q}{2} + 2 + \frac{72}{q}, \ AVC_o = \frac{q}{2} + 2, \ \text{and} \ MC_o = q + 2,$$

as drawn in Figure 9.5 in solid black.

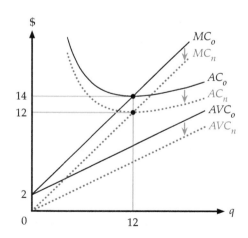

Figure 9.5   Impact of a subsidy on costs

When this firm receives a per-unit subsidy of $2 per unit sold, its new cost function becomes the old cost function less the total subsidy received:

$$c_n(q) = c_o(q) - 2q = \frac{q^2}{2} + 72.$$

Then its corresponding cost curves are

$$AC_n = \frac{q}{2} + \frac{72}{q}, \ AVC_n = \frac{q}{2}, \ and \ MC_n = q.$$

As shown in Figure 9.6 with the blue dotted lines, all three new cost curves are translates of the original cost curves, where every point on any old curve has moved down vertically by $2. In particular, the minimum AVC quantity (i.e., the shutdown quantity) is unchanged at zero; the shutdown price is $2 lower. Similarly, the output at which the AC attains a minimum remains unchanged at 12 units, but the minimum AC level is now $2 less at $12 per unit instead of $14. Since MC_n lies below MC_o, the firm's inverse supply is lower, signifying that at any price, it is willing to sell more than before.

Since taxes are the opposite of subsidies, we may conclude analogously that a per-unit tax on a firm's output raises all the cost curves vertically by the amount of the tax.

9.4   Perfect Competition in the Long Run

In a competitive environment where there are no barriers to entry or exit by firms and all firms are more or less identical, a typical firm's short run profit level is a good indicator of what will happen in the long run. If a firm is making supernormal profits in the short run, this attracts new entrepreneurs to enter this industry until the increased competition squeezes a typical firm's profit to zero at which point entry ceases since a typical entrepreneur only makes normal profits. Conversely, if a typical firm is making losses in the short-run and this situation persists indefinitely, then eventually firms begin to exit this industry until the reduced competition raises a typical firm's profitability to zero.

To see how this plays out, consider a competitive industry where there are 40 identical firms each with a cost function

$$c(q) = \frac{q^2}{2} + 2q + 72.$$

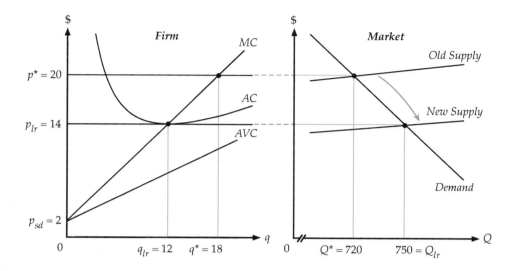

Figure 9.6   Firm and market interaction

The market demand for the product is given by $Q^d(p) = 820 - 5p$. To find the market equilibrium price in the short run which is determined by the intersection of demand and supply, suppose that the market price is p and derive a firm's individual supply curve by setting $p = MC$:

$$p = q + 2,$$

so $q^s(p) = p - 2$ for $p \geq 2$. This is shown in the left hand panel of Figure 9.6 by the rising MC curve above the shutdown price of $2.

Since there are 40 identical firms, the market supply is $Q^s(p) = 40q^s(p) = 40p - 80$. Setting the market demand equal to the market supply, we get

$$820 - 5p^* = 40p^* - 80,$$

or the market equilibrium price is $p^* = \$20$ which is shown in the right hand panel of Figure 9.6. Thus a typical firm produces 18 units of output and the market equilibrium quantity traded is 720 units. It is also easy to calculate a typical firm's profit: $TR = 20 \times 18 = \$360$, while $TC = c(18) = \$270$, so $\pi^* = \$90$ and there are supernormal profits in the short run, a fact that can be visually discerned by noting that $p^* > AC$ for producing 18 units in the left hand panel of Figure 9.6.

When there are supernormal profits in the short run, there will be entry by new firms in the long run until a typical firm makes normal profits.

Therefore, in the long run, the market price is such that each firm makes normal profits. Recall from section 9.1 that for a firm to make normal profits, we require $p = AC$; since a competitive firm produces where $p = MC$ (Rule 1), a firm earns normal profits when it produces at the point where $p = MC = AC$, i.e., at the minimum AC point. Therefore, to calculate the long-run price, p_{lr}, follow these two steps that exploit the fact that the MC passes through the minimum AC.

1. Set the MC equal to the AC and derive the long-run quantity, q_{lr}.

2. Substitute q_{lr} into either the MC or the AC to derive the long-run price, p_{lr}.

From step 1, set $MC = AC$:

$$2 + q_{lr} = \frac{q_{lr}}{2} + 2 + \frac{72}{q_{lr}},$$

and solve for $q_{lr} = 12$. From step 2, substitute into the MC function to get ◀ ◿ $p_{lr} = \$14$. Therefore, in the long run, the market price will settle at $p_{lr} = 14$ and each firm will produce $q_{lr} = 12$.[3]

But this means that there will be sufficient entry by new firms so that the market supply curve shifts to the right (as shown in the right panel of Figure 9.6) until the price drops from \$20 to \$14. Substituting $p_{lr} = 14$ into the market demand, we obtain the long run market quantity of $Q_{lr} = 750$. Since each firm produces 12 units of output in the long run and all firms are identical, there must be $750/12 \simeq 62$ firms in the market after entry. In other words, starting from the short-run equilibrium price of \$20 when typical firms are making supernormal profits, it will require 22 more firms to enter this market for the price to drop to the long-run level of \$14 in order for each firm in the industry to earn a normal profit. Until this happens, there will remain an incentive for firms to enter.

An analogous (but converse) story can be told in the case of short-run losses by firms. In this case, firms will exit the industry until the market supply shifts sufficiently to the left to raise the long run market equilibrium price to the point where typical firms are making normal profits.

---

[3]Note that finding the long-run quantity and price is analogous to the two-step procedure for finding the shutdown quantity and price outlined earlier in section 9.2.3. The only difference is that in the long-run scenario we use the AC rather than the AVC.

Exercises

9.1. Daniel Archer's Midland farm produces corn. His cost function (where total cost is measured in cents) is calculated to be

$$c(q) = \frac{q^3}{480} - \frac{q^2}{2} + 100q + 1000$$

where q is the output level (measured in bushels). The market price of corn is 220 cents per bushel which Midland farm, as a competitive producer, takes as given. How many bushels will Daniel produce? What is Midland farm's shutdown price?

9.2. In Takeout Town, there are 45 identical pizza delivery firms, each firm having the cost function $c(q) = 0.5q^2 + 4q + 162$ where q is the quantity of pizzas produced by a typical firm. The market demand curve is given by $Q^d(p) = 820 - 5p$.

(a) Find a firm's individual supply curve $q^s(p)$ and the market supply curve $Q^s(p)$. Calculate the market equilibrium price p^* and quantity Q^*. Calculate the firm output q^* and profit level.

(b) What will be the long-run price p_{lr} after entry or exit? Calculate the approximate number of firms in the long run (round down to the nearest integer).

9.3. In the market for a product, there are 100 identical competitive firms, each firm having the cost function $c(q) = 50 + 5q + 0.5q^2$ where q is the quantity of output in tons produced by each firm. The market demand curve is given by $Q^d = 1660 - 20p$.

(a) Find the market equilibrium price p^* and quantity produced by each firm, q^*.

(b) A permanent increase in demand shifts the market demand to $Q^d = 1920 - 20p$. What will be the approximate price p^{**} (up to two decimal places) in this market in the short run?

(c) Given the permanent increase in demand, how many firms will there be in this market in the long run after entry or exit?

9.4. In the market for manhole covers, there are 120 identical firms, each firm having the cost function $c(q) = 0.5q^2 + 4q + 18$ where q is the number of manhole covers produced by each firm. The market demand curve is given by $Q^d(p) = 1720 - 100p$.

(a) Find a firm's individual supply curve $q^s(p)$ and the market supply curve $Q^s(p)$. Calculate the market equilibrium price p^* and quantity Q^*. Calculate the output q^* that each firm produces and a typical firm's profit level.

(b) The government imposes a tax of \$1 per manhole cover produced on each firm. What will be the long-run price p_{lr} after entry or exit? If the tax remains in place, calculate the approximate number of firms in the long run (round down to the nearest integer).

9.5. In the market for soy beans, there are 520 identical farms, each farm having the cost function $c(q) = 0.5q^2 + 3q + 32$ where q is the quantity of output in tons produced by each farm. The market demand curve is given by $Q^d(p) = 4640 - 100p$.

(a) Find a firm's individual supply curve $q^s(p)$ and the market supply curve $Q^s(p)$. Calculate the market equilibrium price p^* and quantity Q^*. Calculate the output q^* that each firm produces and the losses made by a typical farm.

(b) In view of the losses, the farmers wish to lobby the government for a price support program. What is the lowest support price acceptable to the farmers?

9.6. There are US cotton farmers and international (non-US) cotton farmers. All farmers are assumed to be perfectly competitive on the world market. The world demand for cotton is given by $Q^d(p) = 12,000 - 100p$.

(a) To begin with, assume that all farmers are identical and the cost function for any farmer, US or international, is given by $c(q) = 0.5q^2 + 162$ where q is the farmer's output. There are 300 US and 200 international farmers. Find a firm's individual supply curve $q^s(p)$ and the world market supply curve $Q^s(p)$ to calculate the world equilibrium price p^*.

(b) The US government decides to give a subsidy to the 300 US cotton farmers after which a US-farmer's cost function becomes $c_u(q_u) = 0.3q_u^2 + 162$. The 200 international farmers have the same cost function as in (a). Assuming that the number of farmers does not change in the short run, find the new world supply $Q_n^s(p)$ and calculate the new world equilibrium price after this subsidy p^{**}.

(c) Calculate the profits of US and international farmers at p^{**}. What will happen to international farmers in the long run?

(d) Assume that the number of US farmers remains unchanged at 300 in the long run. Calculate the approximate number of international farmers that will be in the cotton market in the long run (round down to the nearest integer).

Chapter 10

Monopoly

A monopoly is a market structure with a single producer, so effectively the firm *is* the industry. Examples of monopolies are many. Bell Telephone (renamed AT&T in 1899) had a monopoly in telecommunication services until it was split up in 1984. The Mac operating system is sold exclusively by Apple just as the Windows operating system is sold exclusively by Microsoft. Monsanto is the only company that makes a genetically modified cotton seed which is worm-resistant. Until 2005, the pharmaceutical company Burroughs-Wellcome (now GlaxoSmithKline) was the only company that produced the antiretroviral drug AZT to treat HIV.

A monopoly can engage in uniform pricing, charging the same price from all of its customers, or it can engage in differential pricing (more traditionally known as price discrimination) and charge different prices from different customers (loosely speaking). The primary difference between a competitive firm and a monopoly is that the former is a price-taker and only has to decide how much to produce, while the latter decides both the price (or prices, in the case of differential pricing) to charge as well as the total quantity to produce.

10.1 Uniform Pricing

Even though a monopoly appears to have an extra degree of freedom over a competitive firm because it can set both the price and the quantity, this freedom is somewhat illusory. This is because the market demand curve curbs its ability to choose an arbitrary quantity-price combination. Setting the price determines how much the monopoly can sell and therefore how much it should produce; setting a quantity determines the maximum price that the monopoly can sell that quantity for. Therefore, a monopoly's problem is to find a quantity-price combination (Q^*, p^*) that lies on the market demand curve so as to maximize its profits.

10.1.1   Profit maximization

In general, let $p = D(Q)$ be an inverse market demand curve. Then the monopoly's profit function is

$$\pi(Q) = D(Q)Q - c(Q),$$

where $D(Q)Q$ is the firm's total revenue and $c(Q)$ its cost function. If there is a profit-maximizing quantity Q^*, the slope of the profit function at that quantity must be zero:

$$\pi'(Q^*) = [D(Q^*) + D'(Q^*)Q^*] - c'(Q^*) = 0,$$

where the term in the square brackets is found using the Chain Rule and represents the marginal revenue. Thus the monopoly quantity produced is found by setting its marginal revenue equal to marginal cost:

$$D(Q^*) + D'(Q^*)Q^* = c'(Q^*). \tag{10.1}$$

The price charged for the output Q^* is found from the inverse demand, so $p^* = D(Q^*)$. Replacing this in (10.1) we obtain

$$p^* + D'(Q^*)Q^* = c'(Q^*).$$

Factoring out p^*, we get

$$p^* \left(1 + D'(Q^*)\frac{Q^*}{p^*} \right) = c'(Q^*). \tag{10.2}$$

From section 1.4.1, recall that the price elasticity of demand at any point (Q, p) on the inverse demand is

$$\varepsilon = \frac{1}{D'(Q)} \cdot \frac{p}{Q}.$$

Let ε^* denote the price elasticity at the monopoly's profit-maximizing quantity-price pair (Q^*, p^*). Replacing this in (10.2), we obtain

$$p^* \left(1 + \frac{1}{\varepsilon^*} \right) = c'(Q^*). \tag{10.3}$$

Note that the left hand side of (10.3) is the firm's marginal revenue which is positive only if $|\varepsilon^*| > 1$. Therefore a monopoly can earn a positive marginal revenue only if its demand is price elastic.

A further algebraic manipulation of (10.3) yields an insightful equation:

$$\frac{p^* - c'(Q^*)}{p^*} = -\frac{1}{\varepsilon^*}. \tag{10.4}$$

The numerator on the left hand side, $p^* - c'(Q^*)$, is the difference between what the monopolist charges and what it costs to produce the last unit and is called the **absolute mark-up**. Note that the right hand side of (10.4) is always positive since the price elasticity is negative. Since p^* is positive, the absolute mark-up is positive: the monopolist charges a price that is greater than the cost of producing the last unit. This ability to charge a price above marginal cost stands in contrast to the case of the competitive firm which chooses an output level so that price equals marginal cost, as we saw in section 9.2.2.

Dividing the absolute mark-up by p^*, we obtain the **relative mark-up**, a unit-free measure of market power known as the **Lerner Index** named after Abba Lerner. The larger this index, the greater a firm's ability to charge above its marginal cost. Note that under perfect competition, the Lerner Index is zero since the presence of many competitors producing the same product makes it impossible to charge a price above its marginal cost.

From (10.4), it follows that the more price-elastic the demand the lower the relative mark-up: goods that are relatively elastic will have smaller mark-ups, since a big mark-up would cause buyers to stop buying this product in large numbers. Conversely, goods with relatively inelastic demands will have a larger mark-up. Thus the price elasticity of demand has implications for monopoly pricing.

10.1.2 Calculating monopoly output and price

There are three steps in calculating a monopoly's profit-maximizing output level and price.

1. From the inverse demand, find the MR.

2. Set the MR from step 1 equal to the MC and solve for the profit-maximizing output level, Q^*.

3. Substitute Q^* into the inverse demand to find the price, p^*.

We illustrate these steps in the case of the two types of demand curves introduced in Chapter 1, a linear inverse demand and a demand curve that displays a constant price elasticity throughout.

Linear demand

The linear inverse demand is given by $p = a - bQ$ where a is the demand intercept and b the slope parameter. Therefore, the total revenue is $TR = pQ = aQ - bQ^2$, so the marginal revenue is the derivative dTR/dQ given by

$$MR = a - 2bQ, \tag{10.5}$$

i.e., the MR for a linear inverse demand has the same vertical intercept as the inverse demand but is twice as steep.

Figure 10.1 shows a monopoly that faces a linear inverse market demand $p = 120 - Q$ whose cost function is $c(Q) = Q^2$. For step 1, use the 'same-intercept-and-twice-the-slope' result of (10.5) above to obtain the marginal revenue, $MR = 120 - 2Q$. In step 2, set $MR = MC$ where $MC = c'(Q) = 2Q$, and solve to get $Q^* = 30$. Finally, in step 3, the price charged is found by substituting $Q^* = 30$ into the inverse demand, so $p^* = \$90$. Note that the price of $90 is quite a bit more than the MC of producing the last unit of output of $60: the absolute mark-up is $30.

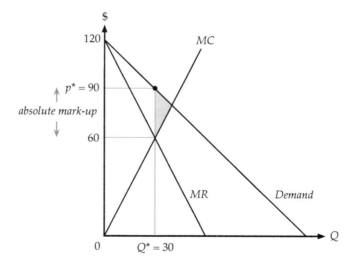

Figure 10.1   Monopoly output and price

Constant-elasticity demand

A demand curve with a constant price elasticity of demand is given by $Q = Ap^{\varepsilon}$ where ε is of course a negative number. Then the inverse demand is $p = (Q/A)^{1/\varepsilon}$ and the total revenue is

$$TR = pQ = A^{-1/\varepsilon}Q^{(1+\varepsilon)/\varepsilon},$$

so the marginal revenue is

$$MR = \left(\frac{1+\varepsilon}{\varepsilon}\right)A^{-1/\varepsilon}Q^{1/\varepsilon}. \tag{10.6}$$

From (10.6) it follows that if the demand is inelastic (i.e., $|\varepsilon| < 1$), then the $(1+\varepsilon)/\varepsilon$ term is negative and so the MR is *always* negative no matter what the level of Q. In this case no monopoly will ever produce since it can never earn a positive marginal revenue. So in order for a monopoly to produce, the demand must be elastic (i.e., $|\varepsilon| > 1$), as was derived earlier in equation (10.3).

Suppose that the demand is $Q = 100p^{-2}$ (so $\varepsilon = -2$) and $c(Q) = Q/10$. For step 1, use (10.6) to derive $MR = 5Q^{-\frac{1}{2}}$. In step 2, set $MR = MC$ where ◀◿ $MC = 1/10$ and solve for the output, $Q^* = 2500$. Finally, in step 3, put $Q^* = 2500$ into the inverse demand function to get $p^* = \$0.20$.

10.1.3 Inefficiency of uniform-pricing monopoly

A central difference between competitive and non-competitive behavior is that under the latter, a firm is no longer a price-taker: it knows that it can influence (if not actually set) the price of its product. When even one firm is not a price-taker, the market outcome is generally Pareto inefficient. Therefore the existence of a monopoly leads to Pareto inefficiency. We illustrate this inefficiency first in a partial equilibrium context and then in general equilibrium.

Inefficiency in partial equilibrium

The standard demonstration of market inefficiency that you probably encountered in your introductory economics class focuses on the gains from trade. In Figure 10.1, if the monopoly were to produce a bit more than 30 units, the additional production has a marginal cost slightly above $60 which is lower than the almost $90 that some consumers are willing to pay for it, as shown by the market demand. Since the buyer value exceeds the seller value, a potential gain from trade does not come about because the monopoly restricts the production to 30 units. In fact, every unit of output from the monopoly production of 30 to the output of 40 where the marginal cost crosses the demand is valued by buyers at a price higher than what it costs the monopoly to produce. Hence, the blue shaded triangle represents foregone gains from trade and is the **deadweight loss of a monopoly**.

Inefficiency in general equilibrium°

To show that a monopoly leads to a Pareto inefficient allocation, consider a two-person Edgeworth box economy where the initial endowment is $\omega = ((0, 10), (10, 0))$, as shown in Figure 10.2. Assume that good 2 is the numéraire so both individuals take $p_2 = 1$ as given. When it comes to good 1, individual a is a price-taker but individual b who controls the entire supply of good 1 behaves like a monopolist: she sets the price p_1 so as to maximize her own utility.

Suppose a's preferences are given by $u^a(x_1^a, x_2^a) = x_1^a + \ln x_2^a$ so her demand function is

$$h^a(p_1, p_2, m) = \left(\frac{m^a}{p_1} - 1, \frac{p_1}{p_2}\right) = \left(\frac{10}{p_1} - 1, p_1\right).$$

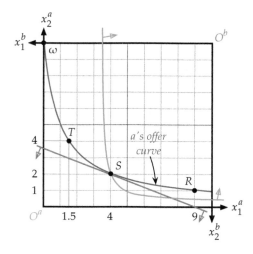

Figure 10.2   Pareto inefficiency of a monopoly

Since $p_2 = 1$ implies $m^a = 10$, if b were to set a price $p_1 = 1$, a would want to buy the bundle $(9, 1)$ at R. Similarly, if $p_1 = 2$, a would demand the bundle $(4, 2)$ at S; if $p_1 = 4$, a would want to purchase the bundle $(1.5, 4)$ at T and so on. Joining these points gives us a's price consumption curve (sometimes called a's **offer curve**) shown in blue in Figure 10.2. We can derive the equation for this offer curve by noting that since $x_1^a = (10/p_1) - 1$ and $x_2^a = p_1$, substituting for p_1 in the first function yields $x_1^a = (10/x_2^a) - 1$, so the offer ◀ ⃟ curve is given by the equation $x_2^a = 10/(x_1^a + 1)$.

Finally, assume that b's preferences are linear and given by $u^b(x_1^b, x_2^b) = 0.4x_1^b + x_2^b$. Because setting the price p_1 leads a to demand a bundle that lies on her blue offer curve, b's objective is to find an allocation on this offer curve that maximizes b's utility. Graphically, this occurs at point S where b's indifference curve is tangent to a's offer curve. To calculate this point algebraically, set the slope of a's offer curve $dx_2^a/dx_1^a = -10/(1 + x_1^a)^2$ equal ◀ ⃟ to the slope of b's indifference curve of -0.4 to obtain $x_1^a = 4$. Then $p_1 = 2$ and $x_2^a = 2$, i.e., $S = ((4, 2), (6, 8))$. In other words, when b sets $p_1 = 2$, b's utility is maximized at $(4, 2)$. However, the allocation S is not Pareto efficient since the indifference curves are not tangent: the marginal rates of substitution are unequal at S since $MRS^a = 2$ and $MRS^b = 0.4$.

10.2 Differential Pricing

Consider the following pricing examples.

- As a student, you can show your identity card and pay $4 for a movie at a local theater while regular people pay $6.

- You are traveling economy class on a flight from New York to Boston. In the course of a conversation with a fellow passenger, you find out that she paid $80 for the flight while you paid $120.

- You debate whether to buy an 16GB iPhone for $199, a 32GB for $299 or a 64GB for $399.

- An Atlanta taxi charges $2.50 for the first eighth of a mile and 25 cents for every subsequent eighth of a mile.

What all of these examples have in common is that different people pay different prices for the same service or product. In the first, your status as a student is used to determine the price you pay; in the second, it may depend on when (e.g., 15 days in advance or last minute) or how (e.g., online versus over the phone) you bought the ticket; in the third, you choose between three different price-quantity bundles; in the last, a passenger pays an amount that varies with the distance traveled. These are all examples of differential pricing (DP).

A precise definition of DP is surprisingly difficult to formulate. The following definition, though not comprehensive, is widely accepted:

> A producer engages in differential pricing if two units of the same commodity are sold at different prices to different individuals, where the price difference cannot be explained by the marginal cost of providing the product.

Thus if a pharmaceutical company with a monopoly over an antidepressant drug charges $65 for a month's supply in the US while it charges $41 in Mexico, and if this price difference cannot be explained by the marginal cost of making them available in each country such as transportation and distribution costs, then this company is engaging in DP.

But charging the same price from all customers does not automatically mean an absence of DP! For example, take Amazon.com's policy of waiving shipping charges for orders in excess of $35. If two customers — one in Anchorage, Alaska and the other in Miami, Florida — order the same encyclopedia set, they each pay the same price but the customer living in Alaska is in essence paying a lower price than the one living in Florida because the shipping charges for the former are likely to be much greater than for the latter. Amazon, by absorbing the shipping charges, is subsidizing one customer more than the other and therefore engaging in DP.

Arthur Pigou, an English economist, is usually credited with the fundamental insight that the aim of DP is for producers to convert as much of the consumer surplus in a transaction into producer surplus by raising the price at which trade takes place. Before we consider how this may be accomplished, we look at the factors that facilitate or hinder DP.

10.2.1   Successful differential pricing

In order for a seller to successfully engage in DP, it is necessary for the firm to have some (1) market power, (2) ability to sort customers, and (3) ability to prevent resale of the product.

For a firm to have market power, it must be able to charge a price above the product's marginal cost, i.e., it must typically be operating under imperfect competition, whether under monopoly, oligopoly, or monopolistic competition. Market power could also arise due to asymmetric or imperfect information, for instance, when buyers are unaware about the pricing of similar products sold by others.

Sorting customers is the ability to tell apart different customers, or groups of customers, or classify one's potential customer base into types of customers. Charging a price above marginal cost means that it may be possible to lower the price for marginal customers and thereby increase sales and profits. In order to lower the price for some customers but not others, the firm has to be able to differentiate among them, or know how much each customer type is willing to pay even if it cannot distinguish one customer type from another.

Finally, it has to be able to prevent resale, for otherwise consumers who could buy at a cheaper price would engage in arbitrage, i.e., offer to sell to those who are being charged a higher price and turn a profit. For some products, resale can be difficult due to the nature of the goods, as in the case of electricity, or services, like haircuts. For others, like textbooks or medicines sold in different parts of the world, resale may be difficult due to geographical distance, transportation costs, or tariffs. In some cases, such as software sold to university students at an educational discount, resale may be prevented by the terms of the contract governing the sale.

10.2.2 A taxonomy of differential pricing

Following Pigou, we classify differential pricing into three categories depending on the ability of a firm to sort its customers (see Figure 10.3). Under perfect sorting, the firm can distinguish among each of its customers and engages in price discrimination in the first-degree (or personalized pricing). With an imperfect ability to tell consumers apart, firms can engage in price discrimination in the second-degree (either bundling or nonlinear pricing, a category that we refer to jointly as menu pricing), or the third-degree (or group pricing). While this classification is neither comprehensive nor sharply delineated (various real-world examples may contain elements drawn from more than one category), it serves the purpose of making sense of many everyday DP practices. We present these in order of increasing complexity from first-degree to third-degree to second-degree.

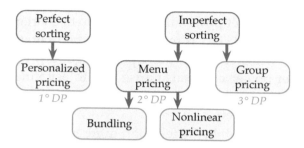

Figure 10.3   Types of differential pricing

Personalized pricing (1° DP)

When a seller knows every consumer's reservation price (the maximum price that each buyer is willing to pay) or reservation utility (the utility received when the consumer does not trade), it can sort its customers perfectly and engage in personalized pricing: the firm charges the maximum possible price from every customer so that the consumer surplus is zero,[1] or, alternatively, the consumer receives her reservation utility. In either event, the consumer is indifferent between accepting the offer or not. Perfect sorting therefore provides a benchmark as to the maximum profit that a firm can make in a given situation.

Group pricing (3° DP)

Suppose a seller has some (but not perfect) information about a customer's type. Specifically, it is able to identify each potential customer as belonging to a group or market segment based on some observable or verifiable characteristic before the purchase takes place. Under group pricing, members of different groups pay different prices, while members within a group pay the same price. For instance, Amtrak offers 15 percent off its everyday fares for students, senior citizens, or veterans. Similarly, the arthritis drug, Lodine, manufactured by Wyeth-Ayerst Laboratories sells for $108 a month when prescribed for humans and $38 when prescribed for dogs. Consumers may be segmented by geography (e.g., buyers in the US versus the EU), age (seniors versus non-seniors), status (student versus non-student), time (first-time versus repeat buyers) and so on.

---

[1] We make the innocuous assumption that when a consumer is indifferent between buying and not buying, she will decide to buy.

Menu pricing (2° DP)

Suppose a seller knows the type distribution of the customers but cannot tell a consumer of one type apart from another. A grocer may know that 20 percent of his customers who buy Coca-Cola want the two-liter bottle and 80 percent want the six-pack, but he does not know whether a particular customer is of the two-liter type or the six-pack type before the moment of purchase. The firm engages in menu pricing by offering a menu of options tailored to the preferences of the customer types.

Menu pricing can take two basic forms, bundling or nonlinear pricing. Under bundling, customers are simultaneously offered a choice among different price-quantity bundles or price-quality bundles. Thus, deciding between a two-liter Coca-Cola bottle and a six-pack, or between an 16/32/64GB iPhone are examples of choices between different price-quantity bundles, while deciding whether to fly economy class or business class is a choice between two price-quality bundles.

Under nonlinear pricing, a consumer faces a price schedule from which a consumer's expenditure can be inferred. In Figure 10.4, the red tariff expenditure line shows the expenditure plotted against the minutes called for a cell phone plan that allows 500 minutes of talk time for $40 per month and charges 20 cents for each minute thereafter. If the price-per-minute were constant, say, 10 cents a minute, the tariff expenditure would be a straight line through the origin. This cell phone plan is an example of *nonlinear* pricing because the per-unit price varies with the quantity. For example, at point

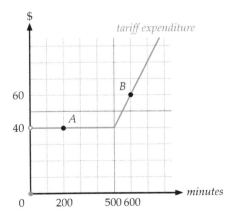

Figure 10.4   Nonlinear pricing

A, the consumer pays $40 for 200 minutes of calls, so the price-per-unit is effectively 20 cents per minute, while at *B* it is 10 cents a minute.[2] In practice, bundling and nonlinear pricing are often combined, as when consumers choose from different calling plans, each with its own tariff expenditure.

10.3   Personalized Pricing

If a seller is able to perfectly sort its consumers, it either knows their reservation prices or reservation utilities. The seller proposes an individualized take-it-or-leave-it offer that leaves a consumer indifferent between purchasing the product or doing without it. Ironically, this kind of DP (in contrast to any other kind of pricing under imperfect competition) turns out to be efficient! We illustrate this in a partial as well as a general equilibrium setting.

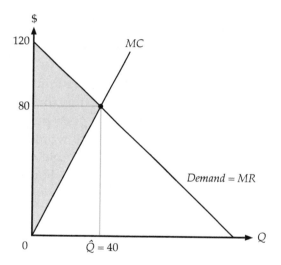

Figure 10.5   Personalized pricing

10.3.1   Efficiency in partial equilibrium

In Figure 10.5, we reprise the example from Figure 10.1 where the inverse demand is $p = 120 - Q$ and the marginal cost is $MC = 2Q$. With perfect sorting, each consumer is charged a price equal to the maximum amount

---

[2]The price-per-minute at any point along the tariff expenditure line is found by joining that point to the origin and figuring out the slope of this line.

she is willing to pay which is given by a point on the inverse demand. Consequently, the demand curve is also the MR of the monopolist that engages in personalized pricing.

Since profits are maximized where $MR = MC$, set the inverse demand equal to the marginal cost to determine the profit-maximizing quantity. Thus, the monopoly produces $\hat{Q} = 40$, charging different consumers different prices ranging from \$120 to \$80 along the inverse demand curve. Because the seller extracts all the consumer surplus, the total surplus consists only of the shaded producer surplus. More importantly, all potential gains from trade have been realized at $\hat{Q} = 40$. Any additional production is undesirable because it is valued below \$80, while its marginal cost of production is above \$80.

10.3.2 Efficiency in general equilibrium°

Consider the same two-person Edgeworth box economy as in Figure 10.2 where the endowment is $\omega = ((0,10),(10,0))$ and a's preferences are given by $u^a(x_1^a, x_2^a) = x_1^a + \ln x_2^a$ and b's preferences by $u^b = 0.4x_1^b + x_2^b$. Then a's reservation utility level is $u^a(0,10) = \ln 10$, shown by the orange indifference curve that passes through ω in Figure 10.6. Keeping a on this indifference curve, maximize consumer b's utility to obtain point E. Then consumer b makes a take-it-or-leave-it offer of approximately 3.22 units of

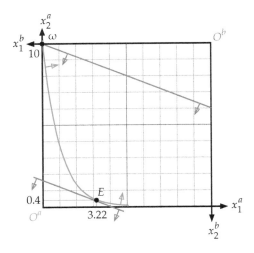

Figure 10.6 Pareto efficient personalized pricing

x_1 in exchange for a giving up 9.6 units of x_2 so as to reach the allocation $E = ((3.22, 0.4), (6.78, 9.6))$. The acceptance of this offer results in a movement from w to E where consumer a is no worse off but b is distinctly better off. Indeed, the point E is both individually rational and Pareto efficient.

10.4   Group Pricing

Consider a firm with two segmented markets for its product. It maximizes profits by producing a total amount Q^* in its production plant and selling Q_1^* units in market 1 and Q_2^* units in market 2 so that $Q_1^* + Q_2^* = Q^*$.

The principle behind the decision of how much to produce and how much to sell in each market is that the marginal revenue from each market must equal the marginal cost. If the marginal revenue from selling the last unit in market 1 exceeds the marginal cost of producing the last unit, i.e.,

$$MR_1(Q_1^*) > MC(Q^*),$$

then producing another unit and selling it in that market would raise profits, so Q^* cannot be the profit-maximizing level of output. Similarly, it is not possible that $MR_1(Q_1^*) < MC(Q^*)$, for in that case producing one unit fewer would also raise profits. Hence, it must be that $MR_1(Q_1^*) = MC(Q^*)$. The same logic holds for the second market as well. Therefore, under group pricing, the following conditions have to hold:

$$MR_1(Q_1^*) = MC(Q^*), \tag{10.7}$$
$$MR_2(Q_2^*) = MC(Q^*), \tag{10.8}$$
$$Q_1^* + Q_2^* = Q^*. \tag{10.9}$$

There are four steps to solve for a firm's profit-maximizing quantities and prices under group pricing using the conditions (10.7)–(10.9).

1. From the inverse demand for each market segment, find the corresponding marginal revenues.

2. Set each marginal revenue equal to the marginal cost.

3. From the equations in step 2, solve for the quantities.

4. Substitute each quantity from step 3 into the corresponding inverse demand to find the prices charged in each market segment.

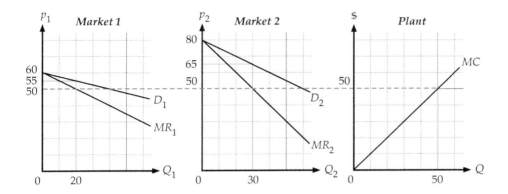

Figure 10.7   Group pricing

To illustrate, suppose a firm's inverse demand curves in each market segment are

$$p_1 = 60 - 0.25Q_1 \quad \text{and} \quad p_2 = 80 - 0.5Q_2$$

shown in the left and middle panels of Figure 10.7. The firm produces in a plant whose cost function is $c(Q) = 0.5Q^2$, where $Q = Q_1 + Q_2$ is the total quantity sold in both markets.

Then from step 1, the marginal revenues in each market are

$$MR_1 = 60 - 0.5Q_1 \quad \text{and} \quad MR_2 = 80 - Q_2.$$

To proceed to step 2, calculate the marginal cost $MC = Q = Q_1 + Q_2$ shown in the right panel of Figure 10.7. Set each of the marginal revenues equal to the marginal cost and simplify to obtain two equations in two unknowns:

$$60 = 1.5Q_1^* + Q_2^* \tag{10.10}$$
$$80 = Q_1^* + 2Q_2^*. \tag{10.11}$$

In step 3, solve for Q_1^* and Q_2^* simultaneously by multiplying both sides of (10.10) by 2 and then subtracting (10.11) from it to obtain $Q_1^* = 20$. Substitute this value in either (10.10) or (10.11) to obtain $Q_2^* = 30$. Therefore the firm produces a total of $Q^* = 50$ units, selling 20 in the first market and 30 in the second. Finally, in step 4, substitute $Q_1^* = 20$ and $Q_2^* = 30$ into their respective inverse demands to find the profit-maximizing prices in each market segment, $p_1^* = \$55$ and $p_2^* = \$65$.

10.4.1   Elasticity and group pricing°

The general principle underlying group pricing is: charge a higher price from those groups whose demand is relatively more inelastic, and charge less from those with more elastic demands. To see this, write the firm's profit function as

$$\pi(Q_1, Q_2) = D_1(Q_1)Q_1 + D_2(Q_2)Q_2 - c(Q)$$

where $D_i(Q_i)$ refers to the inverse demand in the ith market ($i = 1, 2$) and $Q = Q_1 + Q_2$. In order to maximize profits, set the partial derivatives $\partial \pi / \partial Q_1$ and $\partial \pi / \partial Q_2$ equal to zero:

$$D_1(Q_1^*) + \frac{\partial D_1}{\partial Q_1}Q_1^* - \frac{\partial c}{\partial Q} \cdot \frac{\partial Q}{\partial Q_1} = 0, \qquad (10.12)$$

$$D_2(Q_2^*) + \frac{\partial D_2}{\partial Q_2}Q_2^* - \frac{\partial c}{\partial Q} \cdot \frac{\partial Q}{\partial Q_2} = 0. \qquad (10.13)$$

Using the fact that $D_1(Q_1^*) = p_1^*$ and $\partial Q / \partial Q_1 = 1$, we may rewrite (10.12) as

$$p_1^* + \frac{\partial D_1}{\partial Q_1}Q_1^* = \frac{\partial c}{\partial Q} \qquad (10.14)$$

which is analogous to equation (10.1). Using the fact that at any point (Q_1, p_1) on the demand curve D_1, the price elasticity of demand is given by

$$\varepsilon_1 = \frac{1}{\partial D_1 / \partial Q_1} \cdot \frac{p_1}{Q_1},$$

we can derive the analogue of equation (10.3):

$$p_1^*\left(1 + \frac{1}{\varepsilon_1^*}\right) = \frac{\partial c}{\partial Q}. \qquad (10.15)$$

In an identical way, from equation (10.13) it follows that

$$p_2^*\left(1 + \frac{1}{\varepsilon_2^*}\right) = \frac{\partial c}{\partial Q}. \qquad (10.16)$$

Since the right hand side is the same marginal cost at Q^* in both (10.15) and (10.16), it follows that if $p_1^* < p_2^*$, then $|\varepsilon_1^*| > |\varepsilon_2^*|$, and vice versa. Therefore, a lower price is associated with a more elastic demand while a higher price is associated with a more inelastic demand.

10.4.2 Welfare and group pricing

A firm's profit under differential pricing will be higher than under uniform pricing. But is differential pricing also in the interest of consumers? Not always. So, in general, if a new market is opened up because of differential pricing (i.e., a group that was priced out of the market under uniform pricing is now willing to buy under group pricing), or if the quantity sold under differential pricing is greater than under uniform pricing, both consumer and producer surplus will increase and society will be better off.

10.5 Menu Pricing: Unit-demand bundling

A detailed treatment of optimal bundling is taken up in Chapter 15. Here, we consider a simpler model of bundling when a consumer will buy at most one unit of a product or do without.

Consider a tomato farmer facing two options: she can grow either organic or regular tomatoes or both. Potential customers are either adults without children (we will call them 'singles') or adults with children (we will call them 'parents') who attach a dollar value of v_o or v_r to a pound of tomatoes depending on whether it is organic or regular. Singles do not care as much for organic tomatoes as parents, as can be seen from the table below: a pound of organic tomatoes is valued at \$6 by parents as opposed to \$3 for singles, while a pound of regular tomatoes is worth \$3.50 to parents as opposed to \$2 for singles.[3]

Customer type	v_o	v_r
Parents	\$6.00	\$3.50
Singles	\$3.00	\$2.00

Each customer will buy at most one pound of tomatoes and has a utility function (or consumer surplus) given by

$$u(j, p_j) = \begin{cases} v_j - p_j & \text{if she buys good } j \\ 0 & \text{if she doesn't buy,} \end{cases}$$

where $j = o, r$. We make the tie-breaking assumption that if any consumer derives the same utility from either tomato variety, i.e., $u(o, p_o) = u(r, p_r)$, she will choose the organic one.

---

[3]Organic and regular tomatoes are vertically differentiated products: if organic and regular tomatoes were priced the same, everyone would prefer to buy the organic product.

Suppose that the farmer cannot tell one customer type from another but knows the type distribution: there are 100 potential buyers of whom x are parents and the rest are singles. The marginal cost of producing a pound of organic tomatoes is $1 as opposed to $0.50 for regular ones. The farmer can either engage in **pure bundling**, which is selling only one variety of tomatoes, or in **mixed bundling** where both kinds are offered, with the organic tomatoes being targeted towards parents and regular ones towards singles. We consider these two types of bundling in turn.

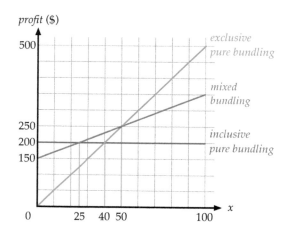

Figure 10.8   Unit-demand bundling

Suppose she engages in pure bundling and produces organic tomatoes only. If she prices to ensure that everyone buys (**inclusive pure bundling**), the maximum she can charge is $3. Since it costs $1 to produce it and all 100 people buy, the profit from sales is $200, as shown by the blue line in Figure 10.8. Alternatively, she can charge $6 which would prevent singles from buying (**exclusive pure bundling**) and earn a profit of $5x$, shown by the diagonal orange line. Comparing profits, the farmer prefers to use inclusive pure bundling if the number of parents are between 0 and 40.[4]

Now suppose the farmer engages in mixed bundling. In order to target the regular tomatoes to singles, she charges $2, which earns her $(2 - 0.50)(100 - x) = 1.50(100 - x)$. Note that parents receive a consumer surplus of $3.50 - 2 = \$1.50$ if they buy regular tomatoes. Therefore, if the

---

[4]It is easy to verify that selling regular tomatoes only earns the farmer less than selling organic ones, whether sold at an inclusive price or an exclusive price and regardless of the number of parents.

farmer charges $6 for organic tomatoes, parents would prefer to buy regular tomatoes since their consumer surplus from organic tomatoes would be zero while that from regular tomatoes is $1.50. In order to ensure that parents buy the organic ones, a price of $4.50 is incentive compatible: parents receive the same utility of 1.50 from either purchase, and, under our tie-breaking assumption, will choose the organic tomatoes. Then the farmer earns $(4.50 - 1)x = 3.50x$ from selling organic tomatoes and her overall profit from mixed bundling is the sum $1.50(100 - x) + 3.50x = 150 + 2x$ which is the green line drawn in Figure 10.8.

Then, Figure 10.8 presents all the options open to the farmer. When x lies between zero and 25, she prefers to engage in inclusive pure bundling. If x lies between 25 and 50, her profit is higher under mixed bundling. Finally, if x exceeds 50, she earns more under exclusive pure bundling.

The steps to solve the mixed bundling problem are summarized below. Let the two types of goods be called high- and low-type goods, and the two types of customers, the high- and low-value customers.

1. Begin with the low-type product which is targeted to the low-value customers. Set the price of the low-type good, p_l, equal to the maximum price that the low-value customers are willing to pay. Low-value customers derive a zero consumer surplus from the product targeted at them.

2. Find the consumer surplus received by the high-value customer from buying the low-type good at the price p_l calculated in step 1.

3. Set the price of the high-type good, p_h, so that the high-value customers receive the same consumer surplus calculated in step 2 from buying the high-type good. High-value customers derive a positive consumer surplus from the product targeted at them.

Exercises

10.1. A monopolist producer faces the inverse demand curve given by $p = 250 - Q$, where p is the price charged and Q is the quantity demanded. The total cost of producing the good is $c(Q) = 50 + 50Q$.

(a) Find the profit-maximizing price and quantity, p^* and Q^*.

(b) Calculate the deadweight loss of this monopoly.

(c) Suppose a per-unit tax of t is imposed on each unit produced by the monopoly. Calculate the new price p^{**} that maximizes the monopoly's profit as a function of t and the derivative dp^{**}/dt. What economic interpretation can you attach to this derivative? Explain!

10.2. A monopoly faces the inverse demand curve given by $p = 10 - Q$, and a constant MC of \$4.

(a) Draw the demand, marginal revenue, and marginal cost curves. Find the price and quantity, p^* and Q^*, that maximize the monopolist's profit.

(b) Suppose the government now regulates the maximum price that the monopoly can charge at \$6. Draw the firm's new marginal revenue given this price restriction and find the new price charged, p^{**}, and quantity sold, Q^{**}.

10.3. A monopolist has two segmented markets with demand curves given by

$$p_1 = 160 - Q_1 \quad \text{and} \quad p_2 = 130 - 0.5Q_2,$$

where p_1 and p_2 are the prices charged in each market segment, and Q_1 and Q_2 are the quantities sold. Its cost function is given by $c(Q) = 2Q^2$, where $Q = Q_1 + Q_2$. Find the monopolists profit-maximizing prices (p_1^* and p_2^*) and outputs sold (Q_1^* and Q_2^*) on each market.

10.4. Wyatt Labs has patented an anti-AIDS drug called Noaidsvir. It produces this drug in two plants, one in the US and another in Canada. The exchange rate between the two countries is assumed to be fixed, so all prices are denominated in US dollars. Drugs produced in Canada cannot be imported into the US to begin with. Prices are unregulated in both countries.

(a) The US demand for Noaidsvir is $p_u = 200 - 0.2Q_u$, where Q_u is the number of doses produced. The total cost of producing the drug in the US plant is given by $c_u(Q_u) = 0.2(Q_u)^2$. What is the profit-maximizing number of doses, Q_u^*, and price, p_u^*, charged in the US?

(b) The Canadian demand for Noaidsvir is $p_c = 120 - 0.2Q_c$. The total cost of producing the drug in the Canadian plant is the same as in the US and is given by $c_c(Q_c) = 0.2(Q_c)^2$. What is the profit-maximizing number of doses, Q_c^*, and price, p_c^*, charged in Canada?

(c) What is the marginal cost of the last dose produced in the US and the last dose produced in Canada? What are the total profits for Wyatt Labs from its US and Canadian operations?

(d) Suppose that Wyatt Labs is now allowed to import the drug from Canada, so it is now a multiplant monopolist with no restrictions on how much it can produce and sell in each country. Assume that there are no additional costs of imports. Note that Wyatt's joint total cost is given by $JTC = 0.1Q^2$, where $Q = Q_u + Q_c$. Calculate the following:

    i. the total number of doses Q_u^{**} and Q_c^{**} that Wyatt Labs should sell in the US and Canada;

    ii. the prices p_u^{**} and p_c^{**} that Wyatt Labs should charge in the US and Canada;

    iii. the total profits from sales in the US and Canada; and

    iv. the marginal cost of producing the last dose in the US and Canada.

(e) What conclusions can you draw from the above analysis? Explain!

10.5. The monopoly producer of a popular laundry detergent, Wave, knows that there are two types of potential buyers, people with children (high-use customers) or single people (low-use customers). There are 100 potential customers each of whom will buy either one box or none at all; of these, x are of the high-use type. It can sell a large box (60 washes) which costs $8 to produce or a small box (40 washes) which costs $6 to produce. High-use customers are willing to pay up to $12 for the large box and $7 for the small one. Low-use customers are willing to pay up to $9.20 for the large box and $6.60 for the small one. The detergent producer knows these valuations but is unable to distinguish between the two types of buyers. Assume that if a consumer obtains the same consumer surplus from buying either good, the consumer will choose the larger box. Draw a graph of Wave's profits under exclusive pure bundling (it sells the large box only), inclusive pure bundling (it sells the small box only), and mixed bundling (it targets the large box to high-use and the small box to low-use customers) and answer the following questions.

(a) For what range of x will Wave prefer to engage in exclusive pure bundling?

(b) For what range of x will Wave prefer to engage in inclusive pure bundling?

(c) For what range of x will Wave prefer to engage in mixed bundling?

10.6. Inkjet printers can be *high volume* (H) or *low volume* (L). There are three types of customers, businesses (type 1), families (type 2), or students (type 3). The number of each consumer type and the maximum price each consumer type is willing to pay is given in the table below; the last row shows the marginal cost of making each type of printer.

Customer type	#	High	Low
Type 1	20	$280	$200
Type 2	40	$220	$160
Type 3	40	$120	$80
MC		$80	$40

(a) *Option H123*: Suppose you wish to sell the high-volume printer only to all customers. Find the price p_H you should charge and calculate your profit, π_{H123}.

(b) *Option H12*: Suppose you wish to sell the high-volume printer to type 1 and type 2 consumers only; type 3 consumers are priced out of the market. Find the price p_H you should charge and calculate your profit, π_{H12}.

(c) *Option H1*: Suppose you wish to sell the high-volume printer to type 1 consumers only; type 2 and type 3 consumers are priced out of the market. Find the price p_H you should charge and calculate your profit, π_{H1}.

(d) *Option H1L2*: Suppose you wish to sell the high-volume printer to type 1 consumers and the low-volume to type 2; type 3 consumers are priced out of the market. Find the incentive-compatible prices, p_H and p_L, and calculate your profit π_{H1L2}.

(e) *Option H1L23*: Suppose you wish to sell the high-volume printer to type 1 consumers and the low-volume to type 2 and type 3 consumers. Find the incentive-compatible prices, p_H and p_L, and calculate your profit π_{H1L23}.

(f) *Option H12L3*: Suppose you wish to sell the high-volume printer to type 1 and type 2 consumers and the low-volume printer to type 3 consumers. Find the incentive-compatible prices, p_H and p_L, and calculate your profit π_{H12L3}.

(g) Are there other targeting options worth considering? If so, what are the associated prices and profit levels from these options? Of all the possible options, including the ones in (a)–(f), which maximize profits?

Chapter 11

Risk

Suppose you own a house worth $400,000$ which has a 1 percent chance of being damaged in a fire, bringing down the value of the house to $300,000$. How much might you be willing to pay to insure against this $100,000$ loss? These kinds of decisions involve risk, a situation where the uncertainty can be captured by objective probabilities, i.e., probabilities for which there is some statistical, experimental, or analytical basis that different people can agree upon.[1] We also want to know how decisions and outcomes differ when different people have different attitudes towards risk.

The most basic decision theory under risk is the expected utility hypothesis developed by John von Neumann and Oskar Morgenstern. In recent years, some alternative theories have been advocated, but we will restrict our attention to the expected utility hypothesis which remains in wide use due to its relative simplicity and analytical tractability. Moreover, the use of the expected utility hypothesis is widespread in game theory, as we will see in Chapter 12.

11.1 Expected Utility

For decision-making under certainty, the commodity space consists of commodity bundles over which a consumer is assumed to have preferences, as seen in Chapter 3. For decision-making under risk, however, the commodity space has to be redefined. We consider the simplest possible set-up that allows us to introduce the main ideas of the expected utility hypothesis.

---

[1]See section A.7.3 in the Mathematical appendix for a review of probability.

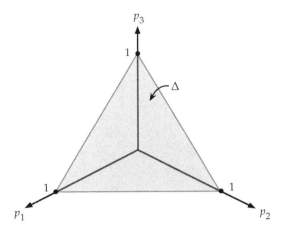

Figure 11.1   Commodity space of lotteries

11.1.1   Commodity space

Assume that a nature-loving consumer can win one of three **prizes** denoted by $X = \{x_1, x_2, x_3\}$. For instance, x_1 may be a camping trip to the Okefenokee swamp in Georgia, x_2 a hiking trip in the Olympic National Park in Washington, and x_3 a safari trip to the Kruger National Park in South Africa.

A **lottery**, written as $p = (p_1, p_2, p_3)$, assigns a probability p_j of winning prize x_j, where the probabilities have to sum to one, i.e., $p_1 + p_2 + p_3 = 1$. Then, a lottery $p = (0.3, 0.5, 0.2)$ gives her a 30 percent chance to win the first prize, a 50 percent chance of winning the second and a 20 percent chance of winning the third; similarly, a lottery $q = (0.2, 0.4, 0.4)$ gives different probabilities of winning the prizes, etc.

The consumer's decision problem under risk is to choose between different lotteries. In other words, her commodity space is the set of all possible lotteries which we denote by Δ consisting of any triplet of fractions (p_1, p_2, p_3) so long as $p_1 + p_2 + p_3 = 1$. Figure 11.1 shows Δ as a two-dimensional plane in three dimensions.[2]

The **Marschak triangle**, named after Jacob Marschak,[3] is a clever way to represent the commodity space Δ in two dimensions and is shown by

---

[2]Mathematicians call this set a **unit simplex**. You may think of it as a special case of the budget with three commodities we encountered in section 2.2.1 but where the prices are between zero and one and the income equals one.

[3]It is also called the Marschak-Machina triangle after the American economist Mark Machina who popularized it.

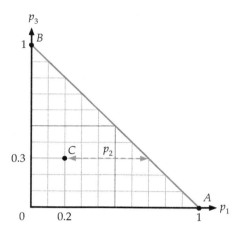

Figure 11.2   The Marschak triangle

the triangle $0AB$ in Figure 11.2. The horizontal axis shows the probability p_1 associated with the worst prize (x_1), while the vertical axis shows the probability p_3 associated with the best prize (x_3). Since the probabilities p_1, p_2, and p_3 add up to one, the point A in the Marschak triangle represents the lottery $(1, 0, 0)$. Similarly, point B shows the lottery $(0, 0, 1)$, while the origin is the lottery $(0, 1, 0)$. The coordinates of a point such as C inside the triangle show the probabilities 0.2 and 0.3 of winning prizes x_1 and x_3; the probability of winning prize x_2 is $1 - 0.2 - 0.3 = 0.5$ and can be inferred from the horizontal length from C to the hypotenuse as shown by the dashed magenta arrow.

11.1.2   Preferences

Under the expected utility hypothesis, we assume that a consumer's preferences over lotteries, $\succsim$, satisfy certain assumptions (called 'axioms'). These are:

vNM1 Reflexivity: for any lottery p in Δ, $p \succsim p$.

vNM2 Totality: for any two lotteries p and q in Δ, either $p \succsim q$, or $q \succsim p$, or both.

vNM3 Transitivity: for any three lotteries p, q and r in Δ, if $p \succsim q$ and $q \succsim r$, then $p \succsim r$.

vNM4 Independence: for any three lotteries p, q and r in Δ, if $p \succsim q$, then for any t in the range $0 < t \leq 1$, $tp + (1 - t)r \succsim tq + (1 - t)r$.

vNM5 Continuity: for any three lotteries p, q and r in Δ, if $p \succsim q$ and $q \succsim r$, then there is some t in the range $0 \leq t \leq 1$ for which $q \sim tp + (1 - t)r$.

The first three axioms should be familiar from Chapter 3 as the requirement for regular preferences. The idea of continuity too is fairly intuitive: if $p \succsim q \succsim r$ so that p is the best of the three and r the worst, then there is some average of the best and worst lotteries that is indifferent to the one in the middle.

The idea of independence (which has been somewhat controversial) is that if p is weakly-better-than q to begin with, then taking any weighted average (or **mixture**) of p with r should remain weakly-better-than the corresponding weighted average of q with r. In other words, the ranking between p and q is independent of any third lottery r when this lottery is averaged with p and q in the same manner.

For example, suppose the lottery $p = (0.2, 0.5, 0.3)$ is at least as good as $q = (0.5, 0.3, 0.2)$, and $r = (0.4, 0.4, 0.2)$. Let $t = \frac{1}{2}$. Then independence requires that the mixture

$$\frac{1}{2}p + \frac{1}{2}r = \frac{1}{2}(0.2, 0.5, 0.3) + \frac{1}{2}(0.4, 0.4, 0.2) = (0.3, 0.45, 0.25)$$

be at least as good as the mixture

$$\frac{1}{2}q + \frac{1}{2}r = \frac{1}{2}(0.5, 0.3., 0.2) + \frac{1}{2}(0.4, 0.4, 0.2) = (0.45, 0.35, 0.2).$$

The **expected utility theorem** of von Neumann and Morgenstern shows that if a consumer's preferences over lotteries satisfy these axioms, then

(a) there is a **von Neumann-Morgenstern (vNM) utility function** $u(x)$ over the set of prizes, X, and

(b) that the consumer's preferences over lotteries can be represented by an **expected utility (EU) function** V, where her utility from lottery p is given by

$$V(p) = p_1 u(x_1) + p_2 u(x_2) + p_3 u(x_3). \tag{11.1}$$

Two remarks about the expected utility theorem are in order. First, this theorem holds for any positive monotonic transformation v of the vNM utility u, so long as $v = au + b$ where $a > 0$. In other words, the preferences over lotteries are unchanged if we replace each of the utilities from the prizes in (11.1) by the transformation $v(x_i) = au(x_i) + b$. However, because a vNM utility cannot be subject to *any* positive monotonic transformation, it is not an ordinal utility function like the utility functions from Chapter 3. Second, because the $u(x_i)$ terms are multiplicative constants, the EU function is linear in the probabilities. As we will see below, this implies that the consumer's preferences over lotteries generate linear indifference curves.

Given that a consumer's preferences over lotteries can be represented by the EU function $V(p)$, we can figure out the shape of her EU indifference curves in the Marschak triangle. Since $p_1 + p_2 + p_3 = 1$, first replace p_2 in (11.1) with $1 - p_1 - p_3$ to obtain

$$
\begin{aligned}
V(p) &= p_1 u(x_1) + (1 - p_1 - p_3)u(x_2) + p_3 u(x_3) \\
&= -p_1[u(x_2) - u(x_1)] + u(x_2) + p_3[u(x_3) - u(x_2)].
\end{aligned} \tag{11.2}
$$

To draw an indifference curve, fix the utility level $V(p)$ at $\bar{V}$. Then (11.2) can be rearranged to obtain

$$
p_3 = \frac{\bar{V} - u(x_2)}{u(x_3) - u(x_2)} + \frac{u(x_2) - u(x_1)}{u(x_3) - u(x_2)}p_1, \tag{11.3}
$$

which is the equation of the indifference curve that yields expected utility $\bar{V}$ in the (p_1, p_3) space of the Marschak triangle. This EU indifference curve is

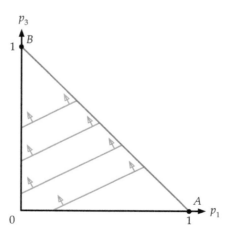

Figure 11.3   EU indifference curves

linear with vertical intercept $[\bar{V} - u(x_2)]/[u(x_3) - u(x_2)]$ and positive slope $[u(x_2) - u(x_1)]/[u(x_3) - u(x_2)]$. Note that the slope of any indifference curve is a constant that depends only the vNM utilities, not on the probabilities of the prizes. The intercept too is independent of the probabilities and increases with the value of $\bar{V}$. Therefore, for larger values of $\bar{V}$, the consumer's EU indifference curves (which are all linear with the same slope) are increasing to the northwest as shown in Figure 11.3 by the direction of the arrows.

11.2 Attitudes towards Risk

From now on, in situations of risk, we shall assume that any consumer is a von Neumann-Morgenstern expected utility maximizer. In this section, assume that the set X consists of monetary prizes with $x_1 = \$6400$, $x_2 = \$9100$ and $x_3 = \$10,000$. Our consumer begins with a wealth of $x_3 = \$10,000$ but there is a 25 percent chance of a fire which would reduce her wealth by $\$3600$ to $x_1 = \$6400$. We can write this lottery as $p = (0.25, 0, 0.75)$: she will either have $\$6400$ with probability 0.25 or she will be left with $\$10,000$ with probability 0.75. Then the expected value of her wealth under the lottery p is $0.75 \times 10,000 + 0 \times 9100 + 0.25 \times 6400 = \$9100$.

Now consider a second lottery $q = (0, 1, 0)$ which yields $\$9,100$ for sure, the same as the expected value of her wealth under lottery p. When two lotteries yield the same expected value of wealth, we say that they are actu-arially fair, so p and q are actuarially fair.

Now we define what it means for a consumer to be risk-averse: a con-sumer is risk-averse if, given a choice between a lottery p or receiving the expected value of p for sure, she prefers the latter. In other words, a risk-averse consumer prefers a sure thing to an actuarially fair lottery. In this instance, a risk-averse consumer would prefer receiving $\$9,100$ for sure over an actuarially fair lottery such as p, so $V(q) > V(p)$.

If a consumer is risk-averse, then her vNM utility function must be con-cave, and vice versa, i.e., risk aversion is embodied in the concavity of the vNM utility. To understand why, note that for our risk-averse consumer, $V(q) > V(p)$ can be explicitly written as

$$u(x_2) > 0.25u(x_1) + 0.75u(x_3) \equiv \bar{u}, \qquad (11.4)$$

where $\bar{u}$ is the weighted average of the utilities $u(x_1)$ and $u(x_3)$.

In the left panel of Figure 11.4, the three prizes are shown along the hori-zontal axis. The left hand side of (11.4) is shown by the point A correspond-

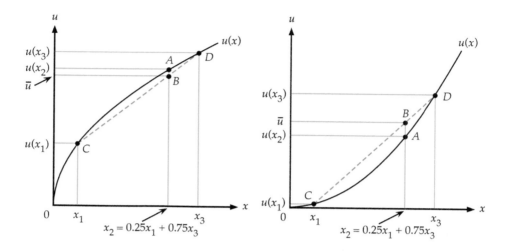

Figure 11.4 Risk-averse and risk-loving vNM utility

ing to the utility from prize x_2; the right hand side of (11.4) is shown by the point B which is the weighted average of $u(x_1)$ and $u(x_2)$. Note that since B assigns a weight of 0.25 to $u(x_1)$ and 0.75 to $u(x_3)$, it lies three-quarter of the length along the chord CD. For $V(q)$ to be greater than $V(p)$, the point A must lie above B which happens only if the vNM utility function is concave.

In the right panel of Figure 11.4, a convex vNM utility function is shown with the same lotteries. Here point A lies below B, i.e., a consumer with such a vNM utility function prefers the risky lottery p to receiving the expected value of that lottery for sure. Such a consumer is called **risk-loving**.

A **risk-neutral** consumer is one whose vNM utility function is linear, of the form $u(x) = ax$ for some $a > 0$. Such a consumer is indifferent between a risky lottery and the expected value of that lottery for certain.

11.3 Stochastic Dominance°

In certain cases, we can compare lotteries and say that a particular lottery is "better" than another. For example, if $q = (1,0,0)$ and $p = (0,0,1)$, we can certainly say that p is better since it yields the best prize (x_3) for sure instead of the worst one (x_1). If one lottery is better than another in some sense, we say that the first **stochastically dominates** the other. There are two important types of stochastic dominance, **first order** and **second order**.

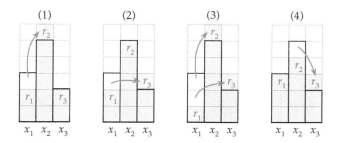

Figure 11.5   First order stochastically dominant lotteries

11.3.1   First order stochastic dominance

Here the set of prizes may be monetary or non-monetary with the usual pro-
viso that the vNM utility ranks x_3 above x_2, and x_2 above x_1. We say that a
lottery r **first order stochastically dominates** (FOSD) q if one of the following
conditions hold:

(i) $r_1 < q_1$ and $r_1 + r_2 = q_1 + q_2$, (i.e., $r_2 > q_2$);

(ii) $r_1 < q_1$ and $r_1 + r_2 < q_1 + q_2$, (i.e., $r_3 > q_3$); or

(iii) $r_1 = q_1$ and $r_1 + r_2 < q_1 + q_2$, (i.e., $r_3 > q_3$).

Each of these cases is illustrated with a specific example in Figure 11.5 as
a probability histogram. In each panel, the bordered black rectangles show
the histogram for the lottery $q = (0.3, 0.5, 0.2)$. The shaded blue histogram
shows the lottery $r = (r_1, r_2, r_3)$. In going from q to r in panel (1), the probability mass shifts from prize x_1 to x_2 as shown by the magenta arrow, corresponding to condition (i). Panels (2) and (3) both correspond to condition
(ii): in (2), the probability mass shifts from from x_1 to x_3, while in (3), it shifts
from x_1 to both x_2 and x_3. Finally, panel (4) corresponds to condition (iii),
where the probability mass shifts from x_2 to x_3.

Therefore, the notion of first order stochastic dominance captures the
idea that lottery r is better than lottery q because the probability mass shifts
from the lower-ranking prize(s) towards the better prize(s), lowering the
chances of getting a worse prize and increasing the chances of getting a
higher-valued prize.

In the Marschak triangle, it is easy to verify when the conditions (i)–(iii)
that ensure first order stochastic dominance hold. In Figure 11.6, any lottery
in the blue shaded area northwest of the lottery $q = (0.3, 0.5, 0.2)$ satisfies one

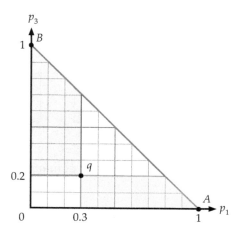

Figure 11.6   First order stochastic dominance in the Marschak triangle

of the three conditions, so any lottery r in the blue area first order stochastically dominates q. (As an exercise, plot the four r lotteries from Figure 11.5 as points in the Marschak triangle in Figure 11.6.) Similarly q first order stochastically dominates any lottery in the pink area.

We saw in section 11.1.2 that any consumer who behaves according to the EU hypothesis has expected utility indifference curves that are always positively sloping and increasing to the northwest as shown in Figure 11.3. Therefore if lottery r FOSD q, then it must be true that $V(r) > V(q)$ *always*, regardless of whether the consumer is risk-averse, risk-loving or risk-neutral.

11.3.2   Second order stochastic dominance

Here the set of prizes *must* be monetary with $x_3 > x_2 > x_1$, so the vNM utility naturally ranks x_3 above x_2, and x_2 above x_1 as usual. Monetary prizes mean that we can now calculate the expected value of a lottery.

A lottery q is a **mean-preserving spread** of r if both lotteries have the same expected value but $q_1 > r_1$ and $q_3 > r_3$, i.e., the probabilities of the tail prizes x_1 and x_3 under lottery q are larger at the expense of the middle prize x_2. Thus q and r have the same mean but q has a higher variance. We say that a lottery r **second order stochastically dominates** (SOSD) q if q is a mean-preserving spread of r. Second order stochastic dominance captures the idea that lottery q has the same expected value but is a "riskier" lottery than lottery r.

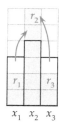

Figure 11.7   Second order stochastically dominant lottery

In Figure 11.7, the idea of a mean-preserving spread and second order stochastic dominance is shown with a probability histogram over the three prizes, $x_1 = \$0, x_2 = \$50$, and $x_3 = \$100$. The black rectangles show the histogram for the lottery $q = (0.3, 0.4, 0.3)$ which has expected value $50. The shaded blue histogram shows the lottery $r = (0.2, 0.6, 0.2)$ which has the same expected value of $50. In going from q to r, probability mass is shifted from the two extreme prizes towards x_2, as shown with the magenta arrows, so that the mean remains unchanged. Then q is a mean-preserving spread of r, and r SOSD q.

The idea of second order stochastic dominance can also be shown in a Marschak triangle for any lottery q. Denote the expected value of the lottery q by $\bar{x}$, i.e.,

$$\bar{x} = q_1 x_1 + q_2 x_2 + q_3 x_3.$$

Substituting q_2 with $1 - q_1 - q_3$ and simplifying, we obtain

$$q_3 = \frac{\bar{x}}{x_3 - x_2} + \frac{x_2 - x_1}{x_3 - x_2} q_1. \tag{11.5}$$

This is the equation for the **iso-expected value line** which shows all combinations of q_1 and q_3 that yield the same expected value of $\bar{x}$. In Figure 11.8, the iso-expected value lines are shown as blue lines. All lotteries that lie on one of these iso-expected value lines yield the same expected value, i.e., they are actuarially fair. Note that these lines have the same slope of $(x_2 - x_1)/(x_3 - x_1)$, and higher iso-expected value lines lie to the northwest, as shown by the direction of the blue arrows.

Now consider lotteries r and q that lie along one iso-expected value line as shown in the right part of Figure 11.8. In moving northeast from lottery r to q, $q_1 > r_1$ and $q_3 > r_3$, so q is a mean-preserving spread of r. Since they have the same expected value, r SOSD q. Thus, given any two lotteries on the

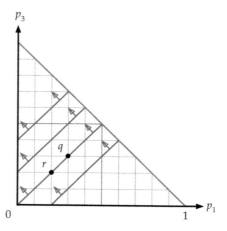

Figure 11.8   Second order stochastic dominance in the Marschak triangle

same iso-expected value line, the one towards the southwest always second order stochastically dominates the other.

In the case of a consumer with vNM EU preferences, we know that risk aversion requires that the vNM utility function $u(x)$ be strictly concave. In the case of three prizes, strict concavity requires that

$$\frac{u(x_2) - u(x_1)}{x_2 - x_1} > \frac{u(x_3) - u(x_2)}{x_3 - x_2}. \tag{11.6}$$

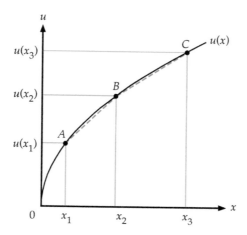

Figure 11.9   Strictly concave vNM utility

In Figure 11.9, strict concavity of the vNM utility function necessitates that the slope of chord AB be more than that of BC. Precisely this idea is expressed in (11.6) whose left hand side is the slope of chord AB, and right hand side is the slope of BC. Rearranging (11.6), we obtain

$$\frac{u(x_2) - u(x_1)}{u(x_3) - u(x_2)} > \frac{x_2 - x_1}{x_3 - x_2}. \tag{11.7}$$

In (11.7), note that the left hand side is the slope of the consumer's EU indifference curves from (11.3), while the right hand side is the slope of the consumer's iso-expected value lines from (11.5). Therefore, (11.7) establishes that when r SOSD q, a risk-averse consumer prefers lottery r over q if, and only if, her EU indifference curves are steeper than the iso-expected value lines.

This is shown in Figure 11.10. The two lotteries q and r lie on the same blue iso-expected value line, and since r lies to the southwest, r SOSD q. When the vNM utility is strictly concave, the orange EU indifference curves are steeper than the iso-expected value line and $V(r) > V(q)$. It can be analogously shown that a risk-loving consumer will have EU indifference curves that are flatter than the iso-expected value lines, so for such a consumer $V(q) > V(r)$, i.e., the riskier alternative is preferred over the less risky one.

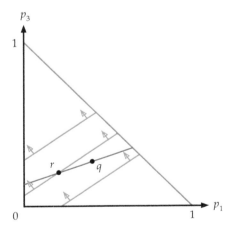

Figure 11.10   Risk-averse EU and second order stochastic dominance

11.4   Pareto Efficient Risk Sharing

To see how two individuals, *a* and *b*, may share risk, consider the simplest possible situation which is known as a **state-contingent claims** environment. There is a single good, *x*, but two states of the world: a 'high' state (H) which occurs with probability *p*, and a 'low' state (L) which occurs with probability $1 - p$. Thus any state-contingent claims bundle, (x_H, x_L) is understood to be a lottery over prizes x_H and x_L with probabilities *p* and $1 - p$.

In Figure 11.11, the horizontal axis shows the amount of good *x* in state H, while the vertical axis shows the amount in state L. (Note that the scales of measurement along the axes are different: each unit along the horizontal axis represents twice as much as along the vertical axis.) The diagonal line C^a is the **line of certainty** along which $x_H^a = x_L^a$, i.e., the consumer receives the same amount in either state. Consumer *a*'s endowment in the two states is given by $\omega^a = (676, 196)$ which lies below the diagonal line C^a, meaning that she is better off in the high state as opposed to the low state.

Assume that *a* is risk-averse and has the vNM utility function $u^a(x^a) = \sqrt{x^a}$. Then *a*'s expected utility from the bundle (x_H^a, x_L^a) is

$$V^a(x_H^a, x_L^a) = p\sqrt{x_H^a} + (1 - p)\sqrt{x_L^a}.$$

In particular, the expected utility from the endowment $\omega^a = (676, 196)$ is

$$p\sqrt{676} + (1 - p)\sqrt{196} = p(26) + (1 - p)(14) = 12p + 14.$$

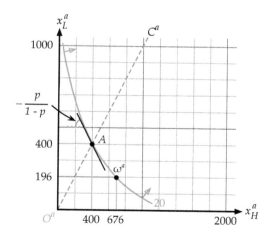

Figure 11.11   State-contingent claims

For example, if each state of the world is equally likely, then $p = 1/2$ and a's expected utility level from ω^a is 20. All the consumption bundles (x_H^a, x_L^a) that yield the expected utility of 20 are represented in Figure 11.11 by the orange EU indifference curve which shows that a's preferences over the bundles is convex. The MRS between the two states is given by

$$MRS^a = \frac{p}{1-p} \cdot \frac{MU_H^a}{MU_L^a} = \frac{p}{1-p} \cdot \frac{\sqrt{x_L^a}}{\sqrt{x_H^a}}. \tag{11.8}$$

Along the certainty line C^a, $x_L^a = x_H^a$ so the MRS equals $p/(1-p)$, i.e., the MRS always equals $p/(1-p)$ along the certainty line, no matter what the utility function. The point $A = (400, 400)$ in Figure 11.11 is the certainty equivalent of the lottery ω^a: it gives the same expected utility as ω^a except that it is risk-free because it lies on the certainty line.

Suppose there is another consumer, person b, with an endowment $\omega^b = (1324, 604)$, so the aggregate endowment is $\omega^a + \omega^b = (2000, 800)$. We now look at the possibility of risk sharing between consumers a and b under two different cases: (i) when a is risk-averse but b is risk-neutral, and (ii) when both are risk-averse.

11.4.1   A risk-averse and a risk-neutral consumer

The Edgeworth box for this state-contingent claims economy is shown in Figure 11.12. Since the initial endowment ω lies below each consumer's line of certainty, both are better off in the high state than in the low state. Consumer a is assumed to be risk-averse as before with the vNM utility of $u^a(x^a) = \sqrt{x^a}$. Suppose that consumer b is risk-neutral with a vNM utility $u^b(x^b) = x^b$. Then b's expected utility is

$$V^b(x_H^b, x_L^b) = px_H^b + (1-p)x_L^b$$

which is linear with $MRS^b = p/(1-p)$ as shown by the green EU indifference curve.

Then the interior contract curve is found by setting MRS^a given by equation (11.8) to $MRS^b = p/(1-p)$. Solving, we obtain $x_L^a = x_H^a$, i.e., the contract curve coincides with the line of certainty, C^a. Therefore, at any (interior) Pareto efficient allocation, consumer a is fully insured against the state-contingent risk.

One such allocation is at A where consumer a is as well off as at ω but consumer b is better off. In this case, the two consumers agree that in the

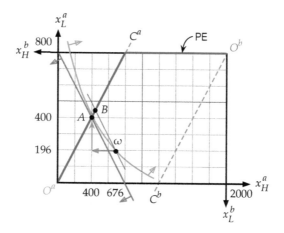

Figure 11.12   Full insurance for consumer *a*

high state, *a* promises to pay 276 units of *x* to *b* (shown by the left magenta arrow from ω), while in the low state, *b* promises to pay 204 units to *a* (shown by the up magenta arrow). Therefore, consumer *a* receives 400 units in either state and so is now fully insured against the risk. Consumer *b* who is risk-neutral ends up bearing all the risk (since she is off her line of certainty) and is strictly better off at *A* than at ω.

Another possible allocation is at *B* where consumer *b* is as well off as at ω, but *a* is better off. In principle, the consumers could agree to any insurance contract so long as they reach an individually rational and Pareto efficient allocation, i.e., any point between *A* and *B* along consumer *a*'s line of certainty.

In summary, we conclude that when one individual is risk-averse and another risk-neutral, the risk-neutral consumer bears all the risk under Pareto efficient risk-sharing and the risk-averse consumer is fully insured. It is often assumed in the literature that those who seek insurance are risk-averse and that the providers of insurance are typically risk-neutral.

11.4.2   Two risk-averse consumers

Consider the same state-contingent claims economy as in the previous section, except that *b*'s vNM utility is $u^b(x^b) = \sqrt{x^b}$, so both consumers are risk-averse. Then the set of Pareto efficient allocations (the contract curve) is shown in Figure 11.13 as the diagonal from O^a to O^b along which the

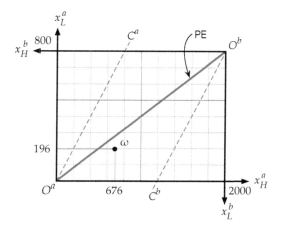

Figure 11.13   Partial insurance

marginal rates of substitution for *a* and *b* are equal. Given that ω is off this diagonal, there is a small segment of the contract curve which is both individually rational and Pareto efficient; one can expect that bilateral nego-tiations would lead to both consumer agreeing to an allocation in this range where *a* agrees to transfer some good *x* to *b* in the high state in exchange for some transfer from *b* to *a* in the low state. But because both consumers *a* and *b* are off their lines of certainty anywhere along the interior diagonal, Pareto efficient risk-sharing implies that each consumer is only partially insured.

Exercises

11.1. In a set of prizes, $X = \{x_1, x_2, x_3\}$, let x_1 be the worst prize and x_3 the best. A consumer has a vNM utility function *u* over *X* where

$$u(x_1) = u_1, \ u(x_2) = u_2 \text{ and } u(x_3) = u_3.$$

The expected utility theorem allows the transformation of *u* into the utility $v = au + b$ where $a > 0$ and *b* is of arbitrary sign. This means that it is always possible to normalize the vNM utility so that the utility from the worst prize is zero and the best prize is one, i.e., $v(x_1) = au_1 + b = 0$ and $v(x_3) = au_3 + b = 1$.

(a) Find the values of *a* and *b* as functions of u_1 and u_3.

(b) Suppose $u_1 = 10, u_2 = 20$, and $u_3 = 50$. Find the values of a and b in the utility transformation $v = au + b$ so that $v(x_1) = 0$ and $v(x_3) = 1$. What is the value of $v(x_2)$?

11.2. Let $X = \{0, 100, 400, 10000\}$ be a set of four monetary prizes. Stowell claims he is a vNM expected utility maximizer and is observed to choose the lottery $(\frac{1}{4}, \frac{1}{4}, \frac{1}{3}, \frac{1}{6})$ over $(0, \frac{1}{4}, \frac{11}{24}, \frac{7}{24})$. Is he truly a vNM EU maximizer as he claims? Explain!

(*Hint*: Normalize the vNM utility function by setting $u(x_1) = 0$ and $u(x_4) = 1$.)

11.3. Consider a set of monetary prizes $X = \{0, 12, 24\}$ and three lotteries:

$$p = \left(\frac{5}{12}, \frac{1}{4}, \frac{1}{3}\right), q = \left(\frac{1}{6}, \frac{3}{4}, \frac{1}{12}\right), \text{ and } r = \left(\frac{1}{3}, \frac{5}{12}, \frac{1}{4}\right).$$

(a) Calculate the expected value of the lotteries p, q, and r. Can you rank them in terms of stochastic dominance? Explain!

(b) Calculate the slope of the iso-expected value lines in the Marschak triangle.

(c) Suppose Lajos has a vNM utility $u(0) = 0$, $u(12) = 0.6$, and $u(24) = 1$. What is the slope of his EU indifference curves in the Marschak triangle?

(d) What can you conclude regarding Lajos' attitude to risk? Explain!

11.4. Jimmie chooses between lotteries defined on a set of monetary prizes $X = \{0, 300, 500\}$. He is a vNM EU maximizer. Answer the following questions.

(a) In a Marschak triangle, plot the following lotteries:

$$a = (0.2, 0.5, 0.3), \ b = (0.7, 0, 0.3), \text{ and } c = (0, 0.5, 0.5).$$

Draw Jimmie's iso-expected value lines that pass through these lotteries.

(b) Assuming that Jimmie's vNM utility is $u(0) = 0$, $u(300) = 10$, and $u(500) = 30$, draw his EU indifference curves that pass through lotteries a, b and c.

(c) Is Jimmie risk-averse, risk-neutral or risk-loving? Explain!

11.5. A consumer's vNM utility over good x is $u(x) = \sqrt{x}$. There are two possible states, high (H) and low (L) that occur with probability 0.4 and 0.6 respectively.

(a) What is this consumer's expected utility of the bundle $(x_H, x_L) = (10000, 100)$?

(b) Calculate the certainty equivalent of $(x_H, x_L) = (10000, 100)$.

11.6. Félix can pursue a life of crime. His probability, p, of getting caught is 0.4. If he gets caught, his wealth in jail is $25; if he is not caught, he enjoys a wealth of $100.

(a) What is Félix's expected wealth?

(b) Suppose Félix's vNM utility of wealth is given by $\sqrt{w}$. What is his expected utility?

(c) What is the level of wealth which would make Félix indifferent between living honestly or choosing a life of crime?

(d) Suppose the judicial system wants to deter crime by increasing the penalties for a life of crime, so Félix's wealth in jail is now $16. To what extent can society reduce law enforcement, i.e., the probability of being caught, p, so that Félix's expected utility is the same as in (b)?

11.7. Consumer a has property worth $1,000,000. With probability 0.1, he will face fire damage which reduces his property's value to $640,000 (a loss of $360,000); with probability 0.9, his wealth remains at its current value of $1,000,000. Consumer a's vNM utility for wealth is given by $u^a(w) = \sqrt{w}$.

Consumer b who runs an insurance company is willing to insure a: she will pay a dollar amount q (called the **coverage**) in the event of fire damage in exchange for a payment r (called the **premium**). If a buys insurance from b, with probability 0.1, a has wealth $640,000 + q - r$, while with probability 0.9, he has wealth $1,000,000 = r$. Conversely, with probability 0.1, consumer b has income $r - q$, while with probability 0.9, she has income r. Consumer b's vNM utility over her income y is $u^b(y) = y$.

(a) What is the expected utility of a when he does not purchase insurance from b? What is the certainty equivalent for this level of expected utility?

(b) Will b provide full coverage (i.e. $q = \$360,000$) in case of fire damage? Explain why or why not.

(c) Suppose b provides full coverage $q = \$360,000$ in case of fire damage. If a buys the insurance, he will then have a sure wealth of $1,000,000 - r$ regardless of whether there is any fire damage or not. Consumer a wants to be at least as well off as when he does not buy insurance. Calculate the maximum premium r^* he will pay.

Chapter 12

Game Theory

Game theory provides tools to model strategic interaction among economic agents. Strategic interaction refers to situations where outcomes depend on the choices of *all* agents. For instance, if Delta Airlines decides to cut its fares from Atlanta to New York with the hope of attracting customers and raising some quick cash, how much money it can raise depends on whether other airlines flying on the same route match Delta's new price or not, because their pricing decisions will influence the number of passengers who choose Delta.

Game theory was pioneered by John von Neumann and Oskar Morgenstern in their 1944 book, *The Theory of Games and Economic Behavior*, the same duo who developed the expected utility hypothesis. John Nash developed the fundamental notion of equilibrium in simultaneous-move games, the Nash equilibrium, in the early 1950s. In the 1960s, John Harsanyi extended game theory to include uncertainty, developing the idea of a Bayesian Nash equilibrium, while Reinhardt Selten expanded the range of game theory by considering sequential games with its corresponding notion of subgame perfect Nash equilibrium. All three were awarded the 1994 Nobel Prize in Economics.[1]

Game theory has become a vast field in its own right. The aim of this chapter is very modest: to present, without formal definitions, just enough game theory in order to model how firms behave under oligopoly (the subject matter of Chapter 13). In particular, only games of complete information (where the structure of the game is commonly known) are covered.

---

[1]Subsequently, in 2005, Robert Aumann and Thomas Schelling also shared the Nobel Prize for their contributions to game theory.

12.1   Static Games

A game consists of three basic elements: the **players**, their **strategies**, and the **payoffs** each player receives as a result of their combined choice of strategies. In a static game, all players decide on their strategies simultaneously without being able to see what others are doing.

To illustrate a static game of complete information, suppose Anna and Bob are given a penny each to play with. They place their pennies on a table simultaneously, choosing whether it faces heads or tails. If the pennies match (i.e., both choose heads or both choose tails), Anna gets both pennies; if they do not match, Bob gets both pennies. Here the players are Anna and Bob and their strategy choices are either heads or tails. The three basic elements — players, strategies, and payoffs — are depicted in Figure 12.1. Such a depiction is called **a normal-form game**.

		Bob	
		Heads	Tails
Anna	Heads	2, 0	0, 2
	Tails	0, 2	2, 0

Figure 12.1   Matching pennies game

Anna (in orange) is the **row player**, choosing either the top row (heads) or the bottom row (tails), while Bob (in green) is the **column player** who chooses either the left column (heads) or the right column (tails). The colored numbers in each cell of the matrix show the payoffs to the players, the first number (in orange) being the payoff of the row player and the second (in green) being that of the column player. For example, in the top left cell when both play heads, Anna gets both pennies (a payoff of 2) while Bob gets nothing (a payoff of 0). Payoffs may be expressed in monetary units or in terms of utility levels.

Two-player games where each has two or more strategies can be easily represented with an appropriate payoff matrix where the number of rows and columns correspond to the number of strategies available to the respective players. To see how a three-player game can be depicted, consider the following example. Three neighboring hotels on an interstate highway, Relax Inn (R), Sleep Motel (S), and Take-Five Lodge (T), cater to business customers. If all offer basic broadband internet access (b), each hotel's market

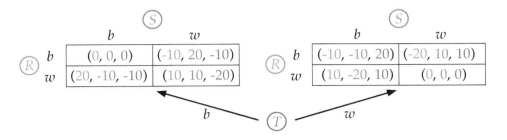

Figure 12.2 Internet service game

share remains unchanged. If only one offers high-speed Wi-Fi internet access (*w*), it gains a 20 percent market share of the business travelers who frequent that area, while the market share of the other two decreases by 10 percent each. If two hotels offer Wi-Fi service, each gains a 10 percent market share at the expense of the remaining hotel whose market share shrinks by 20 percent. If all three switch to Wi-Fi, their market share remains unchanged. This game is depicted in Figure 12.2 with the change in market shares as payoffs.

Here *R* is the orange row player, *S* the green column player, and *T* the blue **matrix player**, choosing the matrix on the left when its internet connection is basic, and the one on the right when it is wireless. The colored payoffs are triples, with the orange number being the payoff to *R*, the green being that of *S*, and the blue being that of *T*.

When *R* plays *b*, for example, its possible payoffs are found by reading across the first row of both matrices: $0, -10, -10,$ and -20, depending on the strategies of the other two. When *S* plays *b*, its possible payoffs can be found in the first column of each matrix, while *T*'s possible payoffs when it plays *b* are found in the four cells of the first matrix.

Finally, note that the payoffs in each cell happen to add up to zero. Such a game is called a **zero-sum game** where one player's gain is always counterbalanced by the loss of some other player or players.[2]

12.2 Solving Static Games

The predictive value of using game theory to model strategic interaction is that it can tell us something about how a game might be played. In this

---

[2]A game where the payoffs in each cell add up to a constant is called a **constant-sum game**; zero-sum games are a special case of a constant-sum game.

section, we introduce two basic solution concepts for solving games, a **dominant strategy equilibrium** which can be applied to certain special games, and a **Nash equilibrium** which can be used more widely.

12.2.1   Dominant strategy equilibrium

A player has a **dominant strategy** if there is one strategy that is the best in terms of this player's payoffs, regardless of what others are doing. To see this, consider a babysitting game where Mahala and Aruna are teenagers who babysit children in their neighborhood, charging either $10 or $15 per hour. The payoffs (in dollars) are given in Figure 12.3.

		Aruna	
		$10	$15
Mahala	$10	50, 50	80, 30
	$15	30, 80	45, 45

Figure 12.3   Babysitting game

If Aruna charges $10, Mahala looks at her payoffs in the first column and concludes that she should also charge $10, receiving the higher payoff of $50 instead of the $30 she would receive if she charged $15. Similarly, if Aruna charges $15, Mahala looks at her payoffs in the second column and concludes that she should charge $10, receiving the higher payoff of $80 instead of the $45 she would receive by charging $15. In other words, *regardless* of what Aruna charges, charging $10 is always the best for Mahala, i.e., it is a dominant strategy. On the other hand, because charging $15 is always worse for Mahala than charging $10, we call charging $15 a **dominated strategy**.

To determine whether a row player has a dominant strategy, pick a particular row and check *all* the payoffs for the row player with the corresponding row payoffs from other strategies. If one strategy dominates (i.e., the set of row payoffs for that strategy exceeds the corresponding payoffs on all other rows), then that is a dominant strategy. For example, in the babysitting game, Mahala's payoffs from charging $10 are 50 and 80, which are larger than the corresponding row payoffs from charging $15 of 30 and 45. So charging $10 is a dominant strategy for her and charging $15 is a dominated strategy.

Similarly, to determine whether a column player has a dominant strategy, pick one strategy column and check all the payoffs along that column with the corresponding payoffs on other columns. It is easy to verify that charging

$10 is also a dominant strategy for Aruna.[3] As an exercise to make sure that you understand this notion, go back to the matching pennies and the internet service games and determine whether any player has a dominant strategy in those games.

A dominant strategy equilibrium (DSE) comes about when players play their dominant strategies. This is an equilibrium of the game because each person has a strategy that is the best no matter what others are doing; no person has an incentive to switch to a different strategy. In the babysitting game in Figure 12.3, ($10, $10) is a DSE; in the internet service game in Figure 12.2, (w, w, w) is also a DSE. However, the DSE solution concept cannot be applied to the matching pennies game in Figure 12.1 because neither player has a dominant strategy. This exposes a shortcoming of this solution: if just one player does not have a dominant strategy, that game cannot have a DSE.

The classic application of this equilibrium concept is in a game called the **Prisoners' Dilemma**. A crime has been committed in a totalitarian state and a police commissioner has imprisoned two suspects in separate jail cells. Each prisoner is given the opportunity to talk to the commissioner (i.e., say that they witnessed the other committing the crime) or remain silent. If a prisoner talks while the other is silent, the one who talks is set free while the other is sent to jail for 20 years. If both prisoners talk, they each receive a lesser 10-year sentence for cooperating with the police. If both prisoners remain silent, they are charged with a minor offense and get a light sentence of 1 year in prison each. The payoff matrix for this game is shown in Figure 12.4 where the years in prison provide negative payoffs to each prisoner.

		Prisoner 2	
		Talk	Be silent
Prisoner 1	Talk	−10, −10	0, −20
	Be silent	−20, 0	−1, −1

Figure 12.4 Prisoners' dilemma

Check that Talk is a dominant strategy for each prisoner, i.e., (Talk, Talk) is a DSE. The Prisoners' Dilemma is a dilemma because when the prisoners

---

[3]Note that the babysitting game is a **symmetric game**. In a two-person symmetric game, if the row and column players are switched (e.g., by making Aruna a row player and Mahala a column player in the babysitting game), the payoff matrix does not change. Consequently, whatever strategy is dominant for Mahala must also be dominant for Aruna.

follow their own self-interest and play their dominant strategies, they end up in prison for 10 years each at the DSE, when instead they *both* would have been better off being in prison for one year *if the two could find a way to remain silent*. But the incentives in this game are structured in such a way that being quiet is never in one's self-interest. Nor does pre-play communication between the prisoners solve this dilemma: even if they verbally agreed to remain silent, each prisoner's incentive to talk is very strong, especially if each believes that the other will remain silent.

The Prisoners' Dilemma motif shows up in many strategic situations and economic games. In order for a game to be a Prisoners' Dilemma, the following conditions must hold:

(a) each player must have a dominant strategy, and

(b) the DSE outcome must yield payoffs that are worse for each player than some other outcome that is potentially possible in the payoff matrix.

12.2.2   Nash equilibrium

Because there are games where all players do not have dominant strategies (as in the matching pennies game), the DSE cannot be used to solve such games. An alternative equilibrium concept is the Nash equilibrium (NE) which has wide applicability in simultaneous games.

At a NE, unilateral deviation does not pay — no player gains by changing her strategy on her own. There are two ways to use this idea and find a NE. The first is the **method of unilateral deviation** which eliminates the possible strategy combinations where at least one player wants to deviate. Any strategy combination that does not get eliminated is then a NE. The second is the **method of mutual best-response** which determines each player's **best-response** to different strategies played by other players. A NE arises when each player's strategy is a mutual best-response: every player maximizes her payoff given what others are doing. Each method is illustrated below.

Method of unilateral deviation

In the cell phone game whose payoff matrix is given in Figure 12.5, Akbar calls Babur on his mobile phone but just as the conversation gets interesting, the call is dropped. He has two choices: to call back, or wait for Babur to call him back. Similarly, Babur has the same options: to call, or wait for Akbar to call him.

Babur

		Call	Wait
Akbar	Call	0, 0	1, 2
	Wait	2, 1	0, 0

Figure 12.5   Cell phone game

If they both call at the same time, they get a busy signal and are unable to continue the conversation, resulting in a utility of zero each. If one calls while the other waits, the one initiating the call gets a utility of 1; the one who waits gets a payoff of 2. If they both wait, the conversation is not resumed, resulting in a utility of zero each.

To use the method of unilateral deviation, list all the possible candidates for a NE:

(i) (Call, Call);

(ii) (Call, Wait);

(iii) (Wait, Call); and

(iv) (Wait, Wait).

Consider each in turn. At (i), Akbar receives a utility of zero. If he deviates to wait while Babur is calling, then his utility jumps to 2, so a unilateral deviation by Akbar pays off. Ergo this cannot be a NE.

Now consider (ii) where Akbar receives a utility of 1. If he deviates (i.e., chooses to wait) while Babur is waiting, his utility decreases to zero, so unilateral deviation does not pay for Akbar. For this to be a NE, Babur must also not want to deviate unilaterally. At (ii), Babur, while waiting, receives a utility of 2, so if he deviates to calling when Akbar is calling, his utility drops to zero. Thus neither player gains from deviation and so this is a NE.

In a similar manner, it can be checked that (Wait, Call) is also a NE,[4] while (Wait, Wait) is not. Hence, there are two Nash equilibria in this game. This exposes a shortcoming of the NE solution: there may be multiple equilibria. In this eventuality, the solution is not *exactly* predictive. In the cell phone game, a NE occurs when one person calls and the other waits, but there is no

---

[4]This should be no surprise since it is a symmetric game.

way to know which player will call and which player will wait. In the real world, there may be some social norms or customs that determine which of the two NE will actually come about. For instance, one plausible norm might be that the one who initiated the call should call back because it is generally easier for the initiator to redial the number.

Method of mutual best-response

To illustrate this method, consider the game given in Figure 12.6 between two players with three strategies each. Here Alito's strategies are up (U), middle (M) and down (D), while Breyer's are left (L), center (C) and right (R). There is no 'story' behind this game; its sole purpose is to show how mutual best-responses can be derived.

		Breyer	
	L	C	R
U	1, 0	1, 2	3, 1
Alito M	2, 3	0, 2	1, 1
D	1, 1	1, 0	1, 1

Figure 12.6   A 3×3 game

First, find Alito's best-response to Breyer's strategies. Suppose Breyer plays left. Restricting attention to the first column (see Figure 12.7 below), the highest payoff for Alito is when he plays middle, so place an asterisk next to his payoff of 2. Now suppose Breyer plays center. Restricting attention to the second column this time, the highest payoff for Alito is 1 when he plays up or down, so place an asterisk next to his payoffs of 1. Finally, Alito's best-response to Breyer playing right is to choose up, yielding a payoff of 3.

		Breyer	
	L	C	R
U	1, 0	1*, 2*	3*, 1
Alito M	2*, 3*	0, 2	1, 1
D	1, 1*	1*, 0	1, 1*

Figure 12.7   Finding best-responses

To find Breyer's best-responses, suppose Alito plays up. Restricting attention to the top row, Breyer's best-response is to play center when he obtains a payoff of 2, so mark this with an asterisk. When Alito plays middle, Breyer's best-response is to play left and obtain 3. Finally, when Alito plays down, Breyer's best-response is to go either left or right, with a payoff of 1 in either case.

A NE is a *mutual* best-response, i.e., the choice of the row player's strategy is the best given the column player's choice, and vice versa. Therefore, any cell where both players' payoffs have asterisks denotes the outcome of a mutual best-response. Hence (U, C) and (M, L) are both Nash equilibria.

Relationship between a NE and a DSE

How are Nash equilibria and dominant strategy equilibria related? A NE is a configuration of strategies where no single player wants to change their strategy given what the other players are doing. At a DSE, no player wants to deviate *regardless* of what the others are doing; in particular, no player will want to deviate when everyone else plays their dominant strategies. Therefore, if a game has a DSE, then that strategy profile is automatically a NE: for instance, (Talk, Talk) in the Prisoners' Dilemma game is also a NE. In other words, every DSE must be a NE, but of course not the other way around (a game can have a NE but no DSE, as in the cell phone game). Thus a DSE is a special case of a NE.

12.2.3   Mixed strategies°

In certain games such as the matching pennies game in Figure 12.1, there appears to be no NE (which implies that there can be no DSE either). While it is true that there is no NE in **pure strategies** — meaning each player chooses a strategy *for sure*, either H or T, with probability 1 — Nash's brilliant discovery was that all games (with finitely many players who have finitely many strategies) always have at least one NE when you allow for **mixed strategies**.

Possibly the best way to make sense of the idea of playing mixed strategies is to imagine that two players will play the same game many times, say 100 times. Suppose Ann chooses to play H and T randomly where 25 times out of 100 she chooses heads and 75 times tails. Then we say that Ann plays H with probability 0.25 and T with probability 0.75 and write this mixed strategy as the list of probabilities of each strategy $(0.25, 0.75)$. If Ann *always* plays H, we can list the probabilities as $(1, 0)$, while if she plays T always, we write it as $(0, 1)$. Thus a pure strategy can be viewed as a special case of a mixed strategy.

Solving the matching pennies game

Suppose we allow for mixed strategies in the matching pennies game. Let Ann choose heads with probability p and tails with probability $1 - p$, while Bob chooses heads with probability q and tails with probability $1 - q$. Since this is a situation of risk, we assume that each player is a von Neumann-Morgenstern expected utility maximizer. Then Ann's expected utility from playing H is

$$E_A(H) = 2 \times q + 0 \times (1 - q) = 2q, \tag{12.1}$$

whereas her expected utility from playing T is

$$E_A(T) = 0 \times q + 2 \times (1 - q) = 2 - 2q. \tag{12.2}$$

Similarly, Bob's expected utility from playing H is

$$E_B(H) = 0 \times p + 2 \times (1 - p) = 2 - 2p, \tag{12.3}$$

while his expected utility from playing T is

$$E_B(T) = 2 \times p + 0 \times (1 - p) = 2p. \tag{12.4}$$

A NE in mixed strategies is one where no one wants to change their own mixed strategy, given the mixed strategy of the other players. In this instance, it means that Ann's choice of p has to be a best-response to Bob's choice of q, and vice versa. In Figure 12.8, we illustrate how to plot the best-response functions for each player.

To figure out Ann's best-response to Bob's choice of randomization, suppose Bob chooses $q = 1$, i.e., he plays heads for sure. Substituting $q = 1$ into equations (12.1) and (12.2) reveals that Ann is better off playing H for sure, i.e., she chooses $p = 1$ to maximize her expected payoff. This is shown in Figure 12.8 by point X where $(p, q) = (1, 1)$.

Next suppose that Bob chooses heads with probability $q = 0.8$. From (12.1), if Ann plays heads, she expects to receive a payoff of 1.6. If she plays tails instead, her expected payoff from (12.2) is 0.4. Clearly, she is better off playing heads for sure, i.e., with probability $p = 1$. Therefore, her best-response to Bob's $q = 0.8$ is to play $p = 1$. This is shown in Figure 12.8 by point Y where $(p, q) = (1, 0.8)$.

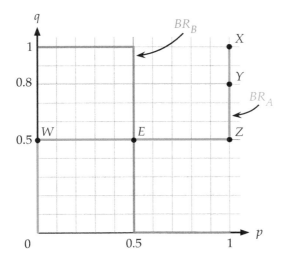

Figure 12.8   Mixed strategies in the matching pennies game

If Bob plays heads with probability $q = 0.5$, Ann's expected payoff from either (12.1) or (12.2) is 0.5 irrespective of what p she chooses. Therefore, her best-response to Bob choosing $q = 0.5$ is to play *any* p, $0 \leq p \leq 1$. In Figure 12.8, this is shown by the horizontal orange line WZ.

Verify that when Bob plays with $q < 0.5$, Ann will choose $p = 0$ since ◀◿ playing tails always yields the highest expected payoff. Thus the orange zigzag line $0WZX$ shows Ann's best-response to Bob's strategies and is labeled as BR_A. In a similar fashion, construct Bob's best-response function marked BR_B which is the mirror image of BR_A since this is a symmetric ◀◿ game. The best-responses cross at $E = (0.5, 0.5)$ which gives the unique NE in mixed strategies.

We write the mixed strategy NE as the list of probabilities associated with each strategy for each player: $((p, 1-p), (q, 1-q)) = ((0.5, 0.5), (0.5, 0.5))$.

Solving the Battle-of-the-Sexes game

Suppose a husband (H) and wife (W) have the choice to go to the football (F) or the opera (O). Their payoffs, given in Figure 12.9, reflect the fact that both partners prefer to be in each other's company rather than being apart. The wife likes both alternatives equally so long as she is in the company of her spouse, but the husband prefers going to the football over the opera. Verify ◀◿ that there are two Nash equilibria in pure strategies, (F, F) and (O, O).

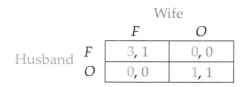

Figure 12.9   Battle-of-the-Sexes game

In addition, however, there is a NE in mixed strategies. Suppose the husband plays F with probability p and O with probability $1 - p$, while the wife plays F with probability q and O with probability $1 - q$. Then the expected payoffs of each player from playing each strategy is given by

$$E_H(F) = 3q, \tag{12.5}$$
$$E_H(O) = 1 - q, \tag{12.6}$$
$$E_W(F) = p, \text{ and} \tag{12.7}$$
$$E_W(O) = 1 - p. \tag{12.8}$$

Equate the expected payoffs for the husband, equations (12.5) and (12.6), and solve to obtain that, when $q = 0.25$, his expected payoff is the same regardless of the value of p he chooses. In Figure 12.10, this is shown by the horizontal orange segment of the husband's best-response function, BR_H.

To figure out the remaining segments of BR_H, set $q = 0$ and $q = 1$. For $q = 0$, compare his expected payoff from (12.5) and (12.6) to conclude that he is better off if he goes to the opera, i.e., if he plays $p = 0$. This yields the point $(0,0)$ in Figure 12.10 as being part of BR_H. Now join the point $(0,0)$ to $(0,0.25)$ to complete one 'leg' of BR_H.

For $q = 1$, his expected payoff is maximized if he goes to the football game, i.e., $p = 1$. This yields the point $(1,1)$ in Figure 12.10. Join $(1,1)$ to $(1,0.25)$ to complete the other 'leg' of BR_H. Since the best-responses are always piecewise linear, we obtain the orange best-response function for the husband.

To find BR_W, first set equation (12.7) equal to (12.8) to obtain $p = 0.5$ at which the wife is indifferent about the value of q she sets. This yields the vertical green line. To find the remaining segments, set $p = 0$ and $p = 1$. In the former case, the wife prefers to go to the opera, so $q = 0$; in the latter, she prefers to go to the football game, so $q = 1$. Now the rest of BR_W can be drawn.

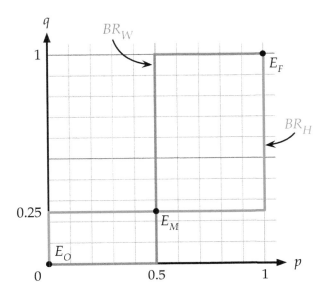

Figure 12.10   Mixed strategies in the battle-of-the-sexes game

Assuming a two-person two-strategy game where the row player chooses probability p and the column player chooses q, the steps for drawing the best-response functions in the case of a mixed strategy NE are summarized below.

1. Begin with the row player. Set the expected value from the first strategy equal to that of the second to find the q value where the row player's best-response is horizontal.

2. Fix $q = 0$ and solve for the p that maximizes the row player's expected payoff (it will be either $p = 0$ or $p = 1$). Use this information to complete one 'leg' of the best-response function.

3. For $q = 1$, find the p that maximizes the row player's expected payoff; it will be the other extreme of the p value from step 2. Use this information to complete the remaining 'leg' of the best-response.

4. Repeat steps 1–3 for the column player, reversing the roles of the p's and q's.

Note that the solution in step 3 does not require any specific calculation and follows automatically from step 2: if the solution to step 2 is $p = 0$, then the solution to step 3 is $p = 1$, and vice versa.

In the battle-of-the-sexes game, the orange and green best-responses of the husband and the wife cross three times, i.e., there are three mutual best-responses or three Nash equilibria. The NE at E_O is $((0,1),(0,1))$, corresponding to the pure strategy NE when both go to the opera. The NE at E_M is the mixed strategy NE $((0.25,0.75),(0.5,0.5))$ when the husband goes to the football game a quarter of the time, while the wife randomizes equally between the two choices. Finally, the NE at E_F is $((1,0),(1,0))$ which is the other pure strategy equilibrium when both go to the football game.

All best-response functions in two-player games with two strategies each are piecewise linear. There are a limited number of ways they can cross, resulting in either one or three Nash equilibria. The idea of a mixed strategy NE can be extended to more than two players and more than two strategies but it is no longer possible to draw best-response functions and derive solutions graphically.

12.3 Dynamic Games

So far, we have only considered simultaneous games. Dynamic games enlarge the scope of game theory by allowing players to move sequentially. Two features are crucial to dynamic games: (i) the timing of play (who gets to move at what point) and (ii) what information the players have when they move. We depict dynamic games using a **game tree** as shown in Figure 12.11; such a depiction is called an **extensive-form game**.

12.3.1 Extensive-form games

Consider the potential entry game played between an incumbent firm (I) in a market and a potential entrant (E) who is threatening to turn the market from a monopoly into a duopoly. In Figure 12.11, the **initial node** is shown by an open circle which is assigned to E, indicating that the entrant moves first. The two **branches** emanating from the initial node are marked d and e signifying the strategies 'Don't enter' and 'Enter'. If the entrant does not enter, the game ends at a **terminal node** with payoffs $(0,4)$, where the first number denotes the payoff to the entrant and the second denotes that to the incumbent. If E does enter, the incumbent gets to make a decision

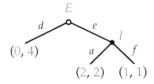

Figure 12.11 The potential entry game

and choose either to 'Accommodate entry' (*a*) or to 'Fight' (*f*). To accommodate entry means that the incumbent accepts the entry of *E* as a *fait accompli*, while to fight signifies that it engages the entrant in a price war. Accordingly, choosing *a* leads to a payoff of (2, 2) while *f* yields (1, 1). Thus, in general, a dynamic game consists of an initial and intermediate nodes, each of which is assigned to a player. At any terminal node, the game ends in payoffs for each player.

In principle, all games — even simultaneous ones — can be written in extensive form. For instance, the matching pennies game is shown in extensive form in Figure 12.12. The dashed line that joins the two nodes assigned to Bob shows that he cannot distinguish between those nodes, i.e., he cannot surmise whether Anna has played heads (*H*) or tails (*T*). Thus he has to choose his own strategy without knowing the true state of the world, i.e., in ignorance of what Anna has played. Of course his payoffs from choosing *H* or *T* are different depending on the true state of the world.

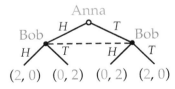

Figure 12.12 Matching pennies game in extensive form

When two or more nodes are joined as in Figure 12.12, we refer to the collection of those nodes as an **information set**. If a player's information set consists of only one node as is the case for player *I* in Figure 12.11, we call it a **singleton information set**. If all information sets in a game are singleton sets, we say that it is a game of **perfect information**. In this chapter, we will restrict attention to games of perfect information all of which can be solved by **backward induction**, as shown in the following section.

12.3.2   Subgame perfect Nash equilibrium

We assume the common knowledge of rationality on the part of all players, which (loosely speaking) means that all players know that at any decision node, if the player at that node has a choice that leads to a strictly higher payoff compared to any other strategy, then she will choose the former.[5] Then a game can be solved backwards, i.e., starting from the "bottom" of the game tree and moving up to the initial node by considering subgames along the way. A subgame (loosely speaking) is a subset of the extensive-form game that contains a singleton initial node and all the nodes below that can be reached from it. Instead of giving a formal definition of a subgame, we will illustrate the notion with a couple of examples.

Solving the potential entry game

Consider the potential entry game. In Figure 12.13, we first identify the subgames. Beginning with the terminal nodes that end in payoffs $(2, 2)$ and $(1, 1)$ there is one subgame labeled as 'Subgame 1' where the relevant decision node is that of I who has to choose between a and f. This is a subgame because there is a single initial node (the one labeled I) and because all subsequent nodes that can be reached (the two terminal nodes that end in $(2, 2)$ and $(1, 1)$ are included. Moving up the game tree, the second subgame is the entire game itself that has the single initial node labeled E and includes all the nodes that follow from this initial node.

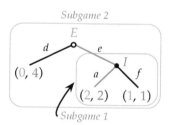

Figure 12.13   Solving the potential entry game

At subgame 1, it is player I's move and the payoff of 2 from playing a is larger than the payoff of 1 from f. From the common knowledge of rationality, I chooses a, as shown by the red branch. This means that if the

---

[5]The formalization of the notion of common knowledge is one of Robert Aumann's many contributions to economic theory, but a precise definition here will take us too far afield.

game were to reach the node labeled I, then it is common knowledge that the game would proceed along the red branch.

Moving up the game tree, at subgame 2, it is player E's move and it can play d and receive a payoff of 0. Alternatively, E can play e in which case we reach I's decision node in subgame 1 and the game proceeds along the red branch and E receives a payoff of 2. From the common knowledge of rationality, it follows that E chooses e, as shown by the red branch emanating from the initial node. Thus the subgame perfect Nash equilibrium (SPNE) is reached when player E plays e and player I plays a, the equilibrium path of the game being shown by the red branches.

Solving the centipede game

The centipede game is shown in Figure 12.14.[6] Initially, there are two piles of cash on a table, one containing \$4 and the other containing \$1. Player 1 can terminate the game (t) and pocket the larger pile of cash, while giving the remaining one dollar to player 2. Alternatively, player 1 can push (p) the pile towards the other player in which case each pile doubles to \$8 and \$2. Now player 2 can terminate the game by taking the larger of the two piles (\$8) and leaving the smaller pile (\$2) for player 1, or continue the game by pushing, in which case the piles double again and player 1 has to choose between terminating or continuing the game. While this sequence of alternating moves could continue for as many rounds as desired, the version in Figure 12.14 ends after four rounds.

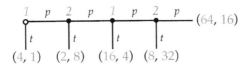

Figure 12.14 The centipede game

In Figure 12.15, the four subgames are shown; they are each nested inside each other. In subgame 1, it is player 2's turn to move and choose between t or p. Then t is a better alternative than p, yielding \$32 as opposed to \$16, as shown by the red branch. Moving backwards in the game, in subgame 2, it is 1's move and t yields her \$16 as opposed to p which (in the continuing subgame along the red branch) yields \$8. Working in this fashion backwards,

---

[6]The name comes from its graphical depiction which somewhat resembles a centipede.

the only SPNE possible in this game is that player 1 chooses to terminate the game at the initial node where player 1 leaves with $4 and player 2 with $1. Many people find this equilibrium prediction to be somewhat at odds with what they would do since both players would be better off if they could continue past the second round.

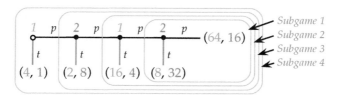

Figure 12.15 Solving the centipede game

Exercises

12.1. Two travelers, returning home from a tropical island where they both purchased an identical antique, discover that the airline has smashed these. The airline manager asks each traveler to write down the compensation desired, any whole number between $2 and $100 (the maximum the manager is allowed to give each traveler). If both write the same number, they each receive that amount. But if, say, $n_1 > n_2$, then the manager gives each the smaller of the two (i.e., n_2) with an adjustment: believing that traveler 1 is lying and traveler 2 is being truthful, the manager punishes traveler 1 by giving $n_2 - 2$ as compensation, while rewarding 2 for his supposed honesty by paying him $n_2 + 2$.

(a) Show the part of the normal-form game when traveler 1 and 2 each write between $95 and $100. Why is $(100, 100)$ not a NE?

(b) Show the part of the normal-form game when traveler 1 and 2 each write between $2 and $10. Is there a NE in this part of the normal-form game?

(c) What is the pure strategy Nash equilibria of this game?

12.2. Consider a fictitious tennis match-up between André Agassi and Björn Borg with Agassi serving to Borg. If Agassi serves to Borg's forehand (*F*), Borg, who has a very strong forehand stroke, wins the point 90 percent of the time if he responds with *F*; if he tries to respond with a backhand stroke (B), he wins 30 percent of the time. If Agassi serves to Borg's backhand (B), Borg wins 40 percent of the time when he plays F but 80 percent of the time when he responds with B. The game is illustrated below.

Borg

		F	B
Agassi	F	10, 90	70, 30
	B	60, 40	20, 80

Draw the mixed strategy best-response functions for the players and determine all the Nash equilibria of this game.

12.3. Two animals are contesting over a food source. Each can be like a 'hawk' (strategy H, willing to fight it out even though it consumes valuable energy) or be like a 'dove' (strategy D, willing to be conciliatory and share resources). The payoffs are given below.

②

		H	D
①	H	-1, -1	8, 0
	D	0, 8	4, 5

Draw the mixed strategy best-response functions for the animals and determine all the Nash equilibria of this game.

12.4. Hunters 1, 2, and 3 decide to go hunting. Each hunter can either hunt for a stag (s) or a hare (h). Hunting a stag is difficult and requires the co-ordination of *all* three hunters — no single hunter, or even two hunters, can catch a stag. Hunting a hare, on the other hand, is easy and any single hunter can catch one on her own. The payoff from catching a stag is 2 each to a successful hunter; the payoff from catching a hare is 1, and the payoff from not catching anything is 0.

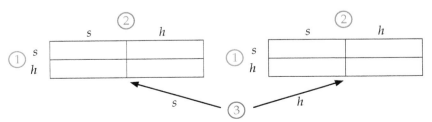

(a) Fill in the payoffs for all three hunters in the cells of the game above.

(b) Find all the Nash equilibria in pure strategies.

(c) Suppose that all the hunters randomize in the same way, i.e., each chooses to hunt a stag with the same probability p and to hunt a hare with probability $1 - p$. Find the symmetric mixed strategy NE.

(*Hint*: In part (c), for hunter 1, the choice of p by the other two hunters must be such that his expected payoffs from stag-hunting or hare-hunting are the same, i.e., $E_1(s) = E_1(h)$.)

12.5. Two pigs, Porky and Squeal, live in a large cage. Porky is a big, lumbering, dominant, male pig while Squeal is a smaller, agile, submissive female. At one end of the cage is a red button, which dispenses food in a trough at the other end. If Porky and Squeal both press the button (strategy P), Squeal gets to the food first and manages to eat some before Porky pushes her aside and eats the bulk of it. If Porky pushes and Squeal does not (strategy N), Squeal manages to get more of the food. If Porky does not push the button but Squeal does, Porky eats everything in the trough before Squeal can get to it. Finally, if neither push the button, they don't receive any food. The utility payoffs from their choices are given below.

		Squeal	
		P	N
Porky	P	4, 2	2, 3
	N	6, -1	0, 0

(a) Find all the pure strategy Nash equilibria of this game.

(b) Suppose Porky plays P with probability p, and N with probability $1 - p$, while Squeal plays P with probability q, and N with probability $1 - q$. Draw the pigs' best-response functions and find all the mixed strategy Nash equilibria of this game.

12.6. Three competing grocery stores, A, B, and C, can run a sale (s) on their items or offer no sale (n). The payoffs from their choices (in millions of dollars) are given below.

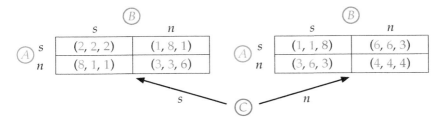

(a) Find all the pure strategy Nash equilibria of this game.

(b) Find a mixed strategy NE where all stores randomize in the same manner, playing s with probability p, and n with probability $1 - p$.

(c) Find all the mixed strategy Nash equilibria where *one* grocery store always chooses n and the other *two* randomize in the same manner, playing s with probability q, and n with probability $1 - q$. (*Hint*: In part (c), let C be the store that chooses n for sure.)

12.7. Firms 1 and 2 must decide whether to enter a new industry. To enter the industry, each firm must choose to build either a plant with a small output capacity (S), or large output capacity (L). A plant with small capacity costs $50 to set up; one with large capacity costs $175. In either case, the marginal cost of production is zero. Firm 1 decides to choose a small capacity (S) or large capacity (L) or not to enter (N). The revenues under the different scenarios are given below.

◇ If neither firm enters, revenues (and hence profits) are zero.

◇ If one small firm enters, its revenue is $80, the other earns zero.

◇ If two small firms enter, each earns revenues of $70.

◇ If one small and one large firm enter, the small firm earns $40 in revenue while the large one earns $160.

◇ If one large firm enters, its revenue is $200, the other earns zero.

◇ If two large firms enter, each earns revenues of $90.

(a) Suppose both firms play a simultaneous game, choosing between S, L or N. Write down the payoffs in the 3×3 normal-form game. What are the Nash equilibria of this game?

(b) Suppose the firms play a sequential game. Firm 2, after observing firm 1's strategy (S, L or N), has to decide whether to choose S, L, or N. Draw the extensive-form game, write down the payoffs and solve for the SPNE.

12.8. Forbes is a monopoly manufacturer who can use laborers to pack his product into boxes or use an expensive set of robotic arms which will reduce the number of workers he hires, but increase his fixed cost. His profit is $900 without the machine and $500 if he buys the machine. Károly is an entrepreneur and is wondering if he should enter this market (which would turn it from a monopoly into a duopoly). If he does not enter, he earns $0. If Károly enters, Forbes earns $400 if he uses labor and $132 with the robot, while Károly earns $300 when Forbes uses labor and makes a loss of $36 if Forbes buys the robotic arms.

(a) Draw the normal-form game with Forbes as the row player who chooses between L (use labor) and R (use robot), and Károly plays S (stay out) or E (enter).

(b) Do either Forbes or Károly have a dominant strategy? Explain.

(c) What is a NE in this game?

(d) Consider the sequential game where Forbes chooses L or R first, followed by Károly choosing S or E. Write down the extensive-form game and find the SPNE.

Chapter 13

Oligopoly

Just as economists make sense of what happens in competitive markets in terms of the market equilibrium that arises from the interaction of demand and supply, in an oligopolistic equilibrium, the behavior of firms corresponds to that of a Nash equilibrium (NE), i.e., each firm is maximizing its profit given the actions of the others.

Oligopolies are usually modeled in one of two ways: firms either choose the quantities they wish to produce (quantity competition), or they choose the prices they wish to charge (price competition). While the game-theoretic ideas are exactly the ones introduced in Chapter 12, the only difference is that the firms typically choose their actions from a *continuum* rather than a finite set of discrete options. For instance, under quantity competition, a firm can choose *any* output ranging from zero to its capacity; under price competition, a firm can charge *any* price ranging from its marginal cost of production to the maximum price that buyers are willing to pay for it.

13.1 Static Quantity Competition

We begin with an example of the classic duopoly model of Augustin Cournot that dates back to 1838 but is still one of the most important ways in which economists think about quantity competition.

13.1.1 Cournot duopoly

Two firms produce a homogeneous good. Firm 1 produces quantity q_1 and 2 produces q_2, so the total quantity produced is $Q = q_1 + q_2$. The firms face an inverse market demand given by $p = 200 - Q$, or $p = 200 - q_1 - q_2$. It costs each firm \$20 to produce each unit of output. We assume that each firm chooses its own output taking as given the other firm's production level.

Graphical representation

One way to find a NE for this problem graphically is to plot each firm's best-response to the other firm's output choice and find a point of mutual best-response. To do so, assume that firm 2 has chosen its output level arbitrarily at q_2. Taking this q_2 as given, firm 1 chooses q_1 to maximize its profit, the difference between its total revenue and total cost:

$$\pi_1(q_1, q_2) = pq_1 - 20q_1 = (p - 20)q_1$$
$$= 180q_1 - q_1^2 - q_1q_2. \tag{13.1}$$

Maximizing (13.1) with respect to q_1, we get

$$\frac{\partial \pi_1}{\partial q_1}(q_1, q_2) = 180 - 2q_1 - q_2 = 0, \tag{13.2}$$

where the value of q_1 in (13.2) maximizes 1's profit for the given q_2. Expressing q_1 as a function of q_2 gives us firm 1's best-response function:

$$q_1 = 90 - \frac{q_2}{2}. \tag{13.3}$$

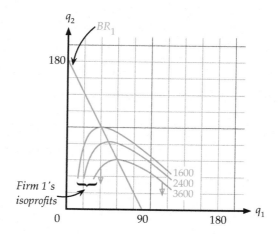

Figure 13.1   Firm 1's best-response function

Firm 1's orange best-response line is plotted in Figure 13.1, showing how much q_1 it should produce in response to different levels of firm 2's output, q_2. Also shown are three of firm 1's isoprofit curves — combinations of q_1 and q_2 that yield a profit level of 1600, 2400 and 3600 dollars — which can be found by setting the left hand side of (13.1) to 1600, 2400 and 3600 respectively. Note that (i) firm 1's best-response line connects the "tops" of its isoprofits, and (ii) firm 1's profits increase to the south as shown by the arrows.

Analogously, maximize firm 2's profit,

$$\pi_2(q_1, q_2) = pq_2 - 20q_2 = (p - 20)q_2 = 180q_2 - q_1q_2 - q_2^2,$$

with respect to q_2 to obtain 2's best-response function:

$$q_2 = 90 - \frac{q_1}{2}. \tag{13.4}$$

Both best-response equations (13.3) and (13.4) are plotted in Figure 13.2 and are labeled as BR_1 and BR_2, the best-response of each firm to the other's choice of output level. Since a NE is a mutual best-response, the point E where BR_1 and BR_2 cross shows the NE quantities for each firm, $(q_1^*, q_2^*) = (60, 60)$. The profit level of each firm is \$3600 and their corresponding iso- profit curves are also shown.

For a different way to understand why $(60, 60)$ is a NE, consider Figure 13.3. Given the inverse market demand $p = 200 - Q$, suppose firm 2 decides to produce $q_2^* = 60$ units. Then the market price (even before firm 1

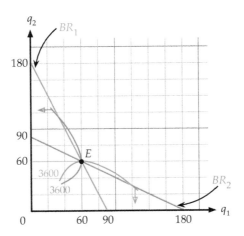

Figure 13.2 The Cournot equilibrium

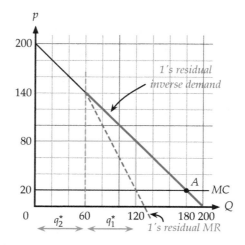

Figure 13.3 The Cournot duopoly market

has produced anything) is at $140 as a result of firm 2's output, and any pro-
duction by firm 1 is going to lead to a total output level in excess of 60 units
and reduce the market price further. In other words, given that firm 2 has
produced 60 units, the demand curve facing firm 1 is the blue segment of the
market demand curve that extends from the coordinate $(60, 140)$ to $(200, 0)$.
We call this firm 1's **residual inverse demand**. From 1's point of view, it is
as if the vertical axis, instead of starting at the $(0,0)$ origin, now begins at
$(60,0)$, as shown by the vertical dashed magenta line.

   To determine how much firm 1 should produce so as to maximize its
profits, set the marginal revenue of its residual demand equal to the marginal
cost of $20. Recall[1] that the marginal revenue must have the same intercept
as the residual inverse demand but twice the slope, as shown by the dashed
blue line. Therefore $q_1^* = 60$ maximizes firm 1's profit when $q_2^* = 60$, i.e.,
it is a best-response to firm 2's output decision. In an analogous way, by
reversing the roles of firm 1 and 2, we can show that if firm 2 takes $q_1^* = 60$
units as given, then $q_2^* = 60$ maximizes 2's profit. Thus $(60, 60)$ is a mutual
best-response or a NE and the total quantity sold on the market is $Q^* = 120$
at a price of $p^* = \$80$.

   When the market inverse demand is linear and firms have identical, constant marginal costs, then each duopolist's output is one-third the output
where the MC crosses the demand at point A in Figure 13.3.

---

[1]See Chapter 10, equation (10.5).

Algebraic derivation

While it is always possible to calculate the Nash equilibrium outputs in a Cournot duopoly from the firms' best-response functions, they can be found in a more straightforward fashion in the case of a symmetric duopoly by following these steps.

1. Write down the profit function of firm 1, π_1.

2. Maximize π_1 with respect to q_1 by deriving the first-order necessary condition at the NE, (q_1^*, q_2^*).

3. Impose symmetry by setting $q_1^* = q_2^* = q^*$.

4. Solve for q^*.

To illustrate, step 1 is given in (13.1). For step 2, find the first-order necessary condition for profit maximization at the NE:

$$\frac{\partial \pi_1}{\partial q_1}(q_1^*, q_2^*) = 180 - 2q_1^* - q_2^* = 0.$$

Imposing symmetry, we get

$$180 - 2q^* - q^* = 0,$$

or, $q^* = 60$.

In the case of an asymmetric duopoly, say where the firms have different costs, the steps above need to be modified slightly.

1. Write down the profit function of each firm.

2. Maximize π_1 with respect to q_1 by writing the first-order necessary condition at the NE (q_1^*, q_2^*), and take all the output terms to one side of the equation.

3. Repeat step 2 for firm 2.

4. Solve for (q_1^*, q_2^*) simultaneously.

Suppose two Cournot duopolists face the inverse market demand $p = 200 - q_1 - q_2$, and where the first firm has a per-unit cost of \$30 and the second of \$10. Then from step 1, the firms' profit functions are

$$\pi_1(q_1, q_2) = (200 - q_1 - q_2)q_1 - 30q_1 = 170q_1 - q_1^2 - q_1 q_2,$$
$$\pi_2(q_1, q_2) = (200 - q_1 - q_2)q_2 - 10q_2 = 190q_2 - q_1 q_2 - q_2^2.$$

From step 2, maximize π_1

$$\frac{\partial \pi_1}{\partial q_1}(q_1^*, q_2^*) = 170 - 2q_1^* - q_2^* = 0,$$

and take all the output terms to the right hand side to obtain

$$170 = 2q_1^* + q_2^*. \tag{13.5}$$

From step 3, similarly obtain

$$\frac{\partial \pi_2}{\partial q_2}(q_1^*, q_2^*) = 190 - q_1^* - 2q_2^* = 0,$$

and

$$190 = q_1^* + 2q_2^*. \tag{13.6}$$

Finally, in step 4, to solve (13.5) and (13.6) simultaneously, multiply the former by 2 and subtract the latter from it to obtain $3q_1^* = 150$, or $q_1^* = 50$. Substitute this in (13.5) or (13.6) to get $q_2^* = 70$.

13.1.2   Cournot oligopoly°

The Cournot duopoly model can be extended to that of an oligopoly with n identical firms by essentially using the same algorithm as the one for a symmetric duopoly.

Suppose the inverse market demand is still given by $p = a - Q$, where $Q = q_1 + q_2 + \ldots + q_n$, and that the marginal cost of production is c per unit. Then a typical firm's profit function — for firm 1, say — is given by

$$\pi_1(q_1, q_2, \ldots, q_n) = pq_1 - cq_1 = (a - c)q_1 - q_1^2 - q_1 q_2 - \ldots - q_1 q_n. \tag{13.7}$$

Given the NE production levels $q_2^*, q_3^*, \ldots, q_n^*$, firm 1 maximizes (13.7) with respect to q_1 to obtain the first-order necessary condition

$$a - c - 2q_1^* - q_2^* - q_3^* - \ldots - q_n^* = 0. \tag{13.8}$$

Since all firms are identical, each will choose the same output level at the NE, so set $q_1^* = q_2^* = \ldots = q_n^* = q^*$. Imposing this symmetry in (13.8), we obtain

$$a - c - (n+1)q^* = 0 \tag{13.9}$$

from where $q^* = (a-c)/(n+1)$. Then the total quantity produced on the market is $Q^* = nq^* = (a-c)n/(n+1)$ and $p^* = (a+cn)/(n+1)$.

Applying this to the specific example in Figure 13.3 where $a = 200, c = 20$ and $n = 2$, then $q^* = (200-20)/3 = 60$, $Q^* = 2q^* = 120$, and $p^* = (200+40)/3 = \$80$ just as we had found graphically.

13.2 Static Price Competition

There are essentially two types of models under price competition, those where the products are identical and those where they are differentiated. The canonical models are those of Joseph Bertrand and Harold Hotelling.

13.2.1 Bertrand duopoly

Firm 1 and firm 2 sell DVDs online at prices p_1 and p_2. Assume that the shipping services are comparable and so shoppers regard one firm's product as identical to the other's. Suppose the inverse market demand is $p = 200 - Q$, where $Q = q_1 + q_2$. Because shoppers can do price comparisons easily using shopbots, if $p_1 < p_2$, then everyone purchases from firm 1, i.e., $q_1 = 200 - p_1$ and $q_2 = 0$. Conversely, if $p_2 < p_1$, then everyone purchases from firm 2, i.e., $q_2 = 200 - p_2$ and $q_1 = 0$. If $p_1 = p_2 = \bar{p}$, then the firms split the buyers equally, i.e., $q_1 = q_2 = (200 - \bar{p})/2$.

Assume that each firm can acquire the DVD from the manufacturer at a constant marginal cost of $10 per DVD. What is a NE in prices, (p_1^*, p_2^*)? For instance, could $(15, 15)$ be a NE? In this case, firm 1 could reduce its price to $14.99 and be the sole seller of the DVD and drive firm 2 out of the market. Likewise, firm 2 could further undercut firm 1's price by a cent to $14.98, kicking firm 1 out. Successive rounds of such undercutting behavior imply that only $(p_1^*, p_2^*) = (10, 10)$ is a NE, i.e., each firm chooses to set its price equal to marginal cost in equilibrium.

This result is known as the **Bertrand paradox**: how is it that marginal-cost pricing requires the presence of many, many firms under perfect competition while under price competition it only requires *two* firms? The paradox can be resolved by examining two underlying assumptions in Bertrand's model:

(i) each firm sells an identical homogeneous product, and (ii) each firm can handle the entire market demand when it undercuts its rival.

If firms sell **differentiated products** — similar, but not identical products — then because of branding or consumer loyalty, one firm could charge above its marginal cost and not be fearful that its entire clientele could be captured by the other firm undercutting its price. In the case of online retail of DVDs, purchasing from Amazon.com may be viewed as buying a different 'product' than from a lesser-known company, perhaps because the former is regarded to be 'more reputable' or because Amazon provides additional services such as future recommendations based on previous purchases. If this is the case, then small price cuts by the lesser-known firm are not likely to woo an Amazon customer away.

If a firm finds it impossible to meet the resulting market demand when it undercuts a rival's price, we say that it faces **capacity constraints**. If firms are capacity-constrained, then pricing at marginal cost is no longer a NE. This is because when firm 2 prices at marginal cost, it will be unable to meet the market demand, and firm 1 will get the overflow of customers that 2 is unable to serve. Consequently, firm 1 could charge a price above marginal cost since it is in no danger of losing these customers to its rival.

13.2.2   Hotelling duopoly

The Hotelling model is one of price competition with differentiated products. Suppose there is a mile-long stretch of a beach whose length is indexed by a number between zero and one as shown in Figure 13.4. A thousand sunbathers are evenly distributed along this stretch on a hot day. Each sunbather would potentially like to consume an icecream which she values at $v = \$8$. There is an icecream seller at each end of this linear market, seller 1 whose location is the orange dot at zero at the extreme left of the mile, and seller 2 shown with the green dot on the extreme right, each selling an identical icecream. For the sake of illustration, suppose seller 1 charges $p_1 = \$6$ while seller 2 charges $p_2 = \$5$ and that these prices are known to every consumer. Each potential buyer has to walk to either icecream seller to make the purchase and incurs a travel cost of $t = \$2$ per mile.

In Figure 13.4, the consumer at point 0 can buy the icecream from seller 1 for $6 (shown by the point A) without incurring any transport cost. Alternatively, the consumer at 0 can walk the mile to seller 2 and pay $5; her **full price** is $7 including the transport cost, shown by point B. Similarly, the

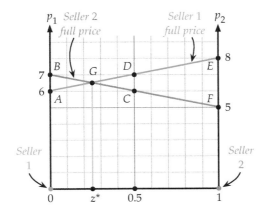

Figure 13.4 The Hotelling market

consumer located at point 1 on the extreme right can buy the icecream from seller 1 for a full price of $8 ($6 + $2 transport cost) shown by point E or from seller 2 for a full price of $5 ($5 + $0 transport cost) shown by point F. Thus for every consumer on the mile-long beach, the point on the orange line shows the full price of buying from seller 1, and the point on the green line shows the full price of buyer from 2. The consumer at point 0.5, for example, pays a full price of $7 (point D) to buy it from 1 and $6 (point C) to buy it from 2. Since C lies below D, this consumer prefers to buy from seller 2. In fact, any consumer between 0 and z^* prefers to buy from seller 1, while any seller from z^* to 1 prefers to buy from 2. Thus, seller 1's share of the market is 25 percent, while seller 2's share is 75 percent.

In Figure 13.4, if seller 1 were to lower its price while seller 2 continues to charge $5, the orange line AG would move down in a parallel fashion and seller 1 would gain market share at the expense of seller 2. Thus charging different prices changes a seller's market share and thereby profits. The solution to the Hotelling duopoly is to find a pair of prices such that each seller maximizes its profits given what the other charges.

Before we can solve the model, let us specify the utility of consumers. A consumer located at some point z along the mile-long beach values the icecream at v dollars and has a utility function given by

$$u(z) = \begin{cases} v - (p_1 + tz) & \text{if she buys from seller 1,} \\ v - (p_2 + t(1-z)) & \text{if she buys from seller 2,} \\ 0 & \text{if she does not buy.} \end{cases}$$

This consumer cares about her consumer surplus: the first line shows her consumer surplus (value minus the full price) when she buys from seller 1, the second line when she buys from seller 2, and the last line when she does not buy. Since an icecream is worth $v = \$8$ to any consumer and the transport cost is $t = \$2$ per mile,

$$u(z) = \begin{cases} 8 - p_1 - 2z & \text{if she buys from seller 1,} \\ 6 - p_2 + 2z & \text{if she buys from seller 2,} \\ 0 & \text{if she does not buy.} \end{cases}$$

The consumer at z^* who is indifferent between buying from either seller derives the same utility whether she purchases from seller 1 or 2:

$$8 - p_1 - 2z^* = 6 - p_2 + 2z^*,$$

or solving

$$z^* = \frac{p_2 - p_1 + 2}{4}. \tag{13.10}$$

Note that every consumer to the left of z^* will find it cheaper to buy from seller 1, while every consumer to her right will want to buy from seller 2. Since a thousand consumers are evenly distributed over the mile, the quantities demanded from each seller will be

$$q_1 = 1000z^* = 250(p_2 - p_1 + 2), \tag{13.11}$$
$$q_2 = 1000(1 - z^*) = 250(p_1 - p_2 + 2). \tag{13.12}$$

Suppose each seller's cost function is $c_i(q_i) = 4q_i$, $i = 1, 2$, i.e., the marginal cost of producing an icecream is a constant $4. Then seller 1's profit function is

$$\pi_1(p_1, p_2) = p_1 q_1 - 4q_1 = (p_1 - 4)q_1$$
$$= 250(p_1 - 4)(p_2 - p_1 + 2). \tag{13.13}$$

Maximizing by choosing price p_1, we find that seller 1's best-response function is

$$p_1 = 3 + \frac{p_2}{2}, \tag{13.14}$$

shown in Figure 13.5 with the orange line labeled BR_1.
    Similarly, maximizing seller 2's profit function

$$\pi_2(p_1, p_2) = 250(p_2 - 4)(p_1 - p_2 + 2), \tag{13.15}$$

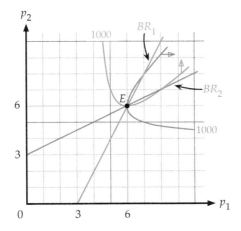

Figure 13.5 The Hotelling equilibrium

with respect to p_2, seller 2's best-response function is

$$p_2 = 3 + \frac{p_1}{2},$$ (13.16)

shown in green. The NE is given by the intersection of the best-response functions at E which can be found by substituting (13.14) into (13.16).[2] Then $(p_1^*, p_2^*) = (6, 6)$, $(q_1^*, q_2^*) = (500, 500)$, and the profits of the sellers are $\pi_1^* = \pi_2^* = \$1000$, as shown by the labels on the respective firms' isoprofit curves.

Note that because this is a symmetric game and both sellers charge the same price of $6 in equilibrium, $z^* = 0.5$ and all consumers in the first halfmile will purchase from seller 1, while the remaining consumers in the second halfmile will buy from seller 2.

To summarize, any symmetric price competition model (and not just the Hotelling model) can be solved by following essentially the same steps as the Cournot equilibrium:

1. Write down the profit function of firm 1, π_1.

2. Maximize π_1 with respect to p_1 by writing the first-order necessary condition at the NE, (p_1^*, p_2^*).

---

[2]Since the sellers are symmetric, in equilibrium the prices charged by each must be the same. So an alternative way to solve for the NE is to impose symmetry $(p_1^* = p_2^* = p^*)$ in (13.14) and solving for p^*.

3. Impose symmetry by setting $p_1^* = p_2^* = p^*$.

4. Solve for p^*.

An asymmetric price competition model is also solved in a manner similar to that of the asymmetric Cournot model:

1. Write down the profit function of each firm.

2. Maximize π_1 with respect to p_1 by writing the first-order necessary condition at the NE (p_1^*, p_2^*), and take all the output terms to one side of the equation.

3. Repeat step 2 for firm 2.

4. Solve for (p_1^*, p_2^*) simultaneously.

In Figure 13.5, the best-response functions in the Hotelling duopoly are positively sloping, unlike the Cournot duopoly best-response functions in Figure 13.2. An upward-sloping best-response function means that as seller 2 raises its strategic variable p_2, seller 1 responds optimally by raising its strategic variable p_1, and vice versa. When the strategic variables move together, we say that those variables are **strategic complements**. In the Cournot case, the strategic variables (quantities) move in opposite directions: if firm 2 raises q_2, firm 1 responds optimally by *reducing* q_1, and vice versa. Here the choices of players are said to be **strategic substitutes**.[3]

13.3   Dynamic Competition

We consider leader-follower models for the Cournot as well as Hotelling duopolies. In the Cournot case, firm 1 chooses q_1 in stage one of the game. This output level is assumed to be publicly observable, so in stage two, firm 2 chooses q_2 *after* having observed q_1. Similarly, in the Hotelling model, seller 1 chooses its price publicly in stage one, whereupon seller 2 sets its price in

---

[3]Games of strategic substitutes and strategic complements have some predictable conse-quences in dynamic games. These consequences are summarized at the end of section 13.3.

stage two. Both are dynamic games of complete information and, as shown in section 12.3.2, they have to be solved backwards for the subgame perfect Nash equilibrium (SPNE).[4]

13.3.1 Stackelberg Cournot duopoly

The steps for solving a Cournot leader-follower model can be summarized as follows.

1. Write down the profit function of the follower, say firm 2, π_2.

2. Maximize π_2 with respect to q_2 and solve for the best-response function, BR_2.

3. Replace q_2 with BR_2 in the profit function of the leader, firm 1.

4. Solve for q_1^*. Substitute in BR_2 from step 2 to obtain $_2^*$.

To illustrate, consider the Cournot duopoly from section 13.1.1 where the inverse market demand is $p = 200 - q_1 - q_2$ and each firm has a marginal cost of \$20. In solving this problem backwards, assume that firm 1 has already produced an output of q_1 in the first stage. Then step 1 consists of maximizing firm 2's profit in the second stage

$$\pi_2(q_1, q_2) = pq_2 - 20q_2 = (p - 20)q_2 = 180q_2 - q_1q_2 - q_2^2$$

with respect to q_2. In step 2, obtain its best-response function

$$q_2 = 90 - \frac{q_1}{2},$$

which is the same best-response we found earlier in (13.4).

Knowing that this is how firm 2 will choose its output in stage two, firm 1 incorporates this information into its profit function (13.1). Therefore in step 3, replace q_2 with (13.4) in (13.1):

$$\pi_1(q_1) = 180q_1 - q_1\left(90 - \frac{q_1}{2}\right) - q_1^2$$

$$= 90q_1 - \frac{q_1^2}{2}. \qquad (13.17)$$

---

[4]The SPNE of a leader-follower game is sometimes called a Stackelberg equilibrium after Heinrich von Stackelberg who was the first to publish it in 1934.

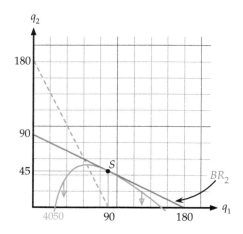

Figure 13.6   The Stackelberg Cournot equilibrium

⚠ ▶   Finally, in step 4, maximize (13.17) to obtain $q_1^* = 90$. Then $q_2^* = 45$, so the SPNE is $(90, 45)$.

Figure 13.6 shows the Stackelberg Cournot solution as the point S. Since firm 2 is the follower, it will choose its output based on the green best-response line, BR_2. Knowing this, firm 1 chooses an output level so as to maximize its profit, i.e., it chooses the highest orange isoprofit that it can reach given BR_2. This is shown by the point of tangency of the leader's highest possible isoprofit to the best-response line of firm 2, the follower. The act of substituting the follower's best-response function into the leader's profit function as was done in deriving (13.17) and maximizing this function is the mathematical equivalent of finding the tangency point S.

⚠ ▶   Then the Stackelberg price is $p^* = \$65$ and firm profits are $\pi_1^* = \$4050$ and $\pi_2^* = \$2025$. When compared to the outcome of the simultaneous game shown in Figure 13.2, in the Cournot leader-follower situation, firm 1 is better off (profits are \$4050 as opposed to 3600) from having moved first, while firm 2, the follower, is worse off (profits are \$2025 as opposed to 3600).

13.3.2   Stackelberg Hotelling duopoly

The steps for solving a Hotelling leader-follower (or *any* price competition) model are analogous to the steps described in section 13.3.1 for solving the Cournot leader-follower model. The only difference lies in the strategic variables that the Hotelling competitors choose (prices) versus those chosen by the Cournot firms (quantities). The four steps are summarized below.

1. Write down the profit function of the follower, say firm 2, π_2.

2. Maximize π_2 with respect to p_2 and solve for the best-response function, BR_2.

3. Replace p_2 with BR_2 in the profit function of the leader, firm 1.

4. Solve for p_1^*. Substitute in BR_2 from step 2 to obtain p_2^*.

Consider the Hotelling model from section 13.2.2. Assume that seller 1 has chosen its price p_1 in the first stage. Then in step 1, seller 2 maximizes its profit $\pi_2(p_1, p_2) = p_2 q_2 - 4q_2$ where q_2 is given by (13.12). In step 2, solve for BR_2 which is the best-response function given by (13.16): $p_2 = 3 + p_1/2$.

In step 3, knowing that this is how seller 2 will choose its price in stage two of the game, seller 1 incorporates this information into its profit function (13.13) by replacing p_2 with (13.16):

$$\pi_1(p_1) = 250(p_1 - 4)\left(3 + \frac{p_1}{2} - p_1 + 2\right)$$

$$= 125(p_1 - 4)(10 - p_1). \tag{13.18}$$

Finally, in step 4, maximize (13.18) to obtain $p_1^* = \$7$ and $p_2^* = \$6.50$, so ◀◢

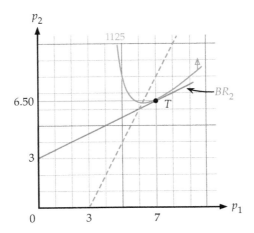

Figure 13.7 The Stackelberg Hotelling equilibrium

the SPNE is $(7, 6.50)$ as shown in Figure 13.7. The Hotelling Stackelberg equilibrium is at the tangency point T which is given by the highest orange isoprofit that firm 1 can attain given the green best-response function of the follower, BR_2. At this point, the Stackelberg quantities are $q_1^* = 375$ and $q_2^* = 625$ and firm profits are $\pi_1^* = \$1125$ and $\pi_2^* = \$1562.50$.

Compared to the outcome of the simultaneous game shown in Figure 13.5 when each firm earned $1000 in profits, both firms now earn higher profits. However, unlike in the Cournot Stackelberg model, the *follower* is relatively better off from having moved second, earning a profit of $1562.50 as opposed to the leader's $1125. The reason for this is that as a follower, it can slightly undercut the market leader's price of $7 by charging $6.50 and gain some extra consumers at the margin, thereby driving up its profit.

The following conclusion is generally valid. When players' choice variables are strategic substitutes, then there is a first-mover advantage in the leader-follower game. However, when players' choice variables are strategic complements, then there is a second-mover advantage in the leader-follower game.

Exercises

13.1. Suppose there are two identical firms, 1 and 2, who compete as Cournot duopolists. The inverse market demand is given by $p = 120 - Q$, where $Q = q_1 + q_2$. Each firm's cost function is given by $c_i(q_i) = q_i^2$, $i = 1, 2$. Calculate the NE quantities, q_1^* and q_2^*, the market price p^*, and firm profits, π_1^* and π_2^*.

13.2. Consider two firms, 1 and 2, which produce an identical product at a marginal cost of $20 per unit for firm 1 and a marginal cost of $10 per unit for firm 2; there are no other costs. They face the inverse market demand curve, $p = 210 - q_1 - q_2$, where q_1 and q_2 are the output levels produced by each firm.

    (a) Suppose both firms produce their output levels simultaneously. What will be the quantities q_1^* and q_2^* produced by firm 1 and firm 2 in a NE? Find the market price p^* and firm profits, π_1^* and π_2^*.

    (b) Now suppose firm 1 is the market leader and produces first. Firm 2, the follower, observes how much firm 1 produces and then chooses its output level. What will be the quantities q_1° and q_2°

produced by firm 1 and firm 2 in a SPNE? Find the market price p° and firm profits, π_1° and π_2°.

13.3. Suppose there are n identical firms in an oligopoly who compete in quantities. The inverse market demand is given by $p = 2520 - Q$, where $Q = \sum_{i=1}^{n} q_i$. Each firm's cost function is given by $c_i(q_i) = 0.5q_i^2 + 32,400$, where $\$32,400$ is the fixed (i.e., sunk) cost of entering this market.

   (a) Calculate the output, q^* produced by a typical firm in a symmetric NE as a function of n. Calculate an expression for the NE profit, π^* as a function of n.

   (b) If there are no barriers to entry, firms will enter the market until a typical firm earns zero profits. How many firms will there be in this market in the long run?

13.4. There are 20 identical firms, each with a cost function

$$c(q) = 0.5q^2 + 30q.$$

The inverse market demand is $p = 250 - Q$, where $Q = \sum_{i=1}^{20} q_i$.

   (a) Calculate the symmetric NE quantity produced by each firm, q^*, and the market equilibrium price, p^*.

   (b) Suppose 10 of the firms receive a $\$22$ per-unit subsidy; call these the low-cost (l) firms. An l-type firm now has a cost function $c_l(q_l) = 0.5(q_l)^2 + 8q_l$. The remaining 10 firms who do not receive a subsidy are the high-cost (h) firms and with cost function $c_h(q_h) = 0.5(q_h)^2 + 30q_h$ as before. Calculate the new Nash equilibrium where all the l-type firms produce q_l°, and the type h firms produce q_h°. Calculate new market equilibrium price, p°.

13.5. Consider an asymmetric Hotelling model where firm 1 has a retail location at the extreme left of a mile-long Main Street, while firm 2 is located at the other extreme. There are 100 consumers who are evenly distributed over this market. The value of the product sold is $v = \$10$ to any consumer. The marginal cost of production is $\$1.40$ per unit to firm 1 and $\$3.20$ to firm 2; there are no other costs. The transportation cost is $\$1$ per mile. Calculate the NE prices (p_1^*, p_2^*), the associated quantities (q_1^*, q_2^*), and profits (π_1^*, π_2^*).

13.6. Consider the Bowley-Dixit duopoly model of price competition where firms 1 and 2 produce similar goods and sell them at p_1 and p_2. The demand for each firm's product is given by

$$q_1 = 120 - p_1 + sp_2 \quad \text{and} \quad q_2 = 120 + sp_1 - p_2,$$

where s is a parameter that governs how similar the products are and $|s| < 1$. If $s = 0$, the goods are totally unrelated and each firm has a monopoly over its good. If $0 < s < 1$, then the products are substitutes (a dollar increase in the price of one good increases the demand for the other). If $-1 < s < 0$, then the products are complements (a dollar increase in the price of one good decreases the demand for the other). Marginal costs of producing either good are assumed to be zero. Suppose $s = 0.8$. Calculate the symmetric NE prices, quantities, and profits.

13.7. There is an original manufacturer that makes a popular software priced at p_o dollars, and a copy-pirate that sells illegal copies of the software for p_c dollars. A potential buyer's value for the software, v, ranges from $0 to $300 — you may think of this range as the length of the market. There are 1500 potential buyers who are evenly distributed over the length of the market, i.e., the density of consumers is 5 persons per dollar. A consumer with valuation v has a utility function $u(v)$ given by

$$u(v) = \begin{cases} v - p_o & \text{if she buys the original software,} \\ vs - p_c & \text{if she buys the pirated software,} \\ 0 & \text{if she does not buy.} \end{cases}$$

The parameter s $(0 < s < 1)$ is fixed and shows the quality of the pirated software. If $s = 1$, the pirated software is as good as the original, and if $s = 0$, the pirated software does not work at all. The copy-pirate sets $s = 0.5$, so the pirated software is neither as good as the original (e.g., because it does not come with support services) but nor is it useless. Consider a leader-follower model of price competition where the monopoly firm produces and sells the software first, followed by the copy-pirate.

(a) The marginal buyer who is indifferent between buying the original software and the pirated copy must get the same utility from either choice. Calculate the valuation v^* of this buyer as a function of p_o and p_c.

(b) The marginal buyer who is indifferent between buying the pirated software and not buying anything must get the same utility from either choice. Calculate the valuation v° of this buyer as a function of p_c.

(c) Any consumer whose valuation lies between v^* and \$300 will want to buy the original software. Using the fact that the density of consumers is 5 persons per dollar, find the total demand for the original software, q_m, as a function of p_o and p_c.

(d) Any consumer whose valuation lies between v° and v^* will want to buy the pirated copy. Using the fact that the density of consumers is 5 persons per dollar, find the total demand for the pirated software, q_c, as a function of p_o and p_c.

(e) Assuming that each firm's cost of production is zero, write down the profit functions for the original manufacturer, $\pi_o(p_o, p_c)$, and the copy-pirate, $\pi_c(p_o, p_c)$. Calculate the SPNE (p_o^*, p_c^*) when the original firm is the leader and the copy-pirate is the follower. Find the equilibrium quantities sold by each firm, (q_o^*, q_c^*) and the profits of the firms, (π_o^*, π_c^*) at the SPNE.

13.8. In a two-tier market, there are two upstream firms, U_1 and U_2, and two downstream firms, D_1 and D_2. Consider the following dynamic game. In stage one, the upstream firms produce y_1 and y_2 quantities of the same good at zero cost and sell it at a wholesale price, w, to the two downstream retailers. In stage two, the two downstream firms sell quantities q_1 and q_2 at a price p to consumers whose inverse market demand is given by $p = 180 - Q$, where $Q = q_1 + q_2$. The only costs incurred by the downstream firms is the per-unit cost, w, of acquiring the goods. Find the SPNE quantities q_1^* and q_2^*, retail price p^*, and wholesale price w^*.

(*Hint:* Suppose that the upstream firms have set the wholesale price w. Solve for the stage two symmetric downstream Cournot quantity, q^*, as a function of w. Then find the total quantity, Q^*, sold downstream; this equals $y_1 + y_2$. Invert this function to obtain w as a function of y_1 and y_2; this is the inverse demand facing the upstream producers in stage one. Finally, solve the stage one upstream symmetric equilibrium.)

Chapter 14

Externalities

An **externality** is the accompanying impact (whether positive or negative) of one agent's consumption or production activity on the utility or technology of another, where this impact is independent of markets or prices. For instance, a smoker's second-hand cigarette smoke that causes a bystander to have an asthma attack is a negative consumption externality. When a nurse gets a flu shot, she not only reduces her own chances of catching the flu, but also reduces the likelihood of transmitting the virus to others, a positive consumption externality. Similarly, the classic example from 1879 England of a confectioner's machinery making it difficult for a cardiologist next door to listen to the heartbeat of his patients is a negative production externality.

Because externalities are external to the workings of markets, the prices at which trades occur do not reflect their additional costs (in the case of negative externalities) or benefits (in the case of positive externalities). Consequently, the First Welfare Theorem typically fails, i.e., in the presence of externalities, the Walras allocation is generally no longer Pareto efficient. We begin by illustrating this inefficiency and then consider three "solutions" that have been suggested to mitigate these problems and that have influenced government policy towards externalities.

14.1 Market Inefficiencies

14.1.1 Consumption externalities

Suppose a and b are the only two consumers in our economy, there are two goods x and y, and a's endowment is $\omega^a = (0,1)$ while b's is $\omega^b = (1,0)$.

242

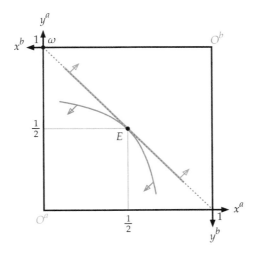

Figure 14.1 Walras equilibrium

Further suppose that their utility functions are given by

$$u^a(x^a, y^a, x^b) = x^a + y^a - 0.5x^b \text{ and } u^b(x^b, y^b) = x^b y^b.$$

Here b's preferences are Cobb-Douglas, but while a's preferences are linear in her own consumption of x^a and y^a, x^b also enters a's utility function as a 'bad'. In other words, consumer a has no part in choosing x^b but derives a negative utility from b's consumption of the x good. So from a's point of view, her indifference curves are linear with slope -1 as shown in Figure 14.1. Therefore, in this Edgeworth box economy, the Walras equilibrium is at point E where both goods are priced at \$1 and $(x^a, y^a) = (1/2, 1/2)$ and $(x^b, y^b) = (1/2, 1/2)$: consumer a gives up half a unit of y for half a unit of x along the dotted blue budget line in Figure 14.1.

However, the allocation at E is not Pareto efficient. To see this, look at this two-person economy from the viewpoint of society or that of a social planner. Such a planner knows that total amount of x in this economy adds up to unity, hence $x^b = 1 - x^a$. Substituting this in a's utility function to obtain $u^a = x^a + y^a - 0.5(1 - x^a) = 1.5x^a + y^a - 0.5$, we obtain a's utility function from the perspective of the social planner: a's indifference curves are linear in x^a and y^a with slope -1.5 as shown by the orange dashed indifference curve in Figure 14.2. In other words, while the **private** MRS^a between the two goods appears to be 1 from a's personal perspective, after the negative externality has been accounted for, the **social** MRS^a is 1.5.

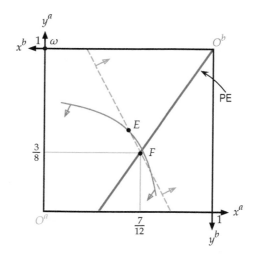

Figure 14.2   Pareto inefficiency

To find the (interior) contract curve for this Edgeworth box economy with externalities, we need to set the *social* marginal rates of substitution for each person equal to each other. For a, we have seen this to be 1.5; for b, it is simply y^b/x^b (the social MRS^b is the same as consumer b's private MRS^b since b is not affected by any externalities). Setting them equal to each other and using the fact that $x^b = 1 - x^a$ and $y^b = 1 - y^a$, we get

$$y^a = -0.5 + 1.5x^a,$$

which is the set of interior Pareto efficient allocations for this economy with externalities and is shown by the blue line in Figure 14.2. Since the Walras allocation E is not on this contract curve, it is not Pareto efficient. To verify this, note that at E, the utility levels of the consumers are $u^a(1/2,1/2,1/2) = 0.75$[1] and $u^b(1/2,1/2) = 0.25$. However, at F where $(x^a,y^a) = (7/12,3/8)$ and $(x^b,y^b) = (5/12,5/8)$, $u^a(7/12,3/8,5/12) = 0.75$ so consumer a is no worse off, but $u^b(5/12,5/8) = 25/96 \approx 0.26$, so b is better off.

14.1.2   Production externalities

An acid factory, A, is located upstream from a fishery, F, along a river. Firm A is allowed to dump some chemical waste into the river which causes the

---

[1]Note that consumer a's utility has three variables because it depends on a's own consumption of both goods as well as b's consumption of good x.

downstream firm F to have to clean up the water before it can be used for pisciculture. Denote the acid output by a and the fish output by f. If acid sells for $36 per unit and firm A's cost function is $c^A(a) = a^2$, then the acid factory's profit function is $\pi^A(a) = 36a - a^2$. Similarly, suppose fish sells for $48 per unit and firm F's cost function is $c^F(f, a) = f^2 + af$. The af term in the cost function captures the impact of the negative externality, indicating that the greater the level of acid production, the greater the cost incurred by the fishery in cleaning up the water. Then the fishery's profit function is $\pi^F(f, a) = 48f - f^2 - af$.

Under free market conditions, firm A maximizes its profit and produces $a^* = 18$ units of acid, earning a profit of $324. Given this level of acid production, firm F maximizes its profit and produces $f^* = 15$ units of fish, earning $225. However, this pair of profit levels is not Pareto efficient because it is possible for at least one firm to earn higher profits without hurting the other.

To see this, imagine that both firms merge. Call this vertically integrated firm M, which has two divisions, the upstream acid division and the downstream fishery division. Then firm M would maximize the joint profit from the divisions, i.e.,

$$\pi^M = \pi^A + \pi^F = 36a - a^2 + 48f - f^2 - af.$$

In doing so, note that M internalizes the externality, i.e., takes into account the negative impact that division A has on division F's profits. Maximizing M's profits with respect to a and f, we obtain

$$\frac{\partial \pi^M}{\partial a} = 36 - 2a° - f° = 0 \tag{14.1}$$

$$\frac{\partial \pi^M}{\partial f} = 48 - 2f° - a° = 0. \tag{14.2}$$

Solving (14.1) and (14.2) simultaneously, we obtain $a° = 8$ and $f° = 20$. Firm M's profits are then $624 which is the largest combined profit possible by the divisions A and F; indeed, we will (loosely) call $a° = 8$ the Pareto efficient level of acid production.[2] If $324 of M's profit is given to A, then A is as well off as before the merger and the fishery is better off with the remaining $300.

But how can the separate firms achieve this Pareto superior situation without merging? One way would be for firm F to convince firm A to reduce its acid production from 18 units to 8 with the assurance that firm F

---

[2]To look at Pareto efficiency more rigorously in this context, we would need a general equilibrium model with at least one consumer and two producers, which is beyond the scope of this text.

would make up the remainder of A's profit and guarantee that firm A continues to make at least \$324. Indeed, it is possible for both firms to be better off relative to the free market profit levels through such bilateral negotiation.

14.2 Three 'Solutions'

There are several ways to mitigate the inefficiencies that arise from externalities, all of them imperfect in some regard. The most crude of these is **direct regulation** which involves the direct intervention by some governmental body (for example, the US Environmental Protection Agency). However, of particular interest are three partial solutions (hence the quotes in the title of this section) associated with the names of Arthur Pigou, Kenneth Arrow and Ronald Coase which have been extremely influential in formulating economic policy when externalities are present. The nature of the intervention differs in the three cases and these are considered in greater detail below.

14.2.1 Pigou: Taxes or subsidies

Pigou's idea is a step removed from direct regulation and uses the notion that appropriately taxing an entity that is imposing a negative externality or subsidizing one whose economic activity is associated with positive externalities can mitigate the problem.

To see how this may work in the context of the production externality from section 14.1.2, suppose a tax of t per unit is imposed on acid production, so firm A's profit function is then $\pi^A(a) = 36a - a^2 - ta$. Then the derivative with respect to a is $36 - 2a - t$, and when $a^\circ = 8$, this derivative equals zero if $t = 20$. Thus a per-unit tax of \$20 induces firm A to maximize its profit by producing the Pareto efficient level of acid production.

Of course this intervention has distributional consequences: firm A's profit plummets to \$64 under Pigovian taxation (down from the free market profit of \$324), while firm F's profit goes to \$400 (up from \$225). As opposed to the total free market firm profits of $\$225 + \$324 = \$549$, the gains from trade under the tax includes the aggregate profit of $\$64 + \$400 = \$464$ plus the tax revenue of \$160, a grand total of \$624.

The biggest limitation of Pigou's idea is that while in principle it can redress the inefficiency arising from an externality, the information necessary to set the tax/subsidy rates appropriately so as not to overshoot or undershoot the target is not readily available. Yet, much of the taxation of harmful substances with significant negative externalities (such as tobacco or alcohol) or the subsidization of flu shots or public education where there are believed to be significant positive externalities is based on this idea and is widely practiced all over the world.

14.2.2   Arrow: Missing markets

An important idea associated with Kenneth Arrow in the context of externalities is that of a **missing market**. For instance, while electricity is a traded product, there is a missing market for the ancillary pollution. By creating an artificial market for the externality, the externality may be turned into a traded commodity and thus 'internalized'. If the market for the externality is perfectly competitive, i.e., all traders behave as price-takers, then presumably the Walras equilibrium where the commodity space has been expanded to include the externality will again be Pareto efficient. We examine two mechanisms for regulating pollution externalities that call for trade in emissions: **emission taxes** and **cap-and-trade**.[3]

Emission taxes

Suppose there are three electric power plants that currently emit 10 tons of sulfur dioxide (SO_2) each into the atmosphere. Each plant faces a total abatement cost (TAC) function given by $TAC_1 = e_1^2/2$, $TAC_2 = e_2^2/4$, and $TAC_3 = e_3^2/6$, where e_j is the emission abatement of plant $j = 1, 2, 3$. Then the corresponding marginal abatement costs are $MAC_1 = e_1$, $MAC_2 = e_2/2$, and $MAC_3 = e_3/3$ as shown in the left panel of Figure 14.3. If the government wishes to reduce the total SO_2 emissions by 12 tons, one way to do this would be through direct regulation by requiring each firm to cut back emissions, say, by 4 tons each. The total cost of reducing pollution through this direct regulation would then be approximately \$14.67 ($= 8 + 4 + 2.67$).

This, however, is not the cheapest way to attain the goal of 12 tons of pollution reduction. If you have studied joint total costs in section 8.4, you will recognize the analogy: we want 12 units of emission reduction to be 'produced' between the three plants in the cheapest way possible. Construct the

---

[3]Cap-and-trade mechanisms have also been implemented to regulate commercial fishing in many parts of the world and prevent overfishing. The regulator establishes a total allowable catch by weight per period of time and allocates individual tradable quotas (ITQs) to fishing operators to limit the extraction.

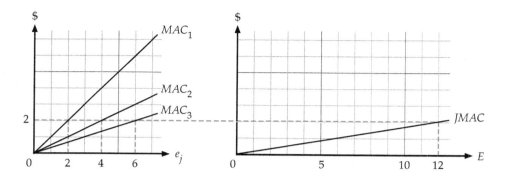

Figure 14.3   Emission reductions

joint marginal abatement cost[4] (*JMAC*) by horizontally summing the three *MAC* curves as shown in the right panel of Figure 14.3. Then $JMAC = E/6$, where $E = \sum_{j=1}^{3} e_j$ is the aggregate emission reduction. For the desired 12 tons of emission reduction, the *JMAC* level is \$2, so the least cost to society of achieving this reduction is when the *MAC* for each plant from the last unit of emission reduced is \$2. Thus the socially cost-efficient emission abatement occurs when $e_1 = 2, e_2 = 4$, and $e_3 = 6$ tons which costs only \$12 in all.

If the government knew the individual *MACs*, then in principle it can engage in direct regulation and ask the first plant to reduce by 2, the second by 4, and the third by 6 tons to achieve this socially cost-efficient emission reduction. However, abatement costs are typically private information known to the power plants and not available to the government. An alternative way to achieve this goal would then be to set an emission tax (i.e., the price of an unit of emission) of \$2 per ton of SO_2.

Then, from the left panel of Figure 14.3, the marginal abatement cost for plant 1, MAC_1, is cheaper than the tax of \$2 per unit for the first two units of emission. Therefore, firm 1 would rather cut back 2 tons of emission than pay the tax on those units. Similarly, firm 2's marginal abatement cost is lower than the emission tax for up to 4 tons of emission, and for up to 6 tons for firm 3. Therefore, firms 2 and 3 would reduce their emissions by 4 and 6 tons respectively instead of paying a tax, bringing about the desired overall reduction in emission in the most cost-efficient manner. Note that the government does not need any of the firms' private information about about

---

[4]This is often called the social marginal abatement cost.

abatement costs; it merely has to raise the emission tax up from zero until the desired level of pollution reduction is attained. This is precisely the idea of a carbon tax that has been under consideration to reduce greenhouse gas emissions.

Cap-and-trade

An alternative to the emission tax is a cap-and-trade regime. To understand this, we need to modify the story above. Suppose the total amount of SO_2 produced by the three plants currently is 30 tons, where plants 1, 2, and 3 respectively produce 12, 10, and 8 tons. The government wants to cap (i.e., limit) the total emission at 18 tons, i.e., reduce pollution by 12 tons. It therefore issues 18 pollution permits, where each permit allows a plant to emit one ton of pollution. These permits are then distributed among the three firms, say, 7 permits being given to plant 1, 5 to plant 2, and 6 to the plant 3, as shown in second and third columns of Table 14.1.[5]

Plant	Pollution level	Permits	Abatement at $3	Trade
1	12	7	3	+2
2	10	5	6	−1
3	8	6	9	−7

Table 14.1   Permit trading at $3 per permit

To understand how the market for pollution permits reaches an equilibrium, suppose the current market price is $3 per permit. Then from MAC_1, $e_1 = 3$ (i.e., plant 1 wishes to abate 3 tons). Similarly, from MAC_2 and MAC_3, plants 2 and 3 wish to abate 6 and 9 tons respectively, as shown in the fourth column of Table 14.1. From the top row of this table, since plant 1 emits 12 tons of pollution for which it has 7 permits from the government plus another 3 it abates, it has a net demand for 2 permits (indicated by the '+2' in the 'Trade' column). Plant 2 which emits 10 tons of pollution, has 5 permits from the government and wishes to abate 6 tons, which leaves it with an excess of 1 pollution permit which it wants to sell (indicated by the '−1' in the 'Trade' column). Verify that plant 3 would want to sell 7 permits. From

---

[5]How these permits are apportioned has distributional consequences — they affect the profit levels of the firms — but has no impact in reducing the level of emissions in the socially cost-efficient manner. In practice, these are sometimes distributed as a proportion of the output of each firm. Alternatively, they can be auctioned off unit by unit to the highest bidder.

the last column in Table 14.1, the net trade is negative, i.e., there is an excess supply of permits when its price is $3 per unit. If the market for emission permits is competitive enough, the permit price will drop to equilibrate demand and supply.[6]

Plant	Pollution level	Permits	Abatement at $2	Trade
1	12	7	2	+3
2	10	5	4	+1
3	8	6	6	−4

Table 14.2   Permit trading at $2 per permit

Suppose then that the price for a pollution permit drops from $3 a ton to $2. Table 14.2 recalculates the last two columns in Table 14.1. Now the demand for permits (3 + 1 by the first two plants) equals the supply of permits (4 by the third plant), so the market equilibrium price for pollution permits is $2 per ton and each plant chooses to abate emissions in a socially cost-efficient manner.

Whether the creation of a market for emission permits would lead to Pareto efficiency or not cannot be addressed in this partial equilibrium example. But in principle, carbon taxes or pollution permits could mitigate the negative effects of the externality.

14.2.3   Coase: Property rights

Ronald Coase, the 1991 Economics Nobel Prize recipient, emphasized the importance of defining property rights in mitigating the problems arising from externalities. He suggested that the role of the government should be limited to assigning property rights and enabling their enforcement in the courts. The affected parties can then mutually negotiate a Pareto efficient outcome provided the transactions costs of doing so are very low. He is probably best known for the so-called Coase "theorem" which he never formally stated but is generally interpreted as follows:

---

[6]One of the limitations of the missing-markets approach is that if there are only a few participants, then firms may behave strategically to manipulate the market price rather than behave competitively as price-takers. Even though this example has only three plants and so the market for permits is thin, we assume that they behave as price takers, driving the permit price down in case of excess supply, and up in case of excess demand.

> The equilibrium level of an externality is invariant of the assign-
> ment of property rights (including the assignment of liability for
> damage) so long as there are no transactions costs or income ef-
> fects.

In other words, if a firm pollutes and causes harm to others, the equilibrium level of the externality will be the same, regardless of whether the
firm has the right to pollute, or the harmed have the right to clean air, or any
other in-between assignment of this right. In this subsection, we analyze the
conditions under which the level of externality may be independent of the
assignment of property rights.

A smoker (a) and a non-smoker (b) are roommates. Their utility functions
are given by $u^a(x_a, s) = x_a + \ln s$ and $u^b(x_b, s) = x_b + 4\ln(1 - s)$, where x is
food (a commodity that both care about), s is smoke that gives a pleasure but
imposes a negative externality on b, where $0 \leq s \leq 1$ (the maximum 'quantity' of smoke is normalized to unity). Suppose that the maximum amount
of smoke can be allocated as pollution rights y_a and y_b to each person, where
$y_a + y_b = 1$. Then we can reformulate the utility functions as standard quasilinear utilities: $u^a(x_a, y_a) = x_a + \ln y_a$ and $u^b(x_b, y_b) = x_b + 4\ln y_b$ with horizontally parallel indifference curves as shown in the Edgeworth box in Fig-
ure 14.4. Therefore, neither consumer has any income effects for y, the good
associated with the externality, which is one of the preconditions for Coase's
"theorem".

Suppose the initial endowment is at $\omega = ((5, 0), (5, 1))$. The value of
$y_a = 0$ at ω indicates that a does not have the right to smoke. Similarly, the
endowment $\omega' = ((5, 1), (5, 0))$ shows the same levels of the x goods for each
person as at ω, but where a has the complete right to smoke. Thus sliding
the endowment point up between ω and ω' along the dashed magenta line
depicts all the alternative property rights regimes possible. The set of (interior) Pareto efficient allocations is given by the tangency of the indifference
curves and is the horizontal blue line in Figure 14.4 with a constant level of
the externality commodity, $y_a = 0.2$.

Now suppose a and b can trade property rights for units of x. Coase
did not specify the negotiating mechanism used by the affected parties, only
that the mechanism be one with zero transactions costs. Since we know
the Walras mechanism for pure exchange economies and it is operated with
zero transactions cost, we may use this specific mechanism to illustrate what
Coase had in mind. We will, therefore, solve for the Walras equilibrium for

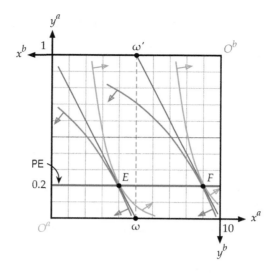

Figure 14.4   The Coase invariance outcome

the case when a has no right to smoke (endowment ω) and also when she does have the right to smoke (endowment ω').

The demands for individuals a and b are

$$x_a = \frac{m_a}{p_x} - 1 \quad \text{and} \quad y_a = \frac{p_x}{p_y}$$

$$x_b = \frac{m_b}{p_x} - 4 \quad \text{and} \quad y_a = \frac{4p_x}{p_y},$$

where p_x is normalized to $1 and $m_a = 5$ and $m_b = 5 + p_y$ at ω. Solving for the Walras equilibrium prices, we obtain $(\hat{p}_x, \hat{p}_y) = (1, 2)$ and the Walras allocation $E = ((4, 0.2), (6, 0.8))$ in Figure 14.4 which is Pareto efficient since it lies on the blue contract curve.

Now consider the case where the initial endowment was at ω' instead. The Walras allocation now is at $F = ((9, 0.2), (1, 0.8))$: b exchanges part of her initial amount of x to buy back some of the smoking rights from a. The outcome is once again Pareto efficient, and because the contract curve is horizontal, the level of the externality does not change with the allocation of the property rights. For different initial allocation of property rights on the magenta dashed line from ω to ω', the Walras allocation will end up somewhere between E and F. While the amount of x each person ends up with will depend on who is purchasing property rights — distributional effects that result from who is 'bribing' the other to either allow smoking or curtail smoking — the level of the externality is always constant at $y_a = 0.2$ which illustrates Coase's "theorem".

The invariance of the level of externality with the allocation of property rights relies on there being a horizontal (interior) contract curve. Quasilinear preferences are sufficient to generate this, but are they necessary? In other words, are there other (non-quasilinear) preferences that give rise to hori- zontal contract curves? The answer is yes, but it is a very a narrow class of preferences.[7] In other words, horizontal contract curves are likely to be un- common. So with arbitrary preferences and no transactions costs, the alloca- tion of the property right *does* make a difference to the *level* of the externality even in theory (though the allocation reached will still be Pareto efficient). Understanding this limits the appeal of Coase's "theorem". Given that ne- gotiations between affected parties typically involve lawyers and court set- tlements, the transactions costs in practice are formidable, further reducing this theorem's applicability.

Exercises

14.1. There are two consumers, a and b, in an economy with two goods x and y, and an initial endowment $\omega = ((0,1),(1,0))$. The utility functions of the consumers are

$$u^a(x^a, y^a, x^b) = x^a + 1.5y^a + 0.5x^b,$$
$$u^b(x^b, y^b) = x^b y^b.$$

They each choose their consumption levels of the goods independently but b's consumption of the x good confers a positive externality on a.

(a) Find the contract curve for this two-person Edgeworth box.

(b) Find a Walras equilibrium. Is it Pareto efficient? Explain why or why not.

14.2. Romeo and Juliet are the only two consumers in an economy with two goods x and y, and Romeo's endowment is $\omega^R = (0,1)$ while Juliet's is $\omega^J = (1,0)$. They each choose their consumption levels of the goods

---

[7]See Chipman and Tian (2011) 'Detrimental externalities, pollution rights, and the "Coase theorem"' in *Economic Theory*, 49, pp. 309–307 for details.

independently. But because they are madly in love, they get satisfaction not only from their own consumption of the goods but also from the other's consumption of both goods:

$$u^R(x^R, y^R, x^J, y^J) = x^R y^R + x^J + y^J,$$
$$u^J(x^R, y^R, x^J, y^J) = x^J y^J + x^R + y^R.$$

(a) Find the contract curve for this two-person Edgeworth box.

(b) Find a Walras equilibrium. Is it Pareto efficient? Explain why or why not.

14.3. In the production externality example from section 14.1.2, suppose the firms are producing $a^* = 18$ and $f^* = 15$ units under free market conditions. Consider two alternative property rights regimes.

(a) Suppose the upstream acid firm is liable for the damage it causes to the downstream fishery: it has to compensate the fishery af. Calculate how many units of acid ($\bar{a}$) and fish ($\bar{f}$) will be produced and the firm profits, $\bar{\pi}^A$ and $\bar{\pi}^F$.

(b) Suppose the upstream acid firm is *not* liable for the damage it causes to the downstream fishery. The fishery is willing to pay a bribe of b dollars to the acid producer for cutting back the production of acid to the Pareto efficient level of $a^\circ = 8$ units. What is the minimum bribe, b_{min}, that firm A will be willing to accept? What is the maximum bribe, b_{max}, that firm F is willing to pay?

(c) Does the Coase "theorem" hold here? Explain why or why not.

14.4. An economy consists of two consumers, labeled a and b. There are two commodities, x and y, that can be traded. Good x is food and is desired by each consumer. However, y is a good for person a but a 'bad' for person b. We interpret y^a as the level of smoke consumed by person a, while $y^b = 1 - y^a$ is the level of remaining clean air consumed by b. The utility functions and demands of each consumer is given in the table below:

Person i	u^i	x^i	y^i
a	$x^a + \ln y^a$	$(m^a/p_x) - 1$	p_x/p_y
b	$x^b + 2\ln y^b$	$(m^b/p_x) - 2$	$2p_x/p_y$

In the table, m^a and m^b refer to the value of each consumer's endowment. The price of y (for the right to smoke or clean air) is normalized to $1; for simplicity, write p_x as just p.

(a) Suppose $w = ((3,0),(3,1))$. Draw the set of interior Pareto efficient allocations in an Edgeworth box for this economy.

(b) Suppose $w' = ((3,0),(3,1))$. We interpret this initial endowment to be the case where person a does not have the right to smoke, i.e., person b has the right to clean air. Suppose a and b can trade food for the right to smoke. Find the Walras equilibrium price of x, $\tilde{p}$, for this economy and the Walras allocation $((\tilde{x}^a, \tilde{y}^a), (\tilde{x}^b, \tilde{y}^b))$. Draw the Walras budget and Walras allocation in the Edgeworth box.

(c) Suppose $w = ((3,1),(3,0))$. We interpret this initial endowment to be the case where person a does have the right to smoke, i.e., person b does not have the right to clean air. Suppose a and b can trade food for the right to smoke. Find the Walras equilibrium price of x, $\hat{p}$, for this economy and the Walras allocation $((\hat{x}^a, \hat{y}^a), (\hat{x}^b, \hat{y}^b))$. Draw the Walras budget and Walras allocation in the Edgeworth box.

(d) Does the Coase "theorem" hold here? Explain why or why not.

14.5. An economy consists of two consumers, labeled a and b. There are two commodities, x and y, that can be traded. Good x is food and is desired by each consumer. However, y is a good for person a but a 'bad' for person b. We interpret y^a as the level of smoke consumed by person a, while $y^b = 1 - y^a$ is the level of remaining clean air consumed by b. The utility functions and demands of each consumer is given in the table below:

Person i	u^i	x^i	y^i
a	$\ln x^a + \ln y^a$	$m^a / 2 p_x$	$m^a / 2 p_y$
b	$\ln x^b + 3 \ln y^b$	$m^b / 4 p_x$	$3 m^b / 4 p_y$

In the table, m^a and m^b refer to the value of each consumer's endowment. The price of y (for the right to smoke or clean air) is normalized to $1; for simplicity, write p_x as just p.

(a) Suppose $w = ((4,0),(4,1))$. We interpret this initial endowment to be the case where person a does not have the right to smoke, i.e., person b has the right to clean air. Suppose a and b can trade food for the right to smoke. Find the Walras equilibrium price of x, $\tilde{p}$, for this economy and the Walras allocation $((\tilde{x}^a, \tilde{y}^a),(\tilde{x}^b, \tilde{y}^b))$. Is this Walras allocation Pareto efficient?

(b) Suppose $w = ((4,1),(4,0))$. We interpret this initial endowment to be the case where person a does have the right to smoke, i.e., person b does not have the right to clean air. Suppose a and b can trade food for the right to smoke. Find the Walras equilibrium price of x, $\hat{p}$, for this economy and the Walras allocation $((\hat{x}^a, \hat{y}^a),(\hat{x}^b, \hat{y}^b))$. Is this Walras allocation Pareto efficient?

(c) Does the Coase "theorem" hold here? Explain why or why not.

Chapter 15

Asymmetric Information

Information asymmetry deals with transactions where one party possesses private information, i.e., information that is not known to the other party. In this chapter, we study two canonical models covering the two basic types of information asymmetry, hidden action and hidden information.

In hidden action (or moral hazard) models, there are two parties called a principal and an agent in a vertical relationship. The principal (henceforth assumed to be female) employs the agent (a male) to undertake some action that she cannot observe. Undertaking the action is costly, so the agent has an incentive to shirk. The principal has to write a contract based on the observable output generated by the agent so as to induce him to undertake an action that is optimal from her perspective. While she runs the risk of not compensating him enough to motivate him to work hard, he runs the risk of working hard but getting inadequately compensated because hard work is not perfectly reflected in the output generated. Thus principal-agent contracts are predicated on optimal risk-sharing between the two parties.

In hidden information (or adverse selection) models, typically there is one principal and many heterogeneous agents. Each agent knows his own type but the principal cannot distinguish one agent type from another. However, she knows the distribution of types and has to design a contract so that the decisions of agents is optimal in terms of her objective.

An example of this is the unit-demand bundling example from section 10.5: the tomato farmer is the principal who faces two types of agents, parents or singles, and has to decide whether to sell organic tomatoes only to everyone (a pooling equilibrium), or produce both organic and regular tomatoes targeting them to parents and singles appropriately (a separating equilibrium), or just producing organic tomatoes for parents only (a **semi-separating equilibrium**).

The study of various aspects of information in economics has burgeoned since the 1970s and several luminaries have received the Nobel Prize in Economics for their contribution: James Mirrlees and William Vickrey in 1996, George Akerlof, Michael Spence and Joseph Stiglitz in 2001, and Leonid Hurwicz, Eric Maskin and Roger Myerson in 2007.

15.1   Hidden Action

Consider a risk-averse agent indexed by a and a risk-neutral principal ("the boss") indexed by b who behave as vNM expected utility maximizers. The agent, who is a salesperson in the store owned by the principal, can choose to be attentive to potential customers when they come in (i.e., exert a high effort level, e_H), or ignore them (exert a low effort level, e_L). The principal cannot observe this effort because she has left the agent in charge of the store. When the principal returns, she finds that either there was a low sales revenue of $x_L = \$300$ or a high one of $x_H = \$500$. However, she cannot infer whether the agent put in a high effort or not. This is because the probability of generating sales of $500 when he has put in the high effort is $p_H = 0.8$, while the probability of generating the same sales when he has put in a low effort is $p_L = 0.4$. In other words, the high outcome is possible regardless of the agent's effort, though the probability is higher when he works hard.

The principal, being risk-neutral, has a utility function that is linear in her income y:

$$u^b(y) = y.$$

Here $y = x - w$ is the difference between the sales revenue and the wage paid to the agent. Because she can only observe the sales revenue, she offers a wage that is contingent on the level of the sales revenue: a low wage of w_L if $x_L = \$300$ is observed, or a high wage of w_H if $x_H = \$500$ is the outcome. This pair of wages (w_L, w_H) is called a **wage contract**. Then her income is either $y_L = x_L - w_L = 300 - w_L$ or $y_H = x_H - w_H = 500 - w_H$, depending on the level of sales revenue observed.

Denoting her expected utility by V^b, the principal's expected utility when the agent undertakes the high effort e_H is

$$V^b_{e_H} = p_H y_H + (1 - p_H) y_L = 0.8(500 - w_H) + 0.2(300 - w_L)$$
$$= 460 - (0.8 w_H + 0.2 w_L). \tag{15.1}$$

Similarly, her expected utility when the agent undertakes the low effort e_L is given by

$$V_{e_L}^b = p_L y_H + (1 - p_L) y_L = 0.4(500 - w_H) + 0.6(300 - w_L)$$
$$= 380 - (0.4 w_H + 0.6 w_L). \tag{15.2}$$

The agent's utility depends on the wage received, w, and the effort, e, exerted:

$$u^a(w, e) = \sqrt{w} - d(e),$$

where $\sqrt{w}$ shows the utility from the wage, and $d(e)$ is the disutility of effort. The disutility from the low effort is $d(e_L) = 4$, while the disutility from the high effort is $d(e_H) = 6$, capturing the notion that a higher level of effort is more distasteful. Also note that because his utility from the wage is concave in w (recall sections 11.2 and 11.4), the agent is risk-averse.

When the agent receives a wage contract (w_H, w_L), his expected utility from undertaking the high effort is

$$V_{e_H}^a = p_H[\sqrt{w_H} - d(e_H)] + (1 - p_H)[\sqrt{w_L} - d(e_H)]$$
$$= 0.8\sqrt{w_H} + 0.2\sqrt{w_L} - 6, \tag{15.3}$$

while his expected utility from undertaking the low effort is

$$V_{e_L}^a = p_L[\sqrt{w_H} - d(e_L)] + (1 - p_L)[\sqrt{w_L} - d(e_L)]$$
$$= 0.4\sqrt{w_H} + 0.6\sqrt{w_L} - 4. \tag{15.4}$$

This wage contract is a take-it-or-leave-it offer made by the principal: if the agent does not accept this contract, he has an outside option (the possibility of doing something other than working for the principal) which yields a reservation utility of $\bar{u} = 8$. The contract once accepted cannot be renegotiated.

15.1.1 Wage contract under full information

In order to understand the impact of asymmetric information, let us see what would be an optimal wage contract when the principal can observe the agent's action. We will call this the first-best wage contract. In this case, because the principal is risk-neutral and the agent is risk-averse, we know from Chapter 11 that she will offer him full insurance, i.e., she will set $w_L = w_H = \hat{w}$. Since the principal can observe the agent's effort, we

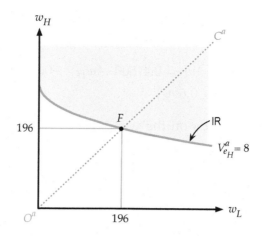

Figure 15.1   First-best wage contract

assume that she is able to enforce an effort level that is the best from her perspective. Therefore, the wage contract is set so that the agent undertakes the high effort, and because he has to choose this effort level voluntarily, this wage contract must leave him as well off as his reservation utility, i.e.,

$$V^a_{e_H} \geq 8. \tag{15.5}$$

Equation (15.5) is called the agent's **individual rationality (IR) constraint.**[1] Writing this out explicitly

$$0.8\sqrt{w_H} + 0.2\sqrt{w_L} - 6 \geq 8, \tag{15.6}$$

replace $w_L = w_H = \hat{w}$ and solve to obtain $\hat{w} \geq 196$. Thus a sure wage of $196 is just sufficient to guarantee that the agent willingly undertakes the high effort and is as well off working for the principal than in his alternative occupation. Given this first-best wage contract $(\hat{w}, \hat{w}) = (196, 196)$, the principal's expected utility can be calculated from (15.1):

$$460 - (0.2\hat{w} + 0.8\hat{w}) = 460 - 196 = 264. \tag{15.7}$$

In Figure 15.1, the axes depict the wages in a contingent claims environment: w_L and w_H are the wages offered in the contract contingent on the observed output being low or high. The expected utility of the agent when the

---

[1]Synonymously, this is sometimes called the agent's **participation constraint.**

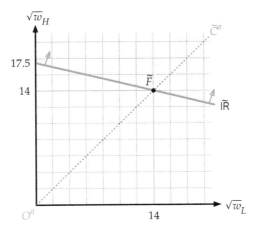

Figure 15.2   First-best utility contract

IR constraint (15.6) holds with equality is labeled IR; the shaded area shows all those wage contracts that satisfy the IR constraint. The line of certainty is the dotted magenta diagonal C^a. Under full insurance, the wage contract $F = (196, 196)$ shows the lowest wage combination that the principal can choose and ensure that the agent undertakes the high effort and obtains his reservation utility.

An alternative graphical depiction of the first-best contract is shown in Figure 15.2 where the axes show the *utility* from the wages, $\sqrt{w}_L$ and $\sqrt{w}_H$, rather than the wages themselves. Rewriting the agent's IR constraint (15.6), we get

$$\sqrt{w}_H \geq 17.5 - 0.25\sqrt{w}_L \qquad (15.8)$$

which is a linear inequality shown by $\tilde{IR}$. The shaded area shows all the contingent utility combinations — and hence (implicitly) all the contingent wage combinations — that satisfy the IR constraint. Since the line of certainty is still the 45° diagonal $\tilde{C}^a$, the point $\tilde{F}$ where it intersects $\tilde{IR}$ represents the first-best wage contract in the space of contingent utilities. Note that the utility of 14 corresponds to a wage of $14^2 = \$196$. Thus Figure 15.1 and Figure 15.2 are two different ways to represent the same situation.

15.1.2   Wage contract under asymmetric information

In the case of asymmetric information where the principal cannot observe the agent's effort, she still wants the agent to take the high effort. So she

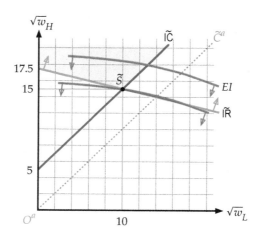

Figure 15.3   Second-best utility contract

must choose a wage contract (w_L^*, w_H^*) so that the agent's IR constraint (15.6) still holds. But now, in addition, she has to make sure that the agent has the incentive to undertake the high effort, i.e.,

$$V_{e_H}^b \geq V_{e_L}^b. \tag{15.9}$$

Equation (15.9) is called the agent's **incentive compatibility (IC) constraint**[2] which shows that the agent's wage compensation is such that he prefers to undertake the high over the low effort. From (15.3) and (15.4), write (15.9) explicitly and simplify to obtain

$$\sqrt{w_H} \geq \sqrt{w_L} + 5. \tag{15.10}$$

Then both the IR and IC constraints, (15.8) and (15.10), can be drawn in utility space as shown in Figure 15.3 by $\tilde{IR}$ and $\tilde{IC}$. Note that both are linear with distinctive slopes: it can be verified that the IR constraint will always have a negative slope of $-(1 - p_H)/p_H$ while the IC constraint will always have a positive slope of 1. The shaded blue area then shows (implicitly) all possible wage contracts that satisfy *both* the IR and IC constraints for the agent simultaneously.

From (15.1), note that maximizing $V_{e_H}^b$ for the principal amounts to the same thing as minimizing her expected wage cost, $0.2w_L + 0.8w_H$. Since we want to plot this in Figure 15.3, the expected wage cost can be rewritten as

---

[2]Synonymously, this is sometimes called the agent's **self-selection constraint**.

$0.2(\sqrt{w_L})^2 + 0.8(\sqrt{w_H})^2$ corresponding to the variables on the axes of the graph. Then fixing the value of the expected wage cost at some level, say $273, and plotting the combination of contingent utilities $\sqrt{w_L}$ and $\sqrt{w_H}$ in Figure 15.3 yields the expected isocost for the principal labeled EI. The arrows indicate the direction in which the expected isocosts are decreasing. By minimizing the expected isocost over the shaded blue area, we obtain the (implicit) optimal wage contract under asymmetric information (also known as the second-best wage contract) at $\tilde{S}$. The wage contract corresponding to point $\tilde{S} = (10, 15)$ is $(w_L^*, w_H^*) = (100, 225)$ which has an expected cost of $200.

From equation (15.1), at this second-best wage contract, the principal's expected utility is

$$460 - (0.8w_H^* + 0.2w_L^*) = 460 - (0.8 \cdot 225 + 0.2 \cdot 100) = 260. \qquad (15.11)$$

Comparing equations (15.7) and (15.11), the principal's expected utility from the second-best wage contract is a bit lower than that from the first-best wage contract. This difference in the principal's utility arises from the additional IC constraint that is necessary under asymmetric information, i.e., when the agent's action is hidden, the principal has to forego some utility relative to when the action is observable in order to get the agent to voluntarily undertake the best action from the principal's viewpoint. This utility foregone by the principal is called the information rent.

Finally, for the sake of completeness, verify that the principal is not better off by letting the agent exert the low effort. In this case there is no incentive compatibility constraint, and the principal only has to ensure that the agent's IR constraint holds, i.e., that he is as well off by putting in the low effort as his outside option:

$$V_{e_L}^a \geq 8. \qquad (15.12)$$

Substituting from (15.4) into (15.12) and realizing that the principal can offer a full insurance contract $(\bar{w}, \bar{w})$, the lowest certain wage she has to offer is $\bar{w} = \$144$. In this case, the principal's expected utility is $236, so she prefers to induce the high effort and go with the second-best contract instead of letting the agent slack off with the low effort.

15.2 Hidden Information

In this section, the prototype model of hidden information studied is a specific model of bundling. However, the principles for solving this bundling

problem are general and can be applied to other problems of hidden information. Several of these principles arise in the mixed bundling case covered
in the unit-demand bundling example in section 10.5. We begin by revisiting
this model with a slight change in notation to underscore the nature of the
principal's maximization problem and its solution.

A principal (the tomato farmer) can sell two types of tomatoes, regular
"low-quality" (type L) or organic "high-quality" (type H), to agents who
may be one of two types: the low-value type L consumer (a 'single'), or the
high-value type H buyer (a 'parent'). There are 100 consumers in all with
x consumers of type H, and hence $100 - x$ consumers of type L. Then the
principal's problem is to find a price pair (p_L, p_H) so as to maximize her
profit $\pi = x(p_H - c_H) + (100 - x)(p_L - c_L)$ subject to the following IR and
IC constraints:

$$V_L(L) - p_L \geq 0, \qquad\qquad (IR_L)$$
$$V_H(H) - p_H \geq 0, \qquad\qquad (IR_H)$$
$$V_L(L) - p_L \geq V_L(H) - p_H, \qquad\qquad (IC_L)$$
$$V_H(H) - p_H \geq V_H(L) - p_L. \qquad\qquad (IC_H)$$

Here (IR_L) states that the regular tomatoes must be priced in such a way
so that the utility of an L-type agent to whom it is targeted is at least as
large as not buying anything; this ensures that an L-type consumer would
be willing to purchase regular tomatoes. Likewise, (IR_H) specifies that the
organic tomatoes must be priced so that the utility of an H-type agent is at
least as much as not buying anything. Equation (IC_L) ensures that the utility
to an L-type agent from buying the low-quality product must be at least as
high as buying the high-quality product, i.e., an L-type consumer prefers to
buy regular tomatoes than switch to organic. Finally, (IC_H) guarantees that
the utility to an H-type agent from buying organic tomatoes is at least as
high as buying the regular tomatoes, so he too is content with the organic
product and would not want to switch.

Given the numbers in section 10.5 and the solution to the mixed bundling
problem of $(p_L, p_H) = (\$2, \$4.50)$, verify that the following are true:

(a) the low-type agent's IR constraint holds with equality, i.e., (IR_L) is
binding and this agent type has a zero consumer consumer surplus;

(b) the high-type agent's IR constraint holds with a strict inequality, i.e.,
(IR_H) is not binding and this agent type has a positive consumer consumer surplus;

(c) the low-type agent's IC constraint (IC_L) is not binding, i.e., this agent type will never want to switch from the low-quality product targeted to him to the high-quality product;

(d) the high-type agent's IC constraint (IC_H) is binding, i.e., this agent type is just about indifferent between switching from the high-quality product to the low-quality one.

Now we extend the unit-demand bundling story to the more general situation when consumers may wish to buy variable units of the good. We explore how the IR and IC constraints as well as the four properties of the solution listed above get modified in this richer context.

Consider a bundling problem with a principal and many agents. The principal is a single seller (female) and the N potential buyers (male) are the agents. The seller knows from market research that the agents can be one of two types, either a low-value or a high-value customer indexed by L or H. There are N_L buyers of the L-type and N_H of the H-type, where $N_L + N_H = N$. There is asymmetric information: each agent knows his type (whether L or H) but the principal does not. Therefore, she cannot resort to group pricing. Instead, she offers her buyers a menu of quantity-tariff bundles (or **packages**) to choose from, $((q_L, t_L), (q_H, t_H))$ — each buyer can either purchase q_L units for a *total* of t_L dollars, or q_H units for t_H dollars.[3] The package (q_L, t_L) is marketed to low-value buyers while (q_H, t_H) is targeted to high-value ones so as to maximize the seller's expected profits.

From the sale to a single agent of a bundle containing q units for a tariff of t dollars, the principal makes a per-agent profit of $\pi = t - c(q)$, where $c(q)$ is the cost of producing the bundle that contains q units of the good. Assume that $c(q) = 0.5q^2$. Note that the marginal cost of production is positive for positive levels of output $(c'(q) = q > 0)$ and increasing $(c''(q) = 1 > 0)$, so a bundle with a larger number of units costs more to produce. By fixing the per-agent profit at some level, in this case $60 and $70, the principal's isoprofit lines are drawn in black in Figure 15.4.[4] Her profits increase in the northwesterly direction.

---

[3]Note that t_L and t_H are *not* per-unit prices. Since we normally use the word 'price' to refer to per-unit price, we will use the word 'tariff' to refer to the price associated with a bundle.

[4]The principal's isoprofit is like an indifference curve in the commodity space of quantity-tariff combinations. Its slope, like that of any indifference curve, is given by the negative ratio of the marginal utilities, which in this instance is $-(\partial\pi/\partial q)/(\partial\pi/\partial t) = -(-c')/1 = c' > 0$, i.e., the slope of the isoprofit is the marginal cost of a bundle. Since the marginal cost increases as q increases, the seller's isoprofit lines curve up as shown in Figure 15.4.

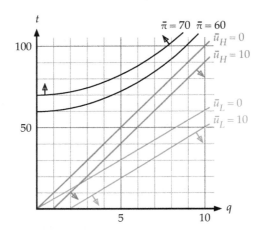

Figure 15.4   Isoprofits and indifference curves

A buyer's utility function is given by $u = \theta_i q - t$, where θ_i is a taste parameter that takes on two values, $\theta_L = 6$ and $\theta_H = 10$, depending on the agent's type $i = L, H$. It represents the marginal utility (in dollars per unit) to a consumer from a bundle containing q units of the good. Then $\theta_i q$ is the dollar-value that a buyer attaches to bundle q and his utility is the consumer surplus from the package (q, t). Fixing the utility level at $\bar{u}$, the equation for a buyer's indifference curve is given by $t = \theta_i q - \bar{u}$, which is linear with vertical intercept $-\bar{u}$ and slope θ_i. Figure 15.4 shows a type-L buyer's indifference curve in orange with a slope of 6, while a type-H buyer's indifference curve has a slope of 10 shown in green for utility levels of zero and 10. Each type's utility increases in the southeasterly direction.

We assume that the buyer's reservation utility is zero, i.e., he gets zero utility if he does not purchase anything. Therefore, if the agent is of the H-type, he will only accept a package if it lies either on the green line $\bar{u}_H = 0$ or to its southeast where his utility is higher. Similarly, an L-type agent will only accept a package that lies on or to the southeast of the orange line $\bar{u}_L = 0$.

15.2.1   Optimal bundling under full information

First, we explore what the optimal packages would be if the seller had full information. If she knows the buyer's type is high, she maximizes her profit function

$$\pi = t_H - c(q_H) = t_H - 0.5q_H^2 \qquad (15.13)$$

by choosing (q_H, t_H) subject to the H-type buyer's IR constraint given by

$$u_H = 10q_H - t_H \geq 0. \tag{15.14}$$

To solve the seller's problem, set the IR constraint (15.14) as an equality to obtain $t_H = 10q_H$. Substitute this in the profit function (15.13) to get $\pi = 10q_H - 0.5q_H^2$. Maximize this with respect to q_H to obtain the first- best quantity $\hat{q}_H = 10$ and $\hat{t}_H = \$100$. The profit from this single sale of the package $(10, 100)$ is $\$50$.

In Figure 15.5, this package is shown by $\hat{A}$ which shows the highest iso-profit curve attainable by the principal given that the H-type agent has to be on or below his green indifference curve labeled $\bar{u}_H = 0$. It should be apparent that if the $\hat{A}$ bundle were to be strictly below the green indiffer-ence curve (thereby giving the agent positive utility), then the corresponding profit of the seller would dip below $\$50$. Therefore at the first-best package, the agent's IR constraint has to hold with equality.

Similarly, if the seller knows the buyer's type is low, she maximizes her profit

$$\pi = t_L - c(q_L) = t_L - 0.5q_L^2 \tag{15.15}$$

subject to the L-type buyer's IR constraint

$$u_L = 6q_L - t_L \geq 0. \tag{15.16}$$

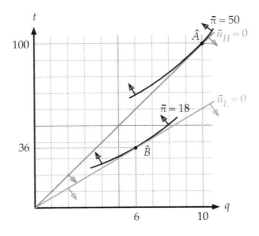

Figure 15.5 First-best packages

Set the IR constraint (15.16) as an equality to obtain $t_L = 6q_L$, substitute this in (15.15), and solve to obtain $\hat{q}_L = 6$ and $\hat{t}_L = \$36$. This package is shown by the point $\hat{B}$.

15.2.2 Optimal bundling under asymmetric information

Separating equilibrium

Under asymmetric information, the seller cannot tell both types of buyers apart and has to offer a menu of quantity-tariff bundles (q_L, t_L) and (q_H, t_H) to choose from. For these packages, each buyer type must satisfy an IR constraint when he buys the package that is targeted towards him:

$$u_L(q_L, t_L) = 6q_L - t_L \geq 0, \qquad (IR_L)$$
$$u_H(q_H, t_H) = 10q_H - t_H \geq 0. \qquad (IR_H)$$

In addition, each buyer type must also satisfy an IC constraint:

$$u_L(q_L, t_L) = 6q_L - t_L \geq 6q_H - t_H = u_L(q_H, t_H), \qquad (IC_L)$$
$$u_H(q_H, t_H) = 10q_H - t_H \geq 10q_L - t_L = u_H(q_L, t_L). \qquad (IC_H)$$

The inequality IC_L states that the utility of an L-type buyer who purchases the package (q_L, t_L) targeted to him must be at least as much as the utility he would have received if he had purchased the 'wrong' package, (q_H, t_H), meant for the H-type buyer. Analogously, the inequality IC_H states that the utility of an H-type buyer who purchases the package (q_H, t_H) targeted to him must be at least as much as the utility he would have received if he switched to the (q_L, t_L) package instead. It is easy to check that the first-best packages $\hat{A} = (\hat{q}_H, \hat{t}_H) = (10, 100)$ and $\hat{B} = (\hat{q}_L, \hat{t}_L) = (6, 36)$ calculated under full information do not satisfy all four constraints by substituting these numbers into the equations above. However, it is more enlightening to verify this graphically. In Figure 15.6, IR_H is satisfied since $\hat{A}$ lies on the indifference curve $\bar{u}_H = 0$; similarly, IR_L is satisfied since $\hat{B}$ lies on the indifference curve $\bar{u}_L = 0$. So is IC_L, since the dashed orange indifference curve through $\hat{A}$ lies *behind* the solid orange indifference curve and yields a lower utility.

However, IC_H does not hold: a type H-buyer prefers $\hat{B}$ over $\hat{A}$ as shown by the dashed green indifference curve through $\hat{B}$ which yields a higher utility. In other words, if the full information packages were to be offered under

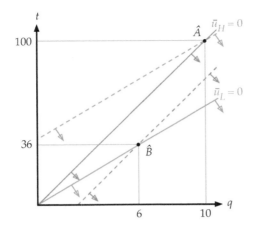

Figure 15.6   First-best IC constraints

asymmetric information, both types of buyers would end up purchasing the low bundle![5]

To calculate the optimal packages (q_L^*, t_L^*) and (q_H^*, t_H^*) under asymmetric information, the seller must maximize her overall profits, Π, with respect to the four unknowns, $q_L, q_H, t_L,$ and t_H:

$$\Pi(q_H, q_L, t_H, t_L) = N_H(t_H - c(q_H)) + N_L(t_L - c(q_L)) \tag{15.17}$$

subject to the $IR_L, IR_H, IC_L,$ and IC_H constraints. Suppose there are 100 potential buyers 80 of whom are type L and the remaining 20 type H. Then (15.17) becomes

$$\Pi(q_H, q_L, t_H, t_L) = 20(t_H - 0.5q_H^2) + 80(t_L - 0.5q_L^2). \tag{15.18}$$

Of the four constraints, the theory of second-best contracts tells us that only two of these four are binding as in the case of unit-demand bundling: the IR_L and the IC_H constraints hold with equality. In addition, this theory tells us that 'there is no distortion at the top', i.e., the H-type agent gets his first-best quantity level at the second-best solution. In our example, this means that $q_H^* = \hat{q}_L = 10$. We will use these three theoretical insights of the optimal second-best solution to solve our problem.

---

[5]Note that this is exactly the same as in the case of unit-demand bundling from section 10.5. Under full information, the price for regular tomatoes is $2.00 and for organic ones is $6.00, but offering these prices will cause both singles and parents to choose regular tomatoes because parents obtain a positive consumer surplus from regular tomatoes, while regular ones yield zero.

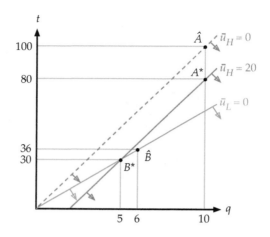

Figure 15.7   Second-best packages

First, set the IR_L to an equality and solve for t_L:

$$t_L = 6q_L. \tag{15.19}$$

Next, set the IC_H to an equality, substitute $q_H = 10$ (using the fact that there is no distortion at the top) and $t_L = 6q_L$ from (15.19) and solve for t_H:

$$t_H = 100 - 4q_L. \tag{15.20}$$

Finally, substitute $q_H = 10$, t_L from (15.19) and t_H from (15.20) into the seller's profit function (15.18) to obtain a reduced-form overall profit function

$$\Pi(q_L) = 80(6q_L - 0.5q_L^2) + 20(50 - 4q_L). \tag{15.21}$$

In other words, the seller's constrained maximization problem with four unknowns can be reduced to an unconstrained maximization of a single variable, q_L. Maximizing (15.21) with respect to q_L and using (15.19) and (15.20), we obtain the second-best solution under asymmetric information to be $(q_L^*, t_L^*) = (5, 30)$ and $(q_H^*, t_H^*) = (10, 80)$.

The second-best packages shown in Figure 15.7 by points A^* and B^* constitute a separating equilibrium because each type of agent gets to purchase a different package. While the H-type buyer gets his first-best bundle containing 10 units of the good, the tariff paid is lower than the first-best one ($80 rather than $100). In other words, an H-type buyer's IR constraint is not binding at the second-best package, i.e., he gets a positive utility at A^*

as shown by the solid green indifference curve for $\bar{u}_H = 20$. However, an L-type buyer's IR constraint is binding at the second-best package, i.e., his utility is zero at B^*. Furthermore both A^* and B^* lie on the same solid green indifference curve, so the H-type buyer's IC constraint is binding. While not illustrated, the IC constraint for the L-type buyer holds since the package A^* lies above his orange indifference curve $\bar{u}_L = 0$ and therefore yields negative utility. Finally, note that the second-best bundle for the L-type buyer is smaller than the first-best bundle (5 units at B^* rather than 6 at $\hat{B}$). Verify ◀ ↵ that the seller's overall profit is $2000.

To summarize, under hidden information, the separating equilibrium has four features:

(a) the low-type agent's IR constraint holds with equality, i.e., (IR_L) is binding and this agent type has a zero consumer consumer surplus;

(b) the high-type agent's IC constraint (IC_H) is binding, i.e., this agent type is just about indifferent between switching from the high-quality product to the low-quality one;

(c) there is no output distortion for the H-type agent, i.e., this agent type receives his first-best bundle;

(d) there is a downward output distortion for the L-type agent, i.e., this agent type receives a lower volume of output.

In order to establish that the menu $((q_L^*, t_L^*), (q_H^*, t_H^*)) = ((5, 30), (10, 80))$ is indeed a separating equilibrium, we need to verify that it is better than the possibility of a pooling equilibrium or a semi-separating equilibrium.

Pooling equilibrium

In a pooling equilibrium, the seller decides to offer only one package $(\bar{q}, \bar{t})$ so as to maximize its overall profit

$$\Pi(q, t) = 80(t - 0.5q^2) + 20(t - 0.5q^2) = 100(t - 0.5q^2) \qquad (15.22)$$

subject to IR constraints (15.14) and (15.16). Since the indifference curve $\bar{u}_H = 0$ lies above the indifference curve $\bar{u}_L = 0$ in Figure 15.5, it follows that if the IR_L is binding, then automatically IC_H will be satisfied. Hence, we only need to maximize (15.22) subject to (15.16) which can be set to equality. This yields exactly the same package as $\hat{B}$ shown in Figure 15.5, i.e., ◀ ↵

$(\bar{q}, \bar{t}) = (6, 36)$ for a profit level of \$1800 which is less than the \$2000 from the separating package. Therefore, the pooling equilibrium is not better than the separating one.

Semi-separating equilibrium

In a semi-separating equilibrium, the seller decides to offer only one package $(\tilde{q}, \tilde{t})$ so as to maximize its overall profit[6]

$$\Pi(q, t) = 20(t - 0.5q^2) \qquad (15.23)$$

subject to the IR constraint (15.14). This yields the same package as $\hat{A}$ shown in Figure 15.5, i.e., $(\tilde{q}, \tilde{t}) = (10, 100)$ for a profit level of \$1,00 which again is less than the \$2000 from the separating package. Hence, the separating equilibrium is optimal.

Exercises

15.1. A risk-neutral principal employs a risk-averse agent who can undertake low effort (e_L) or high effort (e_H). The agents utility function is $u(w, e) = \sqrt{w} - d(e)$ where $d(e_L) = 4$ is the disutility of the low effort and $d(e_H) = 10$ is that of the high effort. The outcome of the effort is either low at \$300, or high at \$800. The probability of the high outcome given the high effort is $p_H = 0.5$, while the probability of the high outcome given the low effort is $p_L = 0.2$. The agents reservation utility level is 10.

(a) Calculate the first-best wage contract, $\hat{w}$.

(b) Calculate the second-best wage contract under asymmetric information, (w_L^*, w_H^*).

15.2. Donald who is risk-neutral owns a retail store. Goofy is the sales person. Goofy can adopt two different sales effort levels, sleepy (e_L) or alert (e_H). His utility from wage w and effort e is given by $u(w, e) = \sqrt{w} - d(e)$ where the disutility $d(e_L) = 0$ and $d(e_H) = 12$.

---

[6]With more than two types of agents, it is possible to have a richer variety of semi-separating equilibria. For example, with three types of agents, it is possible that the highest type gets offered one package and the remaining two types get offered a different package, an outcome that is sometimes called **bunching** or **partial pooling**.

The probability of high monthly sales is 0.1 when Goofy exerts effort e_L, while the probability of high monthly sales when he exerts effort e_H is 0.7. He can earn \$3600 at some other store, giving him a reservation utility of 60. Donald (who is too busy sailing with his nephews) cannot monitor Goofy's effort, and offers him a wage contract (w_L, w_H) contingent on monthly sales: Goofy receives w_L if sales are low at \$10,000, and w_H if they are high at \$12,000.

(a) Write Goofy's IR constraint when Donald wants Goofy to be alert.

(b) Write Goofy's IC constraint when Donald wants Goofy to be alert.

(c) Solve for the optimal wage contract (w_L^*, w_H^*) when Donald wants Goofy to be alert.

(d) Solve for Donald's expected profit under the optimal wage contract when Donald wants Goofy to be alert and contrast this with his profit level when he wants Goofy to be sleepy. What compensation scheme will Donald choose?

(e) Solve for Donald's expected profit under the optimal wage contract when Goofy becomes more productive: the probability of high monthly sales increases to 0.45 when Goofy exerts effort L, while the probability of high monthly sales when he exerts effort H increases to 0.75. Compare Donald's new profit level with the case when he wants the more productive Goofy to be sleepy. What conclusions can you draw from parts (d) and (e)?

15.3. Gloria owns a made-to-order clothing store in Peasantville. The store is run by Gloria's French tailor, Pierre, whose job is to select the cloth and designs, tailor the suits, greet customers and generate sales. Sales depend on how persuasive and attentive Pierre is. The mood of customers can be categorized into three states: s_L (wants to buy a specific item only) with probability 0.3, s_M (wants to buy a specific item but may buy something else) with probability 0.5, and s_H (willing to spend if he feels that the merchandise and service is good) with probability 0.2. Pierre can adopt three sales styles: curt and haughty (e_L), a bit curt but more patient (e_M), or very patient and friendly (e_H). The net cash inflows (gross receipts less materials and other costs, except Pierre's compensation) from the weekly sales are either \$1000 or \$2000 contingent on customer type and sales effort as shown in the table below:

	s_L	s_M	s_H
e_L	1000	1000	1000
e_M	1000	1000	2000
e_H	1000	2000	2000

Pierre does not know what type of customer he is dealing with before he adopts a sales style. Gloria is risk-neutral, while Pierre is risk-averse and has a utility function given by $u(w, e) = \sqrt{w} - d(e)$, where his disutility from effort is given by $d(e_L) = 1, d(e_M) = 6$, and $d(e_H) = 18$. Pierre's reputation is well known and he has standing offers of alternative employment that will provide him a utility of at least 10.

(a) Suppose Gloria installs a customer complaint system from which she can determine ex post the type of customer who came to shop. For each of the possible actions e_L, e_M, and e_H, design the full information wage that would implement that action. Calculate Gloria's expected profits to determine which action she should induce Pierre to take.

(b) Assume that Gloria can only observe net cash inflows and that neither Pierre's actions nor the type of customer can be observed. Determine the contract (w_L^*, w_H^*) that would induce Pierre to take action e_H.

(c) Show that the action e_M cannot be implemented because the two incentive compatibility constraints cannot be satisfied.

(d) Calculate Gloria's expected profit and determine which action she should implement.

15.4. A manufacturer of flash drives has a profit function $\pi = t - q^2$ where t is the price charged for a flash drive and q^2 is the cost of producing a drive whose capacity is q gigabytes. A consumer of type θ has a utility function $u = \theta q - t$, where θ takes on a value of 8 for H-type consumers, or 6 for L-type consumers. There are 100 consumers of each type. A consumer gets zero utility if she does not buy.

(a) Calculate the optimal bundles, $(\hat{q}_L, \hat{t}_L)$ and $(\hat{q}_H, \hat{t}_H)$, under full information.

(b) Calculate the optimal bundles, (q_L^*, t_L^*) and (q_H^*, t_H^*), under asymmetric information.

15.5. Consider a bundling problem where the principal is the seller of a good with a value function $v = t - 2q$ where t is the price charged for a bundle and $2q$ is the cost of the bundle that contains q units of the good. A buyer of type θ has a utility function $u(q, t) = \theta\sqrt{q} - t$, where θ is either 16 or 20 with probability 0.5 each. The buyers reservation utility is zero.

(a) Calculate the optimal bundles, $(\hat{q}_L, \hat{t}_L)$ and $(\hat{q}_H, \hat{t}_H)$, under full information.

(b) Calculate the optimal bundles, (q_L^*, t_L^*) and (q_H^*, t_H^*), under asymmetric information.

Chapter 16

Public Goods

A good is said to be **rival** if one person's consumption of it precludes the consumption by someone else, and **excludable** if a person can be prevented from consuming the product. By considering the extent to which these two properties are present or absent leads to a useful taxonomy of different types of goods.

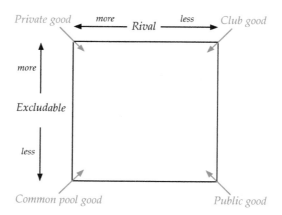

Figure 16.1 Types of goods

In the square in Figure 16.1, the horizontal axis shows degrees of rivalry ranging from rivalrous to non-rivalrous as we move from left to right; similarly, the vertical axis shows degrees of excludability from non-excludable at the bottom to excludable at the top. Then the northwest corner represents **private goods**, goods that are largely rival and excludable. The corner itself may be regarded as a **pure private good** that is entirely rival and excludable.

Many consumption items such as an aspirin tablet or a wristwatch fall into this category, as well as intangibles such as internet domain names. Some rivalrous goods (e.g., a hamburger) get used up in consumption while others (e.g., a hammer) are durable.

Club goods, such as a gym membership or going to the theater or subscribing to cable television, occupy the northeast corner area. Here the good is largely (or completely) excludable but once we have the requisite membership, ticket or subscription, many can enjoy the product at the same time. Hence, these goods are non-rival but excludable. The southwest corner area represents common pool goods, a good that is rival but not excludable such as a lake where consumers cannot be excluded from fishing, or a public land where any neighboring cattle owner's livestock can graze. In both cases, the goods are essentially rival (one's consumption of it leaves less for others) and largely non-excludable so long as the laws allow open access.

In this chapter, we focus on pure public goods, goods that lie in the southeastern corner of the box that are both completely non-rival and non-excludable. An example of such a public good would be the protection and security provided by national defense expenditures which are simultaneously enjoyed by all within the boundaries of a nation and without exclusion. Broadcast television may also be thought of as a pure public good within the range of the transmitter: many people can watch it simultaneously without any degradation in the signal and no one is excluded. Other public goods that conceptually lie in this southeastern area (but not at the corner) are impure public goods subject to congestion effects, e.g., a neighborhood park or a highway — a consumer's enjoyment of it depends on how many others are using it at the same time.[1]

Even though the precise boundaries between these four types of goods — private, club, and public as well as common pool goods — are somewhat fuzzy, the classification by the properties of rivalness and excludability is conceptually useful. You may enjoy puzzling as to where in Figure 16.1 to place a city's police services, or your economics professor's classroom lectures, or the pizzas ordered by a professor to be shared with her students, or any other good or service you can think of.

---

[1]These congestion effects may be regarded as a negative externality if a consumer's enjoyment decreases when too many others are also consuming the same good. However, for some products (such as social media websites or the adoption of a common computing platform) a consumer's enjoyment may increase as the number of other users increase. These positive externalities are called network effects.

In the following sections, we parallel the development of the general equilibrium model of pure exchange from Chapter 6 but in the context of an economy with a public good.

16.1   The Kolm Triangle

Consider the simplest possible public goods environment consisting of two consumers (indexed as usual by a and b) and two goods, x and y. Here x is a private good and its consumption level by each consumer is indicated by x^a and x^b. However, y is a pure public good. So if y units of the public good are available, we do not need to attach a superscript to denote the consumption level of each consumer: each individual consumes the entire y units since the good is non-rival and non-excludable. Thus a consumption bundle for consumer i is written as (x^i, y).

Each consumer i has a characteristic e^i which consists of *three* pieces of information specific to her: her preferences as represented by a utility function u^i, her endowment w^i, and a technology T^i. We write $e^i = (u^i, w^i, T^i)$.[2] The endowment is a commodity bundle $w^i = (w_x^i, 0)$ where w_x^i shows the total amount of good x that person i possesses initially, while zero indicates that neither individual comes into the world with any stock of the public good, so the public good has to be produced. Assume that each consumer has access to the same technology (i.e., $T^1 = T^2$) given by the linear production function $y = x$, i.e., each unit of the private good, x, can be converted into a single unit of the public good, y. Then an allocation is a triple (x^a, x^b, y) where

$$x^a + x^b + y = w_x^a + w_x^b. \tag{16.1}$$

Equation (16.1) is the resource constraint for the Kolm triangle economy which shows that the total consumption of the private and public goods by both individuals equals the total endowment of the private good available.

A consumer's utility function u^i is defined over her consumption bundle (x^i, y). When we graph indifference curves, we will plot the private good along the horizontal axis and measure the public good along the vertical. However, if the utility function is differentiable, there is one big deviation from the past that takes some time to get used to: the marginal rate of substitution between the two goods is now defined in terms of how much of the

---

[2]Compare this with the characteristic for a consumer in the private goods pure exchange economy of section 6.1.

private good a consumer is willing to give up to get an additional unit of the public good, i.e.,

$$MRS_{yx}^i = \frac{\partial u^i / \partial y}{\partial u^i / \partial x^i}.$$

In Chapter 3, the marginal rate of substitution MRS_{xy} could be taken to be the negative of the slope of an indifference curve. However, because the public good is on the vertical axis and the private good on the horizontal, MRS_{yx} is the reciprocal of the negative slope of an indifference curve.

As in section 6.1, the economy, e, is the configuration of consumer characteristics: $e = (e^a, e^b)$. Here e is our prototype of a two-person economy with one private good and one public good. Just as the Edgeworth box is the appropriate tool to study resource allocation in a two-private good two-person pure exchange economy, the **Kolm triangle** (named after Serge-Christophe Kolm) is the analogous tool in a one-private-one-public good economy with a linear production technology.

The Kolm triangle is an equilateral triangle and, as such, has a unique property illustrated in Figure 16.2 that we will exploit. Pick any two points like R and S inside (or on the edges) of this triangle and draw perpendicular lines to each edge of the triangle: r_1, r_2, and r_3 from point R, and s_1, s_2, and s_3 from point S. Then the sum of the length of these lines is the same, i.e., $r_1 + r_2 + r_3 = s_1 + s_2 + s_3$.

To see this, join point R to the vertices A, B, and C and suppose that each edge of the equilateral triangle has length ℓ. Then, the area of the equilateral triangle, Δ, can be written as the sum of the areas of the three smaller tri-

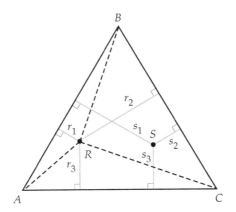

Figure 16.2 Equilateral triangle property

angles: $\Delta =$ area $RAB +$ area $RBC +$ area RAC. Since the area of a triangle equals one-half the base times the height, we obtain

$$\Delta = \frac{1}{2}(AB)r_1 + \frac{1}{2}(BC)r_2 + \frac{1}{2}(AC)r_3$$

$$= \frac{1}{2}\ell(r_1 + r_2 + r_3),$$

so $r_1 + r_2 + r_3 = 2\Delta/\ell$. Using the identical logic with point S, we obtain $s_1 + s_2 + s_3 = 2\Delta/\ell$ as well, which establishes the property.

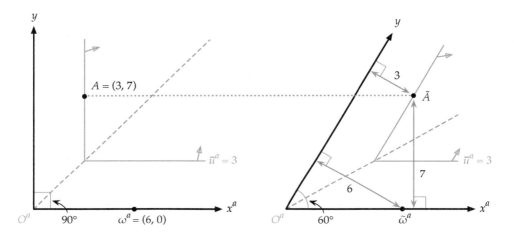

Figure 16.3   Rectangle to oblique coordinates

Suppose consumer a has an endowment $w^a = (6,0)$ and Leontief preferences given by the utility function $u^a(x^a, y) = \min\{x^a, y\}$, so the private and public goods are perfect complements as shown in the left hand panel of Figure 16.3. The right hand panel shows the same commodity space, but where the vertical axis is slanted at a $60°$ angle. This changes the coordinate system in the following manner. A point such as $A = (3,7)$ in the left panel is now shown by $\tilde{A}$ in the right panel where the quantity of y is still measured by the vertical distance from $\tilde{A}$ to the horizontal axis, but the quantity of x is measured by the length of the perpendicular line from $\tilde{A}$ to the slanted axis.[3] The endowment of a, w^a, in the left panel is now shown by $\tilde{w}^a$ in the right panel. Note that the Leontief indifference curve for $\bar{u}^a = 3$ is transformed predictably under the new coordinate system: the two 'legs' of the

---

[3] Any point (x, y) in the left panel is now transformed to the new coordinates $(\tilde{x}, y)$ in the right panel, where $\tilde{x} = \frac{2x+y}{\sqrt{3}}$.

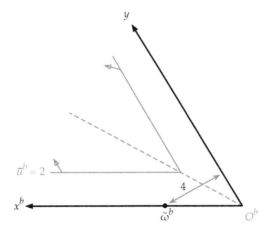

Figure 16.4 Consumer *b*

indifference curve which were parallel to the standard Euclidean axes in the left panel are still parallel to the new axes in the right panel.

To keep things simple, suppose consumer *b* has an endowment of $\omega^b = (4,0)$ and identical Leontief preferences to those of consumer *a* given by the utility function $u^b(x^b, y) = \min\{x^b, y\}$ which looks similar to the right panel of Figure 16.3. Horizontally flipping this, we obtain Figure 16.4 where the indifference curve for $\bar{u}^b = 2$ is shown along with the endowment of 4 given by the perpendicular line from $\tilde{\omega}^b$ with length 4.

Overlapping the right panel from Figure 16.3 with Figure 16.4 and moving them towards each other until the point $\tilde{\omega}^a$ coincides with $\tilde{\omega}^b$ — shown by the point ω in Figure 16.5 — completes the Kolm triangle. The origin for person *a* is given by the left vertex of the triangle, while the right vertex is the origin for person *b*. Person *a*'s Leontief indifference curves are increasing to the northeast, while person *b*'s are increasing to the northwest.

This is where the property of equilateral triangles introduced earlier becomes important. Any point in the triangle represents an allocation of the form (x^a, x^b, y). For instance, $\omega = (6,4,0)$ shows the initial endowment for this economy where *a* has 6 and *b* has 4 units of the private good (shown by the length of the perpendicular arrows from ω) and there is no public good at all. Point $R = (2,3,5)$ shows the allocation where *a* consumes 2 units of the private good, *b* consumes 3 units of the private good, and both individuals consume 5 units of the public good, i.e., consumer *a* converts four of her 6 units of endowment of the private good into the public good using

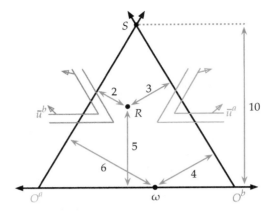

Figure 16.5   The Kolm triangle

the technology, while b converts one unit of her 4 units of endowment to bring the total quantity of the public good to 5. Point S shows the allocation $(0,0,10)$ where neither individual consumes any of the private good — they both consume the maximum amount of the public good possible when the entire aggregate endowment $w_x^a + w_x^b = 10$ of the private good has been converted into the public good.

16.1.1   Individually rational allocations

To derive the individually rational allocations for this public-good economy, note that each consumer has access to the technology for producing y, i.e., each person can convert any amount of her endowment of the private good into the public good. In other words, each consumer has her own **personal transformation frontier (PTF)** where one unit of x can be given up to obtain a unit of y.

Because person a has an endowment $w^a = (6,0)$ and access to the technology that converts one unit of the private good to one unit of the public good, in the standard Euclidean coordinates, person a's PTF would be a 45° line running from $(6,0)$ to $(0,6)$. With the oblique coordinates in Figure 16.6, a's PTF is shown by PTF^a which runs from $\tilde{w}^a$ to T along the blue 60° line. The highest indifference curve that a can reach on her PTF is at $F = (3,3)$ yielding utility $\bar{u}^a = 3$. Then any consumption bundle that yields a utility level of 3 or higher is individually rational for consumer a and is shown by the blue shaded area that extends to the northeast.

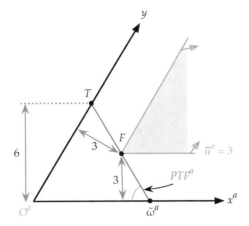

Figure 16.6   IR allocations for *a*

In Figure 16.7 the individually rational allocations for this Kolm triangle economy are shown. From Figure 16.6, the set of all consumption bundles that are at least as good as what *a* can attain on her own lie to the northeast of *F* between the two 'legs' of *a*'s orange indifference curve. Similarly, the set of all consumption bundles that are at least as good as what *b* can attain on her own lie to the northwest of *G* between the two 'legs' of *b*'s green indifference curve. The blue shaded triangle marked IR shows all the allocations that are individually rational, i.e., allocations where both consumers simultaneously are at least as well off than what they could achieve on their own.

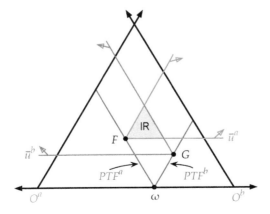

Figure 16.7   IR allocations

16.1.2   Pareto efficient allocations

To obtain Pareto efficient allocations, use the same algorithm as in section 6.2.2: first fix consumer b at a certain utility level — say, at $\bar{u}^b$ given by the green indifference curve in Figure 16.8 — and then maximize the utility of a. The highest utility consumer a can reach is at H. Verify that any movement

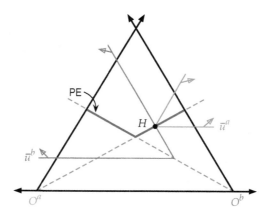

Figure 16.8   Pareto efficiency with Leontief preferences

from H inside the Kolm triangle makes at least one person worse off. Then fix a different utility level for consumer b and repeat the process. Doing this repeatedly yields the blue V-shaped set of Pareto efficient allocations marked PE.

In general, with smooth indifference curves, interior Pareto efficient allocations in the Kolm triangle can be found in the same manner as in the case of an Edgeworth box economy, by plotting the points of tangency of the consumers' indifference curves. In Figure 16.9, each individual's utility is assumed to be Cobb-Douglas of the form $u^i(x^i, y) = x^i y$, and one such point of tangency of the consumers' indifference curves is shown at C.

However, there is an important difference between the tangency of indifference curves inside a Kolm triangle and inside an Edgeworth box: here, tangencies between indifference curves do *not* imply that the marginal rates of substitution of the consumers are equal! To derive the necessary condition for Pareto efficiency in the presence of a public good, we look at Figure 16.9 in greater detail in Figure 16.10.

The left panel of Figure 16.10 shows consumer a's indifference curve $\bar{u}^a$ under standard Euclidean coordinates; point C in the Kolm triangle in the

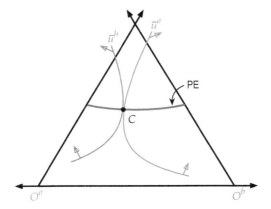

Figure 16.9 Pareto efficiency with Cobb-Douglas preferences

right panel corresponds to point $A = (k, h)$ where a consumes k units of the private good and h units of the public good. At A in the left panel, the slope of the indifference curve is $-h/(l - k)$. Recall from section 16.1 that the marginal rate of substitution is the negative reciprocal of this, i.e., $MRS^a_{yx} = (l - k)/h$. In the right panel as well, the marginal rate of substitution for consumer a at C is then $(l - k)/h$. Analogously for consumer b at C, $MRS^b_{yx} = (s - r)/h$. In the right panel of Figure 16.10, note that $l + s = w^a_x + w^b_x = k + r + h$ from the resource constraint (16.1). Then adding

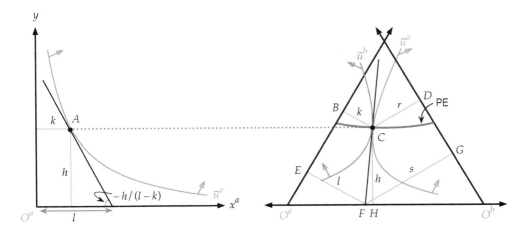

Figure 16.10 Tangency of indifference curves in a Kolm triangle

the marginal rates of substitution for a and b together, we obtain

$$\frac{l-k}{h} + \frac{s-r}{h} = \frac{(l+s)-(k+r)}{h} = \frac{(w_x^a + w_x^b) - (w_x^a + w_x^b - h)}{h} = \frac{h}{h} = 1.$$

In other words,

$$MRS_{yx}^a + MRS_{yx}^b = 1. \tag{16.2}$$

This is a special case of the more general Samuelson condition (named after Paul Samuelson, the first American to win the Nobel Prize in Economics in 1970) for Pareto efficiency when there is a public good. The Samuelson condition states that at a Pareto efficient allocation with one private and one public good, the marginal rates of substitution for the consumers has to add up to the marginal rate of transformation:

$$MRS_{yx}^a + MRS_{yx}^b = MRT_{yx}. \tag{16.3}$$

In the specific instance of the Kolm triangle economy, it takes one unit of the private good x to produce one unit of the public good y, so the MRT_{yx} in equation(16.3) is 1.

The Samuelson condition for Pareto efficiency has a simple economic interpretation: when there is a public good, the sum of the marginal benefits from the public good, $MRS_{yx}^a + MRS_{yx}^b$, must equal the marginal cost of producing this public good, MRT_{yx}, at a Pareto efficient allocation.

16.1.3   Deriving the Samuelson condition°

We have seen in Chapter 6 and in section 16.1.2 that a Pareto efficient allocations is found by fixing one consumer's utility level and maximizing the utility of the remaining consumer subject to the availability of the goods. We will follow the same strategy here to derive the general Samuelson condition (16.3).

In this subsection, it is convenient to put the public good, y, along the *horizontal* axis and the private good on the vertical axis. Given the resources and technology, suppose that the economy's PPF is given by the equation $x = T(y)$ as shown in Figure 16.11. We wish to find a production point of the two goods on the PPF and allocate it between the two individuals so as to reach a Pareto efficient allocation. In order to do so, fix consumer b's utility level at some level $\bar{u}^b$ as shown by the green indifference curve; let the equation of this line be $x^b = U(y)$.

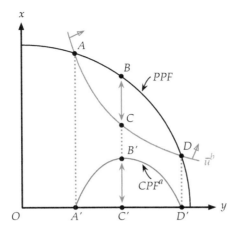

Figure 16.11 Deriving CPF^a

If the availability of the two goods in this economy is at A and consumer b were to attain her utility of $\bar{u}^b$, then she would consume OA' units of the public good and the entire amount AA' of the private good. In this case, a's consumption bundle is given by the point A' where there is no private good left for her to consume, but because y is a public good, a can consume the same level, OA', of it as b. In other words, given that individual b consumes at point A, the point A' shows the corresponding consumption point for consumer a.

Similarly, if the availability of the two goods were to be at B and individual b consumes at point C, she gets OC' units of the public good and CC' of the private good thereby attaining her utility of $\bar{u}^b$. From the total amount BC' of the private good available, subtract the quantity CC' consumed by b to obtain individual a's consumption bundle B', i.e., $BC = B'C'$. Repeating this for all points along the PPF from A to B to D, we can trace the **consumption possibility frontier** for a (labeled CPF^a) shown by the blue curve $A'B'D'$. The CPF^a shows the quantity of x^a available to consumer a when consumer b is guaranteed a utility level $\bar{u}^b$. It is given by the equation

$$x^a = T(y) - U(y). \tag{16.4}$$

In Figure 16.12, we maximize consumer a's preferences shown by the orange indifference curves subject to the consumption possibilities available to her, CPF^a. This yields point G which is a Pareto efficient allocation. Here b receives utility $\bar{u}^b$, both individuals consume OH units of the public good,

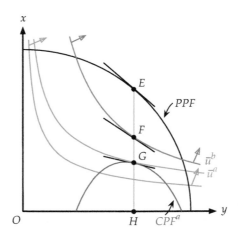

Figure 16.12   The Samuelson condition

while a consumes GH and b consumes FH units of the private good. Since $GH = EF$, the total availability of the two goods is given by point E on the PPF.

To derive the Samuelson condition, note that a's orange indifference curve is tangent to the CPF^a at G. Since the CPF^a is given by (16.4), its slope must equal a's marginal rate of substitution at G:

$$T'(y) - U'(y) = MRS_{yx}^a, \qquad (16.5)$$

where the left hand side is the slope of CPF^a and y is fixed at OH. But T' is the MRT_{yx} at point E, while U' is b's marginal rate of substitution at F. Hence, rearranging (16.5) yields the general Samuelson condition (16.3) which is a necessary condition for Pareto efficiency in the presence of a public good.

16.2 Lindahl Equilibrium

In 1919, Erik Lindahl proposed a way to allocate resources in an economy with a pure public good. The resulting equilibrium parallels the notion of a Walras equilibrium in an economy with private goods only. As seen in Chapter 6, at a Walras equilibrium in an economy with private goods, the prices per unit charged for any good are the same for everyone but the consumption levels of the goods are specific to each person. In an economy with a public good, Lindahl proposed a solution where the prices per unit charged for the public good are specific to each person but its consumption level is the same across all individuals and where the cost of production of the public good is shared by each consumer in accordance with her marginal benefit.

16.2.1 Graphical representation

Consider the Kolm triangle economy with consumers a and b. A **Lindahl equilibrium** consists of **Lindahl prices** $(\hat{p}, \hat{q}^a, \hat{q}^b)$ — here $\hat{p}$ is the per-unit price of the private good and $\hat{q}^a$ and $\hat{q}^b$ are the per-unit personal prices for the public good for consumer a and b — and a **Lindahl allocation** $(\hat{x}^a, \hat{x}^b, \hat{y})$ such that

(a) the consumption bundle $(\hat{x}^a, \hat{y})$ maximizes u^a subject to the budget constraint $\hat{p}x^a + \hat{q}^a y \le \hat{p}w_x^a$;

(b) the consumption bundle $(\hat{x}^b, \hat{y})$ maximizes u^b subject to the budget constraint $\hat{p}x^b + \hat{q}^b y \le \hat{p}w_x^b$; and

(c) the resource constraint holds:

$$\hat{x}^a + \hat{x}^b + \hat{y} = w_x^a + w_x^b.$$

Therefore, a Lindahl is equilibrium consists of prices — a price for the private good and a pair of personalized prices for the public good — and an allocation of private goods for each consumer and a common level of the public good so that each consumer maximizes her utility given her budget constraint, and the resource constraint for the economy holds.

For the Kolm triangle economy where the initial endowment is $w = (6,4,0)$ and where each consumer $i = a, b$ has the same Cobb-Douglas utility function $u^i = x^i y$, the Lindahl allocation is shown in Figure 16.13 by point $E = (3,2,5)$. The utility levels attained by the consumers are $\hat{u}^a = 3 \cdot 5 = 15$ and $\hat{u}^b = 2 \cdot 5 = 10$. The calculation of the Lindahl allocation and Lindahl prices is shown in the next section.

16.2.2 Algebraic derivation

With a standard Cobb-Douglas utility function $u^i = x^i y$ and a budget constraint given by $px^i + q^i y \le m^i$, the demand for the private good is $x^i = m^i/(2p)$ and the demand for the public good is $y = m^i/(2q^i)$, where the income $m^i = pw^i_x$ is the value of the endowment of the private good. The private good is taken to be the numéraire good, so fix $\hat{p} = 1$. Then given the initial endowment $w = (6, 4, 0)$, $\hat{x}^a = 3$ and $\hat{x}^b = 2$. Since the total amount of the private good available is 10 units and 5 of it are consumed by a and b, the remaining 5 units must be converted into the public good in order for the resource constraint (16.1) to hold. Therefore $\hat{y} = 5$, and the Lindahl allocation is $(\hat{x}^a, \hat{x}^b, \hat{y}) = (3, 2, 5)$ as shown by point E in Figure 16.13.

To calculate the Lindahl prices, note that the demand for each consumer of the public good is 5. Then $m^a / (2\hat{q}^a) = 5$, and since $m^a = \hat{p}w^a_x = 1 \cdot 6 = 6$, $\hat{q}^a = \frac{3}{5}$. Similarly, $\hat{q}^b = \frac{2}{5}$, so the Lindahl prices are $(\hat{p}, \hat{q}^a, \hat{q}^b) = (1, \frac{3}{5}, \frac{2}{5})$. Verify that a's marginal rate of substitution at the Lindahl allocation, i.e., the marginal benefit from the public good, is $\frac{3}{5}$, while that of b is $\frac{2}{5}$, so the Samuelson condition (16.2) holds. Indeed, as in the case of the Walras equilibrium, a Lindahl equilibrium allocation is individually rational and Pareto efficient.

While the Lindahl equilibrium appears to solve the allocation and distribution problem when there is a public good, it does not present a practical solution. This is because a consumer pays a personalized price for the public good based on the marginal benefit derived, i.e., her MRS_{yx}. These personalized prices equate the individual valuation of the public good to the cost of providing the public good, thereby satisfying the Samuelson condition for Pareto efficiency. However, it works only if everyone behaves truthfully. In the presence of public goods whose consumption people cannot be excluded

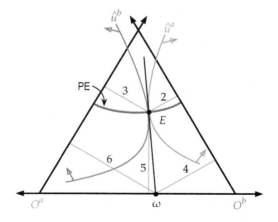

Figure 16.13   Lindahl allocation

from, everyone has an incentive to behave as if their benefit from the public good is less than what it truly is, a problem known as the free rider problem.

Nevertheless, the Lindahl equilibrium establishes the existence of individually rational and Pareto efficient allocations in the presence of public goods. Whether these desirable allocations can be attained through other mechanisms has been an active and important area of research.

16.3 Voluntary Contribution Mechanism°

Many public goods are provided for by individuals who make private contributions (e.g., to charity or to fund public radio programming in the US). In this section we consider a voluntary contribution mechanism in a Kolm triangle economy where each consumer decides independently how much to contribute towards a public good. The level of the public good is determined by the total contribution of both individuals, while the level of the private good consumed is what is left with each consumer after she has contributed.

16.3.1 Graphical representation

Consider a Kolm triangle economy where the initial endowment is $\omega = (10, 8, 0)$ and where each consumer $i = a, b$ has the same Cobb-Douglas utility function $u^i = x^i y$. If each consumer contributes (or 'gifts') an amount g^i of the private good, then the total quantity of the public good produced is the sum of their individual gifts, i.e., $y = g^a + g^b$. The amount of the private good consumed by each is what remains after the contribution: $x^i = \omega^i_x - g^i$, or more specifically, $x^a = 10 - g^a$ while $x^b = 8 - g^b$.

Even though each individual chooses how much to contribute independently (i.e., non-cooperatively, without consulting the other), how much consumer a wishes to contribute depends on how much b contributes and vice versa. For example, if b chooses not to contribute at all, i.e., $g^b = 0$, then a can choose to produce the public good on her own along her personal transformation frontier labeled PTF^a_0 which passes through her initial bundle at ω in Figure 16.14. Her preferences are maximized at R along PTF^a_0, so she contributes $g^a = 5$ when $g^b = 0$.

Similarly, when b contributes $g^b = 4$, individual a's initial bundle moves from ω to L where, in addition to the 10 units of the private good, she now enjoys 4 units of the public good provided for by b. If she chooses to convert

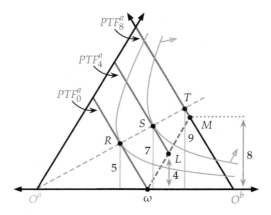

Figure 16.14   Deriving *a*'s best-response

some of her private good into additional units of the public good, she would move along her new personal transformation frontier labeled PTF_4^a which passes through L.[4] Along PTF_4^a, she maximizes her utility at S. Since there are 7 units of the public good at S, of which 4 were provided for by b, a contributes $g^a = 3$ when $g^b = 4$. If b were to contribute all of her endowment of the private good, $g^b = 8$ and individual a's initial bundle moves from ω to M. She then maximizes her utility at point T where $y = 9$, so $g^a = 1$.

Points R, S and T in Figure 16.14 show the optimal gifts by a in response to b's contributions of zero, 4, and 8 units. By considering all the possible gifts that b could make between zero and 8 units, we obtain the best-response function for a by joining the utility-maximizing points along the dashed magenta line from R to T, shown in Figure 16.15 by the orange line, BR_a.

In an analogous manner, b's best-response to a's contributions can be derived by considering various levels of g^a and figuring out how much b would like to contribute so as to maximize her utility. For instance, when $g^a = 0$, consumer b would choose to produce some public good of her own along her personal transformation frontier PTF_0^b at point G in Figure 16.15. By considering other levels of contribution to the public good by a, we find that the utility-maximizing points for b range along the green line from G to H to I,[5]

---

[4]Note that the dashed blue line from ω to M is parallel to the left edge of the triangle. Therefore, at *any* consumption bundle on this dashed line, the amount of the private good consumed by a is the same as at ω; only the amount of the public good consumed increases, from zero at ω to larger and larger positive amounts as one moves northeastwards.

[5]Once b's best-response hits PTF_0^a, it can be shown that her best-response follows PTF_0^a.

which is b's best-response function, BR_b.

The Nash equilibrium in contributions occur where the two best-responses intersect at E, the **voluntary contribution equilibrium allocation**. By looking at the indifference curves for a and b that pass through E, it should be apparent that the allocation E is individually rational but not Pareto efficient.

16.3.2 Algebraic derivation

To derive the voluntary contribution equilibrium allocation algebraically, begin with consumer a's utility $u^a = x^a y$. Because a contributes g^a towards the public good, she consumes $x^a = 10 - g^a$. Then u^a can be rewritten as $u^a = (10 - g^a)(g^a + g^b)$, where $g^a + g^b = y$. Because we seek a Nash equilibrium in the contributions $(\bar{g}^a, \bar{g}^b)$, maximize $u^a = (10 - g^a)(g^a + g^b)$ with ◀◢ respect to g^a to obtain a's best-response:

$$g^a = 5 - \frac{1}{2}g^b. \tag{16.6}$$

Similarly, maximize $u^b = (8 - g^b)(g^a + g^b)$ with respect to g^b to obtain b's best-response:

$$g^b = 4 - \frac{1}{2}g^a. \tag{16.7}$$

Solving, we obtain the Nash equilibrium contributions of $(\bar{g}^a, \bar{g}^b) = (4, 2)$. ◀◢ Then the voluntary contribution equilibrium allocation shown by E in Figure 16.15 is $(\bar{x}^a, \bar{x}^b, \bar{y}) = (6, 6, 6)$.

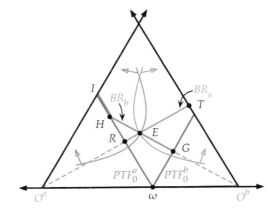

Figure 16.15 Voluntary contribution equilibrium

16.3.3   Neutral income redistributions

A classic result with respect to the voluntary contribution mechanism states that redistributions of income across individuals does not alter the equilibrium allocation so long as those who were contributing before the redistribution continue to contribute afterwards.[6]

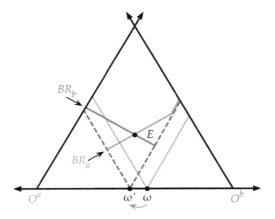

Figure 16.16   Redistribution neutrality

In Figure 16.16, some of person a's endowment is given to person b. Such a transfer from one person to another is called an income redistribution and is shown graphically by a movement to the left of the initial endowment from ω to ω'. Then each consumer's personal transformation frontier (when the other does not contribute) slides over to the left as shown by the dashed blue lines. The best-responses are then modified at the ends as shown, but their intersection point at E does not change. This means that the Nash equilibrium is unchanged and the voluntary contribution allocation remains at $E = (6, 6, 6)$. In other words, the level of the public good does not change because each consumer adjusts her gift by the amount of the transfer.

To see a concrete example of this, consider the new endowment $(8, 10, 0)$, where a has transferred 2 units of the private good to b from $\omega = (10, 8, 0)$. Calculate the best-responses and verify that the new Nash equilibrium contribution levels are $(\bar{g}^{a\prime}, \bar{g}^{b\prime}) = (2, 4)$. In other words, each person adjusts her contribution by the amount of the transfer: a contributes 2 units less and

---

[6]See Warr (1983) 'The private provision of a public good is independent of the distribution of income,' in *Economics Letters*, 13, pp. 207–211, and Bergstrom, Blume and Varian (1986) 'On the private provision of public goods,' in *Journal of Public Economics*, 29, pp. 25–49.

b contributes 2 units more than before, leaving the voluntary contribution allocation unchanged at $(6,6,6)$.

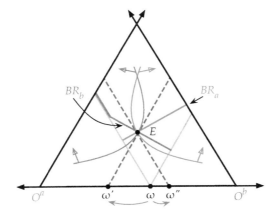

Figure 16.17 Limits of neutrality

To explore the extent to which income redistributions leave the voluntary contribution allocation unchanged, in Figure 16.17 we show the indifference curves of the two consumers through E. Move the initial endowment from $\omega = (10,8,0)$ to $\omega' = (6,12,0)$ by transferring 4 units of the private good from a to b. Then a consumes all of her original endowment of the private good of 6 units and contributes nothing towards the public good, while consumer b contributes 6 units towards the public good, leaving the equilibrium allocation unchanged at E. Hence, 4 units is the most that consumer a can transfer to b while retaining the neutrality property of the redistribution.

Finally, to calculate the maximum that b can transfer to a while retaining the neutrality property, do the converse: move the initial endowment from $\omega = (10,8,0)$ to $\omega'' = (12,6,0)$ so that b transfers 2 units to a thereby consuming her original endowment of the private good of 6 units and contributing nothing towards the public good. In Figure 16.17, this is shown by the dashed blue line that passes through ω'' and E. Therefore, any redistribution between ω' and ω'' shown with the magenta arrows leaves the voluntary contribution equilibrium allocation unchanged.

This neutrality result shows that, at least in theory, small transfers between contributors do not effect the level of the public good. If this were to be true in practice, then one implication would be that if a richer nation were to transfer resources to a poor country to enable the latter to produce a public good — say, cleaner air in the form of lowering greenhouse gases —

the level of the public good would remain at the same level.[7] In this case, transfers of resources from richer contributors to poorer ones may leave the level of greenhouse gases unchanged and so would be futile.

Exercises

16.1. Consider a two-person economy with one private good x and one public good y. Person a's endowment is $\omega^a = (1,0)$; person b's endowment is $\omega^b = (1,0)$. For each of the following pairs of preferences, draw the set of individually rational and Pareto efficient allocations in separate Kolm triangle graphs.

(a) $u^a(x^a, y) = \min\{x^a, y\}$ and $u^b(x^b, y) = x^b + y$

(b) $u^a(x^a, y) = x^a + y$ and $u^b(x^b, y) = x^b + y$

(c) $u^a(x^a, y) = \min\{x^a, y\}$ and $u^b(x^b, y) = x^b$

16.2. Two consumers, a and b, have preferences over a private good x and a pure public good y. Their utility functions and corresponding demand functions (where p is the price of x, and q^a, and q^b are the individual-ized prices for the public good) are given in the table below:

Person	Utility	Demand for x	Demand for y
a	$x^a y$	$m^a / (2p)$	$m^a / (2q^a)$
b	$(x^b)^2 y$	$2m^b / (3p)$	$m^b / (3q^b)$

The initial endowment is $\omega = (4, 9, 0)$. As usual, one unit of the private good can be converted into one unit of the public good. The price of the private good p is normalized to $\$1$. Calculate the Lindahl allocation, $(\hat{x}^a, \hat{x}^b, \hat{y})$, and the Lindahl prices, (q^a, q^b).

16.3. Three consumers, a, b and c, have preferences over a private good x and a pure public good y. Their utility functions and corresponding demand functions (where p is the price of x, and q^a, q^b and q^c are the individualized prices for the public good) are given in the table below:

---

[7]This assumes that both the rich and the poor nations were contributing towards the public good to begin with. If the number of contributors enlarges or shrinks as a result of the transfer, then the neutrality result will not hold in general.

Person i	u^i	x^i	y^i
a	$x^a + \ln y^a$	$(m^a/p_x) - 1$	p_x/q^a
b	$x^b + 2\ln y^b$	$(m^b/p_x) - 2$	$2p_x/q^b$
c	$x^c + 3\ln y^b$	$(m^c/p_x) - 3$	$3p_x/q^c$

The initial endowment is $w = (w^a_x, w^b_x, w^c_x, w_y) = (6,3,9,0)$. As usual, one unit of the private good can be converted into one unit of the public good. The price of the private good p is normalized to \$1. Calculate the Lindahl allocation, $(\hat{x}^a, \hat{x}^b, \hat{x}^c, \hat{y})$, and the Lindahl prices, (q^a, q^b, q^c).

16.4. Consider a two-person economy with one private good, x, and one public good, y. One unit of x can be transformed into one unit of y. Person a's endowment is $w^a = (4,0)$; person b's endowment is $w^b = (8,0)$. The utility functions are $u^a(x^a, y) = x^a y$ and $u^b(x^b, y) = (x^b)^2 y$. Person a can contribute an amount $0 \le g^a \le 4$ towards the production of the public good, while person b can contribute an amount $0 \le g^b \le 8$.

(a) Calculate the Nash equilibrium contribution $(\bar{g}^a, \bar{g}^b)$ and the resulting allocation in a voluntary contribution equilibrium.

(b) Is the allocation you calculated in (a) Pareto efficient? Justify your answer with appropriate calculations.

(c) What is the maximum amount of x that can be taxed from person b and transferred to person a without changing the level of the public good you calculated in (a)? Explain!

(*Hint*: Suppose t is the amount taxed and transferred from person b to a. Then a's endowment of the private good changes to $4 + t$ while that of b changes to $8 - t$. Calculate the new levels of contribution $(\bar{g}^a, \bar{g}^b)$ and use the fact that the new level of the public good, $\bar{g}^a + \bar{g}^b$, must equal the old level, $\bar{g}^a + \bar{g}^b$.)

16.5. Consider a common-pool resource problem, sometimes referred to as the 'tragedy of the commons'. There are 10 identical fishermen on a lake. The production function for fish is $Q = \sqrt{X}$, where Q is the total catch, and $X = \sum_{j=1}^{10} x_j$ is the total labor effort of all the fishermen. The total catch is therefore subject to diminishing returns. Suppose each fisherman gets a share of the total catch that is in proportion to the labor effort supplied, i.e., $q_i = (x_i/X) \cdot Q$. In other words, the labor effort of others imposes a negative externality on any one fisherman by reducing his share of the output. Then fisherman 1's profit function is given by

$$\pi_1(x_1, x_2, \ldots, x_{10}) = pq_1 - wx_1 = px_1 X^{-1} - wx_1,$$

where p is the per-unit price of fish and w the per-unit price of labor effort. Set $p = 1$ and $w = 1/2$ for this problem.

(a) Solve for the symmetric Nash equilibrium, x^*, when each fisherman chooses his labor effort independently of the others. Find the total quantity of fish caught, Q^*. Approximate your answers to two decimal places.

(b) A social planner maximizes the aggregate profit of all the fishermen, $\sum_{j=1}^{n} \pi_j$ by choosing the effort levels $(\hat{x}_1, \ldots, \hat{x}_{10})$. Since all fishermen are identical, find the symmetric solution, $\hat{x}$, and the total quantity of fish caught, $\hat{Q}$, approximated to two decimal places.

(c) How does the level of output Q^* compare to that from the social planner's problem, $\hat{Q}$?

Mathematical Appendix

This chapter provides a bare-bones refresher of the mathematical background that is required to follow this book. Sections A.1–4 review basic material that is covered in a one-semester calculus class. Section A.5 and A.6 introduces multivariate calculus which we use throughout this book. Section A.7 covers a miscellany of concepts.

A.1 Functions

A **function** $y = f(x)$ takes each element from one set called the **domain** and assigns it a single element from another set called the **co-domain**. For example, let $y = 2x$ be a function where both both x and y are real numbers. Then, the real number line is the domain from where the x's are chosen and

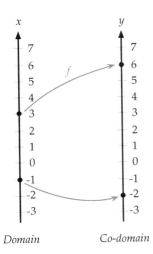

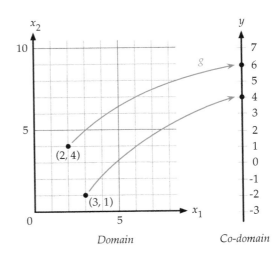

Figure A.1   Functions

assigned an element y in the co-domain, which is also the real number line. In the left panel of Figure A.1, the number 3 in the domain is assigned to 6 in the co-domain, and –1 to –2 under the function f given by $y = 2x$. The right panel of Figure A.1 shows a function of two variables of the form $y = g(x_1, x_2)$ given by $y = x_1 + x_2$ which takes the two-dimensional Euclidean space as its domain and assigns each element (x_1, x_2) to a new element in the co-domain of the real number line.

For the function f, it is more usual to turn the domain clockwise by 90° and draw a **graph** of the function, where each point on the graph is the coordinate $(x, f(x))$ as shown in Figure A.2.

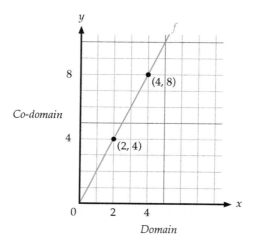

Figure A.2   Graph of a function

When a function of a single variable is written as $y = f(x)$, we call x the **independent variable** and y the **dependent variable**. Multivariate functions have more than one independent variable. For example, a function like $y = h(x_1, x_2, x_3)$ has three independent variables, x_1, x_2, and x_3, and one dependent variable, y. The most common function of a single variable is the **linear function** which has the form

$$y = a + bx, \tag{A.1}$$

where a is called the **vertical intercept** and b the **slope**. In Figure A.3, the graphs of three linear functions are drawn. In the left panel, $a = 7$ and $b = 0$; in the middle panel, $a = 4$ and $b = 1/2$; and in the right panel, $a = 8$ and $b = -2$. For a linear function, the slope refers to how much the

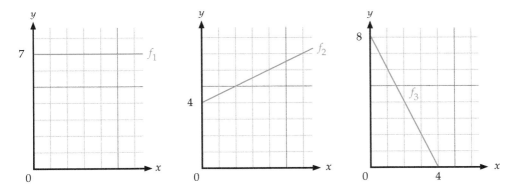

Figure A.3   Linear functions

y value changes when the independent variable changes by an unit, and it is the same no matter what the value of x. For instance, in Figure A.3, as x increases by one unit in the left panel, the y value does not change because the slope is zero; in the middle panel, the y value increases by $1/2$, and it *decreases* by 2 in the right panel.

For a nonlinear function, the slope of the function at a particular x is given by the slope of the tangent of the graph at that point. In the left panel of Figure A.4, a parabola is drawn where, for example, the slope of the tangent at A for $x = 2$ is positive while the slope of the tangent at B for $x = 6$ is negative. This illustrates the main difference between linear and nonlinear

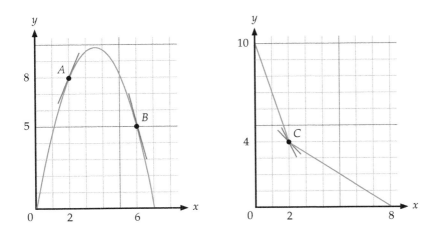

Figure A.4   Nonlinear functions

functions: linear functions have the same constant slope for *any* x, while the slope of a nonlinear function changes with the value of x.

The main purpose of calculus is to find a way to calculate the slope of any function. This requires the function to be **differentiable**, which (in intuitive terms) means that (a) one can draw the tangent at any point on its graph, and (b) the value of that tangent is unique, i.e., there are no kinks. For example, the piecewise linear function in the right panel of Figure A.4 is not differentiable at the kink point C since there is no unique 'tangent' there — the short blue line segments show two of the infinitely many possible 'tangents'.

A.2 Single Variable Calculus Review

Given a function of a single variable, $y = f(x)$, the slope of the graph at some point $\bar{x}$ can be found by taking the **derivative** of this function, written as dy/dx or df/dx or f', and evaluating it at $\bar{x}$. The act of taking derivatives is called **differentiation**. In this section, we review the rules of differentiation for some specific functions followed by some general rules about differentiation that are used in this book.

A.2.1 The specific rules

The polynomial function rule

Given the polynomial function $y = x^n$ where n is a real number, the derivative of the function is given by

$$\frac{dy}{dx} = nx^{n-1}. \tag{A.2}$$

For example, for the parabolic equation, $y = x^2$, we obtain the slope at any point x in the domain as the derivative $dy/dx = 2x$ by using equation (A.2) where $n = 2$. Thus when $\bar{x} = 1$, the slope of the function is 2.

For the equation $y = 1/x$, we may rewrite this as $y = x^{-1}$ and use (A.2) to derive $dy/dx = -1/(x^2)$.

The exponential function rule

The number e is a unique real number which is defined as the limit of the expression $(1 + 1/n)^n$ as n approaches infinity. It is approximately equal to

2.71828. The exponential function is $y = e^x$ is unique in that its derivative equals itself, i.e.,

$$\frac{dy}{dx} = e^x. \qquad (A.3)$$

The logarithm function rule

The logarithm of a number is the exponent to which another number, the base, must be raised to produce that number: if $v = b^w$, we say that with b as the base, w is the logarithm of v, written $\log_b(v) = w$. If we use the base 10 for example, then the logarithm of $y = 1000$ is 3 since $1000 = 10^3$. If the base is e, then when $v = e^w$, we say that w is the natural logarithm of v, written as $\ln v = w$.

For the natural logarithm function $y = \ln x$, its derivative is

$$\frac{dy}{dx} = \frac{1}{x}. \qquad (A.4)$$

For any other logarithm function $y = \log_b x$ with $b > 0$, its derivative is

$$\frac{dy}{dx} = \frac{1}{x \ln b}. \qquad (A.5)$$

In this book, we will only consider natural logarithms.

A.2.2 The general rules

The product-by-a-constant rule

Given a real number c, if $y = cf(x)$, then

$$\frac{dy}{dx} = cf'(x), \qquad (A.6)$$

i.e., the derivative of a function multiplied by a constant equals the derivative of the function times the constant.

For instance, if $y = 10x^2$, then $dy/dx = 20x$ using (A.2) and (A.6). In the case of the linear equation $y = 5x$, its derivative can be similarly calculated to be 5, a constant — which is no surprise, since a linear equation has a constant slope regardless of the value of x.

For a constant function such as $y = 7$ drawn in the left panel of Figure A.3, we may rewrite it as $y = 7x^0$ (since $x^0 = 1$). Using (A.2) and (A.6), the slope of this function is therefore zero everywhere.

The sum-of-functions rule

Suppose $y = f(x) + g(x)$ is the sum of two functions, $f(x)$ and $g(x)$. Then

$$\frac{dy}{dx} = f'(x) + g'(x). \tag{A.7}$$

Therefore, if $y = 10x^2 + 7x$, its derivative is $dy/dx = 20x + 7$ using (A.2), (A.6) and (A.7). This rule extends to the sum of three or more functions.

Note that the the the sum-of-functions rule also extends to the *difference* of functions. To see this, note that if $y = h(x) - k(x)$, we can rewrite this as $y = h(x) + (-1)k(x)$. Then by virtue of (A.6) and (A.7), we obtain $dy/dx = h'(x) - k'(x)$.

The product-of-functions rule

Suppose $y = f(x) \cdot g(x)$ is the product of two functions $f(x)$ and $g(x)$. Then

$$\frac{dy}{dx} = f'(x) \cdot g(x) + f(x) \cdot g'(x). \tag{A.8}$$

As an example, if $y = (10x^2 - 7x)(x^3 + 5)$, one way to calculate the derivative is to multiply everything out first and then use (A.2), (A.6), and (A.7). However, it is usually easier to use (A.8) to obtain

$$\frac{dy}{dx} = (20x - 7)(x^3 + 5) + (10x^2 - 7x)(3x^2)$$

and then simplify.

The quotient-of-functions rule

Suppose $y = f(x)/g(x)$ is the quotient (or ratio) of two functions, $f(x)$ and $g(x)$, where $g(x) \neq 0$ for any x, so that the ratio is well defined. Then

$$\frac{dy}{dx} = \frac{f'(x) \cdot g(x) - f(x) \cdot g'(x)}{[g(x)]^2}. \tag{A.9}$$

Consider the ratio $y = 1/x$, where $f(x) = 1$ and $g(x) = x$. We solved this using polynomial function rule earlier. We can now verify that we get obtain the same result if we use (A.9) instead:

$$\frac{dy}{dx} = \frac{0 \cdot (x) - 1 \cdot 1}{x^2} = -\frac{1}{x^2}.$$

The function-of-a-function rule

Suppose $y = f(x)$ and $z = g(y)$, so we can write z as the *function of a function* of x: $z = g(f(x))$. In other words, z depends *indirectly* on x, and we wish to calculate the derivative dz/dx. Then the function-of-a-function rule (also known as the **Chain Rule**) is

$$\frac{dz}{dx} = \frac{dz}{dy} \cdot \frac{dy}{dz} = g'(f(x)) \cdot f'(x). \tag{A.10}$$

For instance, let $z = (3x^2 - 2x + 7)^5$. Defining $y = 3x^2 - 2x + 7$, we can write $z = y^5$. Then from (A.10),

$$\frac{dz}{dx} = 5y^4 \cdot (6x - 2) = 5(3x^2 - 2x + 7)^4 \cdot (6x - 2).$$

A.3 Concave and Convex Functions

Suppose x' and x'' are any two points in the domain of a function $y = f(x)$. Define x_w as the weighted average of x' and x'', i.e., $x_w = w \cdot x' + (1 - w) \cdot x''$, where $0 < w < 1$. Then the function $y = f(x)$ is **strictly concave** means that

$$f(x_w) > w \cdot f(x') + (1 - w) \cdot f(x'') \tag{A.11}$$

for *any* value of w, $0 < w < 1$.

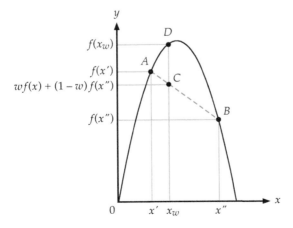

Figure A.5 A strictly concave function

In Figure A.5, a strictly concave function is drawn where the points x' and x'' are chosen arbitrarily for the purpose of illustration. The weight w is 0.75, so $x_w = 0.75x' + 0.25x''$. The height of point C is the right hand side of (A.11) which is the weighted average of the heights of A and B (i.e., $f(x')$ and $f(x'')$), while the left hand side of (A.11) is given by the height of D. In other words, a function is strictly concave if, when we take any two points on the graph of the function and join them with a straight line to make a chord, the graph of the function for any point in-between lies strictly above the chord. In this instance, the chord is shown as the dashed magenta line joining A and B.

A function $y = f(x)$ is concave means that

$$f(x_w) \geq w \cdot f(x') + (1 - w) \cdot f(x'') \tag{A.12}$$

for *any* value of w, $0 \leq w \leq 1$. Therefore, a function is concave if, when we take any two points on the graph of the function and join them with a straight line, the graph of the function for any point in-between lies *on or above* the chord.

For the points x' and x'' in the domain in the left panel of Figure A.6, we obtain the points A and B on the graph of the function. For the weight $w = 0.5$, the point x_w is the average of x' and x'', hence the point C is halfway on the dashed magenta chord joining A and B. The height of point C, f_w, refers to the average of $f(x')$ and $f(x'')$, i.e., it is the right hand side of inequality (A.12). It is apparent that the graph in between A and B lies strictly above

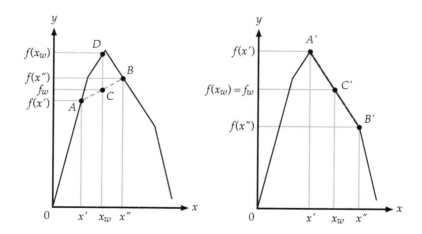

Figure A.6   A (not strictly) concave function

the dashed magenta chord, just as in Figure A.5. But in the right panel, x' and x'' have been chosen differently, so that the corresponding points on the graph are A' and B'. With $w = 0.5$, the function value at x_w, $f(x_w)$, *equals* the average of $f(x')$ and $f(x'')$ — the graph between A' and B' coincides with the dashed magenta chord joining them. Because the chord joining *any* two points on the graph sometimes lies strictly below the graph (as in the left panel of Figure A.6) and sometimes coincides with it (as in the right panel of Figure A.6), this function is not strictly concave but just concave.

A function that is concave but not strictly concave must have a graph that contains a linear segment. In particular, note that by the definition given in inequality (A.12), it is easy to verify that any straight line function $y = a + bx$ ◄ ◿ must be concave and cannot be strictly concave.

Finally, to define a **strictly convex** or **convex** function, simply reverse the inequalities in (A.11) and (A.12).

A.3.1 Second-order derivatives

If a function $y = f(x)$ can be differentiated twice, then we refer to those derivatives as **second-order derivatives**. For instance, if $f'(x)$ is the slope of the function $f(x)$, then df'/dx is the derivative of the derivative. It is written as $f''(x)$ or d^2y/dx^2 and has the interpretation of being the slope of the slope.

For functions that are twice differentiable, it is easy to find out whether they are concave or not. A function is concave if and only if its second derivative is less than or equal to zero, i.e., if a function $f(x)$ is concave, $f''(x) \leq 0$ for all x in the domain, and vice versa. For example, the function $f(x) = ax$ is concave since $f''(x) = 0$.

The intuition for this second derivative test for concavity is shown in Figure A.7. As the values of x increase from x_1 through x_4 for example, the slope of the slope along the graph goes from being positive (such as at point A) to zero (at B and C) to being negative (at D). In other words, the slope of the slope decreases as x increases (going from a large positive number to a smaller positive number to zero to a larger and larger negative value in absolute terms), i.e., $f''(x) \leq 0$ as we move from left to right along the domain of the function.

Is there a similar derivative test for strictly concave functions? Not exactly: if a function's second derivative is negative everywhere, then it is strictly concave, i.e., $f''(x) < 0$ for all x implies that $f(x)$ is strictly concave. For example, if the function $f(x) = \sqrt{x}$ is defined for $x > 0$, it follows

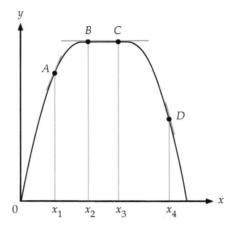

Figure A.7   Concavity and derivatives

⚠️▶ that the second derivative $f''(x)$ is always negative, so the function is strictly concave.

However, the converse is not true: a strictly concave function may not have a negative second derivative everywhere! For example, the function $f(x) = -x^4$ defined for $-\infty < x < \infty$ can be verified to be strictly concave by graphing. While it has $f''(x) = -4x^3 < 0$ for all $x \neq 0$, the second derivative at $x = 0$ is $f''(0) = 0$.

A.4   Single Variate Optimization

One of the many uses of calculus in economics is in the maximization of functions of a single variable. An example of this would be where a firm's profit level depends only on the level of production and the problem is one of finding the profit-maximizing level of output. We assume that we have a function $f(x)$ defined over positive values of the single variable x. If x^* maximizes the function, we refer to x^* as the **maximizer** and to the value attained, $f(x^*)$, as the **maximum**. We now present four important theorems in this context.

Theorem 1. *Suppose $f(x)$ is once-differentiable and attains a maximum at $x^* > 0$. Then $f'(x^*) = 0$.*

Theorem 1 is known as the **first-order necessary condition (FONC)** for a maximum and states that at a maximizer, the slope of the function must be zero, as can be seen in Figure A.7 at x_2 or x_3 both of which are maximizers.

Note that this is only a *necessary* condition, not a sufficient condition, i.e., it does not guarantee that the function is maximized. To see this, consider $f(x) = (x - 2)^2$ for which the first derivative equals zero at $x^* = 2$. But the function attains a *minimum* at this point, not a maximum.

Theorem 2. *Suppose $f(x)$ is twice-differentiable and attains a maximum at $x^* > 0$. Then $f''(x^*) \leq 0$.*

Theorem 2 is known as the **second-order necessary condition** (SONC) for a maximum and states that at a maximizer, the second derivative of the function must be negative or zero. In particular, it cannot be guaranteed that the second derivative at that point is *always* negative — it may equal zero.

To see this, suppose $f(x) = 100 - (x - 2)^4$. Verify by graphing that it attains a maximum of 100 when $x^* = 2$, but $f''(2) = 0$.

Theorem 3. *Suppose $f(x)$ is once-differentiable and concave. If there is an $x^* > 0$ where $f'(x^*) = 0$, then x^* maximizes the function.*

Theorem 3 is known as the **first-order sufficient condition** (FOSC) for a maximum and states that if a concave function attains a zero slope at some x^* in the domain, then x^* is a maximizer.

Figure A.8 shows a concave function for which the slope is zero at x^*. Then x^* is a maximizer because concavity ensures that the graph of the function lies below the horizontal tangent drawn at the maximum point. Of

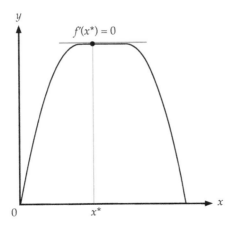

Figure A.8 FOSC for a maximum

course, the maximizer x^* is not unique in this instance — there are infinitely many other maximizers to the left and right of x^* since the graph has a flat top.

This theorem is probably the one that is most commonly invoked in this book to calculate the maximizer of a function. For example, given the function $f(x) = 100 - (x - 2)^4$, it is easy to check that $f''(x) = -12(x - 2)^2 \leq 0$, and hence $f(x)$ is concave. If the first derivative equals zero at some x^*, we can write $f'(x^*) = -4(x^* - 2)^3 = 0$. Solving, we obtain the value of $x^* = 2$ where the function has a zero slope. Then from Theorem 3, $x^* = 2$ maximizes this function.

Theorem 4. *Suppose $f(x)$ is twice-differentiable and there is an $x^* > 0$ where $f'(x^*) = 0$ and $f''(x^*) < 0$. Then x^* maximizes the function locally.*

Theorem 4 is known as the second-order sufficient condition (SOSC) for a maximum and states that if a function attains a zero slope at some x^*, and the function is strictly concave around that point, then x^* maximizes the function in a sufficiently small region around x^*.

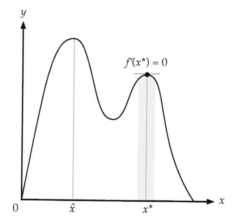

Figure A.9   SOSC for a local maximum

Figure A.9 shows a function where the premise of Theorem 4 holds at x^*: (a) the slope of the function is zero, and (b) the second derivative is negative, i.e., the function is strictly concave in some narrow band around x^* shown in yellow.[8] Since no other restrictions are imposed on the overall shape of the

---

[8]Formally, $f''(x^*) < 0$ implies that there is a sufficiently small $\varepsilon > 0$ such that $f''(x) < 0$ for all x satisfying $x^* - \varepsilon < x < x^* + \varepsilon$.

function, the best that can be said is that x^* maximizes $f(x)$ *locally*, i.e., the function attains a maximum for all x in a small enough neighborhood to the left and right of x^*. Therefore, the premise of Theorem 4 does not guarantee that the point x^* maximizes the function over the entire domain of the function. For instance, in Figure A.9, there is a (unique) *global* maximum that is attained at $\hat{x}$, i.e., $f(\hat{x}) > f(x)$ for all x in the domain of the function.

A.5   Multivariate Calculus

Suppose a function has two independent variables, x_1 and x_2. We may write it as $y = f(x_1, x_2)$, where y is the dependent variable. The graph of such a function is a two-dimensional surface in three-dimensional Euclidean space. For example, an aerial view of the graph of the function $y = 18 - (x_1 - 3)^2 - (x_2 - 3)^2$ in three dimensions is depicted in Figure A.10, where y is measured vertically (axis not shown) and the green lines show the outline of the two-dimensional, dome-shaped surface of the graph.

A.5.1   Partial derivatives

Just as in the case of a function of a single variable, the notion of a slope in the case of two variables has to do with a tangent to the surface, except we now consider a *tangent plane*. In Figure A.10, the tangent plane on the surface at $f(3, 3) = 18$ is outlined as a blue quadrilateral which is parallel to the two-dimensional (x_1, x_2) plane.

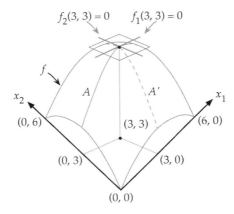

Figure A.10   Graph of a function of two variables

More specifically, in the multivariate case, we are interested in knowing how changing one independent variable changes the dependent variable *when all other independent variables are kept fixed*. So if we were to keep the x_2 variable fixed at 3, and ask how changing x_1 affects the dependent variable y, then we need to take a slice of the green surface along the red solid curve labelled A in Figure A.10, where the cut is parallel to the x_1 axis. The slope of the red solid curve as x_1 increases is called a **partial derivative** and written as

$$\frac{\partial f}{\partial x_1}(x_1, 3), \quad \text{or} \quad f_1(x_1, 3),$$

where $\partial f/\partial x_1$ (or f_1) is read as "the partial derivative of f with respect to x_1". The '3' in the parenthesis indicates that x_2 is fixed at 3.

Conversely, x_1 could be fixed at any number and we could ask how changing x_2 affects the dependent variable y. Doing this for $x_1 = 3$ yields the slice along the red dashed curve labelled A' and the slope along that edge is the partial derivative of f with respect to x_2, written as

$$\frac{\partial f}{\partial x_2}(3, x_2) \quad \text{or} \quad f_2(3, x_2).$$

Partial derivatives are calculated by treating the variables that are not being changed as constants. Suppose $y = x_1^2 - 3x_1x_2 + 3x_2^3 - 20$. In calculating $\partial y/\partial x_1$, treat every occurrence of x_2 in the function as a constant:

$$y = x_1^2 - 3x_1\bar{x}_2 + 3\bar{x}_2^3 - 20,$$

where the bar over a variable indicates that its value is fixed. The equation above is now a function of a single variable, x_1, and can be differentiated according to the rules covered in section A.2. In writing the final expression, remove the bars over any variable:

$$\frac{\partial y}{\partial x_1} = 2x_1 - 3x_2.$$

Similarly, to calculate, $\partial y/\partial x_2$, treat every occurrence of x_1 in the function as a constant:

$$y = \bar{x}_1^2 - 3\bar{x}_1x_2 + 3x_2^3 - 20,$$

so the partial derivative with respect to x_2 is

$$\frac{\partial y}{\partial x_2} = -3x_1 + 9x_2^2.$$

Sometimes it is more convenient to write the partial derivative $\partial y/\partial x_1$ as f_1, and $\partial y/\partial x_2$ as f_2.

All partial derivatives may be calculated in this way. Verify that for the function in Figure A.10, $y = 18 - (x_1 - 3)^2 - (x_2 - 3)^2$, the partial derivatives are

$$\frac{\partial y}{\partial x_1} = -2(x_1 - 3) \quad \text{and} \quad \frac{\partial y}{\partial x_2} = -2(x_2 - 3).$$

As a final example, consider a function of three variables:

$$y = \frac{x_1^2 - 5x_2}{x_3}.$$

Now in calculating any partial derivative, treat the other *two* variables as constants. It is helpful (though not essential) to rewrite the function as $y = (x_1^2 - 5x_2)(x_3)^{-1}$. Then the partial derivatives are

$$\frac{\partial y}{\partial x_1} = \frac{2x_1}{x_3}, \quad \frac{\partial y}{\partial x_2} = -\frac{5}{x_3}, \quad \text{and} \quad \frac{\partial y}{\partial x_3} = -\frac{(x_1^2 - 5x_2)}{x_3^2}.$$

A.5.2 Total differentials

Given a function $y = f(x_1, x_2)$, how can we approximate by how much y changes when *both* x_1 and x_2 change very, very slightly? The total differential of y gives us the answer for infinitesimal changes in the variables:

$$dy = \frac{\partial y}{\partial x_1}dx_1 + \frac{\partial y}{\partial x_2}dx_2. \tag{A.13}$$

Equation (A.13) says that the total change in y, dy, can be found by multiplying the partial derivative of each variable $(\partial y/\partial x_i)$ by the change in that variable (dx_i) and adding them.

A.5.3 Second-order partial derivatives

For a twice-differentiable function $y = f(x_1, x_2)$, second-order partial derivatives can be defined as follows. There are two first-order derivatives, $\partial y/\partial x_1$ and $\partial y/\partial x_2$. Each of these can be differentiated with respect to the variables

x_1 and x_2, yielding four second-order partial derivatives. These can be written explicitly as

$$\frac{\partial}{\partial x_1}\left(\frac{\partial y}{\partial x_1}\right) = \frac{\partial^2 y}{\partial x_1^2},$$

$$\frac{\partial}{\partial x_2}\left(\frac{\partial y}{\partial x_1}\right) = \frac{\partial^2 y}{\partial x_2 \partial x_1},$$

$$\frac{\partial}{\partial x_1}\left(\frac{\partial y}{\partial x_2}\right) = \frac{\partial^2 y}{\partial x_1 \partial x_2},$$

$$\frac{\partial}{\partial x_2}\left(\frac{\partial y}{\partial x_2}\right) = \frac{\partial^2 y}{\partial x_2^2}.$$

They may also be written more simply as f_{11}, f_{12}, f_{21}, and f_{22} respectively, where f_{ij} refers to partial derivative of the ith first-order partial derivative, f_i, with respect to variable x_j. The derivatives f_{12} and f_{21} are also known as **cross-partial derivatives**.

For instance, consider the function $f(x_1, x_2) = x_1^2 - 3x_1x_2 + 3x_2^3 - 20$. Then the first-order partial derivatives are

$$f_1 = 2x_1 - 3x_2 \quad \text{and} \quad f_2 = -3x_1 + 9x_2^2,$$

and the four second-order partial derivatives are $f_{11} = 2, f_{12} = -3, f_{21} = -3$, and $f_{22} = 18x_2$. Note that $f_{12} = f_{21}$. This is a general property known as **Young's Theorem** which says that if a multivariate function is twice-differentiable, then the cross-partial derivatives f_{ij} and f_{ji} must be equal.

A.6 Multivariate Optimization°

Just as in the case of single variate optimization, there are four theorems corresponding to Theorems 1–4, the first- and second- order necessary and sufficient conditions. We state these for a function of two variables, $f(x_1, x_2)$, defined over positive values of x_1 and x_2.

Theorem 1'. *Suppose $f(x_1, x_2)$ is once-differentiable and attains a maximum at (x_1^*, x_2^*). Then $f_1(x_1^*, x_2^*) = 0$ and $f_2(x_1^*, x_2^*) = 0$.*

The FONC for a maximum in the case of a function of two variables requires that each partial derivative evaluated at the maximizer equals zero. In Figure A.10, the function drawn attains a maximum when $(x_1^*, x_2^*) = (3, 3)$. The tangent plane at the maximum is shown as a blue quadrilateral which is parallel to the (x_1, x_2) plane. The slope of the blue plane along the x_1 axis is the slope of the solid magenta line that goes from the southwest to the northeast direction and shows the partial derivative $f_1(3,3)$ which is zero, as Theorem 1' requires. The slope of the blue plane along the x_2 axis is the slope of the magenta line that runs from the southeast to the northwest and is the partial derivative $f_2(3,3)$ which is also zero.

Theorem 2'. *Suppose $f(x_1, x_2)$ is once-differentiable and attains a maximum at (x_1^*, x_2^*). Then $f_{11} \leq 0, f_{22} \leq 0$, and $f_{11}f_{22} - 2f_{12} \geq 0$, where each second-order derivative is evaluated at (x_1^*, x_2^*).*

The SONC of Theorem 2 becomes a bit more complicated when there are two variables and requires restrictions on all the second-order derivatives as given in Theorem 2'.

Theorem 3'. *Suppose $f(x_1, x_2)$ is once-differentiable and concave. If there is an (x_1^*, x_2^*) where $f_1(x_1^*, x_2^*) = 0$ and $f_2(x_1^*, x_2^*) = 0$, then (x_1^*, x_2^*) maximizes the function.*

Theorem 3' is a straightforward extension of the FOSC of Theorem 3 to the two-variable maximization case. A function of two variables is concave if and only if (a) $f_{11} \leq 0$, (b) $f_{22} \leq 0$, and (c) $f_{11}f_{22} - 2f_{12} \geq 0$.

Theorem 4'. *Suppose $f(x_1, x_2)$ is twice-differentiable and there is an (x_1^*, x_2^*) where $f_1(x_1^*, x_2^*) = 0$, and $f_2(x_1^*, x_2^*) = 0$. Furthermore $f_{11} < 0, f_{22} < 0$, and $f_{11}f_{22} - 2f_{12} > 0$, where each second-order derivative is evaluated at (x_1^*, x_2^*). Then (x_1^*, x_2^*) maximizes the function locally.*

Finally, the SOSC for a local maximum when there are two variable requires certain restrictions on all cross-partial derivatives but is otherwise analogous to Theorem 4.

A.7 Miscellanea

In this section, we take up a three mathematical ideas that are used in various chapters: convex sets, homogeneous functions, and a very elementary (and partial) introduction to probability.

A.7.1 Convex sets

A set is said to be a convex set (or a weakly convex set) if the line segment joining *any* two points in that set lies within the set.

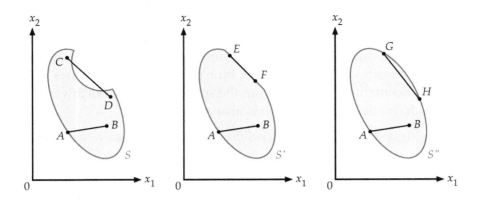

Figure A.11   Non-convex, weakly and strictly convex sets

In the left panel of Figure A.11, the blue shape S is not a convex set: the line segment joining points A and B lies within the set, but this is not true for another pair of points such as C and D. In the middle panel, the set S' is weakly convex because no matter which two points from the set are picked, the line segment joining them is in the set. Note that the line joining points E and F lies on the boundary of S' which is included in S', so the definition of convexity is not violated.

A set is said to be a **strictly convex set** if the line segment joining any two points in that set lies *inside* and not on the boundary of the set. In the right panel of Figure A.11, for any pair of points like A and B or G and H, the line segment joining them lies *strictly* within S'' and can never overlap with the boundary as was the case with points E and F in the middle panel. This set is therefore strictly convex.

A.7.2   Homogeneous functions

A function $f(x_1, x_2, \ldots, x_n)$ is **homogeneous of degree r** if it is the case that for any scale factor $t > 0$,

$$f(tx_1, tx_2, \ldots, tx_n) = t^r f(x_1, x_2, \ldots, x_n).$$

This says that starting from an initial level of the independent variables, $(x_1, x_2, \ldots, x_n)$, scaling their values by the positive factor t changes the function value by the factor t^r.

As an example, suppose $f(x_1, x_2) = x_1 + x_2$. Then if each variable is scaled up by a factor t, then $f(tx_1, tx_2) = tx_1 + tx_2 = t(x_1 + x_2) = tf(x_1, x_2)$.

Therefore, this function f is homogeneous of degree 1 (since the exponent of t in the last term is 1). What this means is that if, say, $t = 3$, i.e., we triple the initial values of x_1 and x_2, then the new function value will be t times the old function value, i.e., thrice the old function value.

For another example, consider the function $g(x_1, x_2) = x_1 x_2$. Then

$$g(tx_1, tx_2) = (tx_1)(tx_2) = t^2 x_1 x_2 = t^2 g(x_1, x_2),$$

and so the function g is homogeneous of degree 2. This means that if $t = 2$ and we double the values of x_1 and x_2, the new function value would be $2^2 = 4$ times the old value. Similarly, if $t = 3$ so the values of x_1 and x_2 were tripled, the new function value would be $3^2 = 9$ times the old value.

A.7.3   Probability and expectation

A random variable, x, is a variable which can take on different values from a set of possibilities, X. For instance, the toss of a coin can take on the value of either head or tail, so $X = \{\text{head, tail}\}$. For the toss of a six-sided dice, $X = \{1, 2, 3, 4, 5, 6\}$. A random variable that takes on finitely many values is called a discrete random variable. In this book, we only consider discrete random variables, so the set $X = \{x_1, x_2, \ldots, x_k\}$ for some finite k, where x_i refers to a specific realization of the random variable.

Associated with each value that the random variable can take is a probability, $p_i \geq 0$, which is the likelihood of occurrence of that particular value. We will assume this probability is *objective* in the sense that everyone agrees to its magnitude, presumably because of data, experiments, or simulations. So for a random variable that can assume k values, the set of probabilities is $\{p_1, p_2, \ldots, p_k\}$, where $p_1 + p_2 + \ldots + p_k = 1$, i.e., the sum of the probabilities across all possible values of the random variable equals one.

Then the expected value of a random variable x, $E(x)$, is the weighted average of possible values using the probabilities as weights:

$$E(x) = p_1 x_1 + p_2 x_2 + \ldots + p_k x_k. \tag{A.14}$$

For example, someone is offered \$10 if a coin toss turns up heads and zero otherwise. Here the random variable is zero or 10 dollars, each occurring with the probability of 0.5 if the coin is fair. The expected value of this random variable is then $0.5 \cdot 10 + 0.5 \cdot 0 = \$5$. If a fair dice is rolled and someone is offered as many dollars as the number of dots that appear on the dice, then the expected value of how much this person will make is

$$\frac{1}{6} \cdot 1 + \frac{1}{6} \cdot 2 + \frac{1}{6} \cdot 3 + \frac{1}{6} \cdot 4 + \frac{1}{6} \cdot 5 + \frac{1}{6} \cdot 6 = \$3.50.$$

An **event** is a particular realization of a random variable from the set X, or of a subset of X. For instance, in the throw of a six-sided dice, the realization of $\{6\}$ is an event; so is the realization of $\{2,6\}$ or some other subset of $X = \{1,2,3,4,5,6\}$. The **conditional probability** measures the probability of an event occurring given that another event has occurred. In the special case when events are **statistically independent**, i.e., the occurrence of one does not affect the probability of the other, the conditional probability of two events occurring is given by the product of the probabilities of the two events.

For example, if we wish to know the probability of getting a 2 on the first throw of a fair dice, followed by a 6, note that these are statistically independent events because the chance of getting a 2 does not impact the chance of getting a 6 thereafter. Therefore, the conditional probability of getting a 2 followed by a 6 is $(1/6) \cdot (1/6) = 1/36$.

Exercises

A.1. For each of the following functions defined for positive values of x, calculate the derivative dy/dx.

(a) $y = 5 + 6x^{1/2} + 2x + \dfrac{x^2}{2}$

(b) $y = \dfrac{2}{\sqrt{x}}$

(c) $y = 6 \ln x$

(d) $y = (2x^3 - 2)(3x^4 - x^{12})$

(e) $y = x^2 (\ln x)$

(f) $y = \dfrac{x}{3 - 2x}$, where $x < 3/2$

(g) $y = (\ln x)^2$

(h) $y = -e^{-2x}$

A.2. Which of the functions in **A.1** parts (a)–(c), (e), (g) and (h) are concave or convex? Are any strictly concave?

A.3. For each of the following functions defined for positive values of x_1 and x_2, calculate the partial derivatives, $\partial y / \partial x_1$ and $\partial y / \partial x_2$.

(a) $y = 6x_1^{1/2} x_2^{1/2} + 2x_1 + 3x_2^2$

(b) $y = \dfrac{4}{\sqrt{x_1} - 3x_2^2}$, where $\sqrt{x_1} > 3x_2^2$

(c) $y = x_1 x_2 - \dfrac{\sqrt{x_2}}{x_2}$

(d) $y = \sqrt{x_1} + \sqrt{x_2}$

(e) $y = \dfrac{\sqrt{x_1} + \sqrt{x_2}}{x_1 x_2}$

A.4. Explain clearly whether each of the following statements is true or false by using the appropriate theorems from section A.4.

(a) The function $y = 60 + 10x + 0.5x^2$ attains a maximum at $x^* = 2$.

(b) The function $y = 60 + 10x + 0.5x^2$ attains a maximum at $x^* = 10$.

(c) The function $y = 56 + 16x - 2x^2$ attains a maximum at $x^* = 4$.

(d) The function $y = (x - 3)^3$ attains a maximum at $x^* = 3$.

A.5. Calculate the degree of homogeneity for each of the following functions defined for positive values of x_1 and x_2.

(a) $y = \sqrt{x_1} + \sqrt{x_2}$

(b) $y = \dfrac{x_1}{x_1 + x_2}$

(c) $y = \dfrac{x_1 x_2}{x_1 + x_2}$

(d) $y = (\sqrt{x_1} + \sqrt{x_2})^2$

(e) $y = x_1 x_2^2 + x_1^2 x_2$

Index

expected utility
    commodity space, 183
    function, 185
    hypothesis, 182
    preference axioms, 184
    theorem, 185
externality
    consumption, 242
    partial solutions for, 246–253
    production, 244

firm's supply curve, 149–151
    shifts in, 151–153
First Welfare Theorem, 101
    externalities and, 242
    proof of, 105
first-order conditions, 308, 309, 314, 315
fixed cost, *see* cost
fixed input, 110
food stamps, 31
free rider problem, 291
function, 299

game, 202
    dynamic, 214–215
    extensive-form, 214
    normal form, 202
    static, 202–203
    zero-sum, 203
general equilibrium, 88
Giffen good, 74, 85
good
    club, 277
    common pool, 277
    complement, 7, 18, 43
    discrete, 24n
    divisible, 23
    excludable, 276
    Giffen, 74, 85
    indivisible, 24n
    inferior, 7, 18, 76, 84
    neutral, 43
    normal, 7, 18, 76
    private, 89n, 276
    pure public, 277
    rival, 276
    substitute, 7, 18, 42, 79

group pricing, 172

Harsanyi, John, 201
Hicks, John, 80
Hicks-Allen decomposition, 80–82
hidden action, 257
hidden information, 257
Hotelling duopoly, *see* duopoly
Hotelling, Harold, 229
Hurwicz, Leonid, 93n, 258

incentive compatibility
    and pricing, 177
    constraint, 262, 264
incidence
    of a subsidy, 13
    of a tax, 12
income consumption curve, 75–77
income effect, 80–85
    negative, 7, 84
    positive, 7, 84
    zero, 67, 77
income elasticity of demand, 18, 79
independent variable, 1, 300
indifference, 36
indifference curve, 40
    expected utility, 186
individual rationality, 91, 101
    constraint, 260, 264
inferior good, *see* good
information rent, 263
information set, 215
input, 110
input Edgeworth box, 120
input intensity, 115
isocost, 126
isoprofit
    for a competitive firm, 145
    for a Cournot duopolist, 225
    for a Hotelling duopolist, 233
    for a principal, 265
isoquant, 112

joint average cost, *see* cost
joint marginal cost, *see* cost
joint total cost, *see* cost

Kolm triangle, 279

CPSIA information can be obtained at www.ICGtesting.com
Printed in the USA
BVOW10s1633250116

3757BVAU00002B/2/P

9 780415 870054